OUR DAILY BREAD

BIBLE SOURCE BOOK

THE WHO, WHAT, WHERE, *WOW*

GUIDE TO THE BIBLE

DAVE BRANON

Discovery House.
from Our Daily Bread Ministries

Our Daily Bread Bible Sourcebook
© 2019 by Discovery House

All rights reserved.

Discovery House is affiliated with Our Daily Bread Ministries, Grand Rapids, Michigan.

Requests for permission to quote from this book should be directed to: Permissions Department, Discovery House, PO Box 3566, Grand Rapids, MI 49501, or contact us by email at permissionsdept@dhp.org.

Unless otherwise indicated, Scripture quotations are taken from The Holy Bible, New International Version,® NIV.® Copyright © 1973, 1978, 1984, 2011 by Biblica, Inc.® Used by permission. All rights reserved worldwide.

Interior design by Rob Williams, InsideOutCreativeArts.com

ISBN: 978-1-62707-924-2

Printed in the United States of America
First printing in 2019

CONTENTS

THE NEW TESTAMENT

INTRODUCTION

Have you ever started a big project full of excitement and enthusiasm, but a few hours or days after you begin, your interest starts to fade?

A few years ago, I decided to paint our house by brush—taking it from dark brown to a nice, fresh tan color. I began with such vigor! But after about three weeks of climbing up and down ladders and interminable back-and-forth brushing, the bloom was off the rose. It became a chore to haul everything out after work, over and over again, so I could slap gallons and gallons of paint on our house until dark.

I worried about having a similar letdown as I began this project: *Our Daily Bread Bible Sourcebook*. We all know how long the Bible is, and the idea of compiling compelling information on all sixty-six books looked a bit daunting.

But, unlike my home improvement project, this task never grew old for me. As I pored over each book of the Bible and sought to dig out fascinating facts about each one, I found myself continuously intrigued and invigorated. As is always the case when I teach, the research and the discovery keep me going. The more I study, the more I learn, and the more interesting the project becomes.

I could share many times when lights went on in my mind as I saw connections in God's Word I had never noticed before. One of those occurred toward the end, as I was working through the Epistles. I started to see connections between the churches of Asia Minor and an event that seemed so far separated from them: the Day of Pentecost. For instance, when I began studying the book of Titus, I discovered that the apostle Paul's letter was going to Crete, an island in the Mediterranean Sea. That doesn't sound like much, but then I realized that Acts 2 mentions that some Cretans were in Jerusalem on the Day of Pentecost—and that they heard the gospel presented in their own language. Could it have been that those very same people traveled back home, shared the gospel, and started a church? And was Paul addressing those people and their children in the faith in his letter to Titus?

Then I looked again at Acts 2 and saw mention of Romans and people from Asia and Pontus—all places where the gospel had spread to because of this miraculous event. And later, the apostles wrote letters to them to explain more about this new faith.

That was just one little connection I discovered. Multiply that by the exciting new (new to me) information I found in all sixty-six books, and you can see why this project, unlike my painting adventure, never grew old.

I hope you share my excitement of discovery as you read the *Bible Sourcebook*. To help you get started, let me explain the contents.

I begin each review of the Bible book with a **Top Ten** list. These are ten facts that relate to the author, the book itself, the times in which it was written, or some other pertinent fact. And who doesn't like top ten lists?

Then we get into the W's:

Who wrote the book and little about the author. I added this section for Old Testament books because it is more given to telling stories than is the New Testament.

What is this book of the Bible about? This is an overview or summary of the key elements of the book.

When did the events of the book take place? The Bible covers several thousand years of history, so it's helpful to be able to plug in the historical context.

Where did the events of the book take place? Geography is often vital to a story, and it enhances our understanding of the Bible when we get a clearer picture of places mentioned in Scripture.

Why is this book in the Bible? What are the book's purposes, and what themes does it explain or explore?

Wow! gives us a unique look at Scripture by revealing some of the particular book's cultural uses, mostly outside of the world of religion. It presents where the contents of the book alluded to in history, politics, literature, movie, the arts, and music. I did not include Wow! references for every book, either because no politician or artist has made a reference, or because I couldn't find one.

Worth Remembering is a listing of valuable verses from each book of the Bible. Of course, every word of Scripture is inspired and valuable, but some verses have special meaning to us. These might be good prompts for Bible memorization.

Wonders from the Past gives us quick looks at archaeological discoveries related to each book of the Bible. It is my hope that this fosters a love for discovery on your own part, for mountains of evidence exists to prove the historicity and accuracy of Scripture.

My work on this project is done (by the way, I also completed my house painting project, in about three months), and you can now dive in and discover new and exciting truths, facts, and lessons from the pages of God's great Book. I hope you enjoy reading it as much as I enjoyed every minute of putting it all together.

— Dave Branon

THE OLD TESTAMENT

GENESIS
Beginnings: The World, Humankind, and the People of God

Top Ten

1. The book of Genesis starts at the beginning of time as we know it and ends in approximately 1806 BC with the death of Joseph.
2. Genesis 3 includes the first hint regarding the gospel of Jesus Christ (vs. 15).
3. Genesis has 50 chapters (fourth most in the Bible) and 1,533 verses.
4. The writer of Genesis, under the influence of the Holy Spirit, used twelve different names for God: Elohim, Yahweh, El Elyon, El Roi, El Shaddai, El Olam, Yahweh-Yireh, Adonai, Shaphat, Abhir, Raah, and Eben.
5. Genesis is the first book of the Pentateuch (Greek for "five scrolls"): Genesis, Exodus, Leviticus, Numbers, Deuteronomy. Jews called this section of Scripture the Torah.
6. Every New Testament writer refers to Genesis. In all, there are upwards of two hundred allusions to Genesis in the New Testament. Genesis 1 through 11 is quoted more than one hundred times in the New Testament.
7. Genesis includes the story of the oldest person who ever lived: Methuselah (Genesis 5:27). Methuselah, Noah's grandfather, died the same year the Flood covered the earth. He was 969 years old. It's not known whether he died in the Flood.
8. The first social institution mentioned in Genesis, the book of beginnings, is marriage (2:21-25).
9. Archaeology has verified such Genesis peoples as the Hittites (Genesis 15:20; 23:5) and the titles given to Joseph in Egypt (Genesis 39:1, 4; 40:2).

10. Adam is referred to several times in the New Testament (see Romans 5:12-14, 1 Corinthians 15:22, Matthew 19:4-6, Jude 14, Luke 3:23-38, 1 Timothy 2:11-15), which verifies him as a historical person.

Who

Who Wrote It

Because of the connections made in Scripture between Moses and the Law, it is generally accepted that Moses is the author. For example, in John 5:46 Jesus said Moses "wrote about me." And on the Emmaus Road, Jesus began "with Moses and all the Prophets" to explain who He was (Luke 24:27). Moses grew up in the home of an Egyptian pharaoh, yet he later led the Israelites out of Egypt and toward Canaan. Moses' brother Aaron and sister Miriam helped him as he led the people to their homeland.

The events recorded in Genesis ended about 300 years before Moses lived. This means he would have received the material for the book through direct revelation of the Holy Spirit (inspiration) and through traditional means of conveying history at the time—probably through oral recitations of earlier events.

Recent studies of ancient writing by Dr. Douglas Petrovich and others indicate that Hebrew writing (which Moses would have used) existed as far back as 1850 BC. This would have been early enough for Moses to record the events of Genesis in writing.[1]

Who's in It

Adam, Eve, Cain, Abel, Noah, Moses, Abraham, Sarah, Hagar, Ishmael, Isaac, Jacob, Esau, Joseph

What

Contained in the pages of Genesis are some of the seminal events in humankind's history. Without a record of creation, we would not know how we got here. Without the story of the Fall, we would not understand why we need a Savior. Without the retelling of the flood story, we would not grasp God's hatred for sin and His grace in providing salvation. Without the details about Abraham and his family, we would not be able to fully understand the sacrificial system that pointed to the true Lamb of God. Genesis provides us that background—establishing our need for a Savior, the promise of a Savior, and the beginnings of the story of the people through whom the Savior would come to earth to save us.

When

Although there is no textual evidence from the book of Genesis as to when it was written, it can be surmised that for Moses to write this book, it would have been compiled in approximately 1440 BC. This was around the time of the end of the Exodus.

Where

The events recorded in the book of Genesis took place in what we loosely refer to as the Middle East. We cannot know exactly where the first geographic location—the garden of Eden—was located. Because the flood, which would have changed the geography dramatically, occurred after this, we cannot use the place names given in Genesis 2:10–14 as evidence for its present location.

We do know about many other places mentioned in Genesis, most notably Canaan, which is most often referred to as the Promised Land. This was the land to which Abram traveled from his home of Ur. And it would be the place where he would begin the Hebrew nation through his son Isaac.

Why

Genesis is foundational to understanding God's story in the Bible. Clearly, it was written to reveal humans' value as those made in God's image, to explain humankind's need of a Savior, and to introduce the family through whom that Savior would someday come.

Genesis sets up for us the primary themes that will be carried through the remainder of the Bible. The first is creation—the record of God speaking the universe and this planet into existence and populating the earth with its wonders, including seas and land and plants, animals, and other living things. It tells of His fashioning of the first man and the first woman. The second theme introduced in Genesis is the fall of humankind—the sin of Adam and Eve that plunged us all into the darkness of evil from which we would need a Savior. The third theme begins to take shape as God's plan for the redemption of humankind is initiated through His chosen people, the Israelites.

Wow!

- On Christmas Eve 1968, Apollo 8 astronauts Bill Anders, Jim Lovell, and Frank Borman, after they had come out from behind the moon and were on their way home, read Genesis 1:1–10 for all the world to hear. Borman ended by saying, "Merry Christmas—and God bless all of you, all of you on the good Earth."
- John Milton's epic seventeenth-century epic poem *Paradise Lost* was based on a retelling of the Adam and Eve story. It is often considered one of the greatest epic poems in the English language.
- One of the most famous paintings in the world, the ceiling of the Sistine Chapel at the Vatican, has as its centerpiece the creation story as rendered by Michelangelo.

Worth Remembering

- In the beginning God created the heavens and the earth (Genesis 1:1).
- "I will put enmity between you and the woman, and between your offspring and hers; he will crush your head, and you will strike his heel" (Genesis 3:15).

- The LORD regretted that he had made human beings (Genesis 6:6).
- "I will make you [Abram] into a great nation, and I will bless you; I will make your name great, and you will be a blessing. I will bless those who bless you, and whoever curses you I will curse; and all peoples on earth will be blessed through you" (Genesis 12:2–3).
- "You intended to harm me, but God intended it for good to accomplish what is now being done, the saving of many lives" (Genesis 50:20).

Wonders from the Past

- British archaeologist Leonard Woolley discovered the ancient city of Ur (Genesis 11:31) in the 1920s.
- A list of Sumerian kings (Sumer was an ancient kingdom located in what is now southern Iraq) dating back to about 2100 BC was discovered. In that list of kings is the mention of a great flood.[2]
- On a series of baked tablets found at Nineveh is recorded the Epic of Gilgamesh, which tells of a great flood and of a man who built a boat to save the animals. The tablet dates to the seventh century BC.[3]
- Near the town of Harran in Turkey are villages that have the same names as Abraham's ancestors: Serug and Nahor (see Genesis 11:22–26).

EXODUS

God's People Escape Egypt, Head for Home

Top Ten

1. Exodus contains the first poetry in the Bible: "The Song of Moses and Miriam" in chapter 15.

2. The time period covered in Exodus is about eighty years.

3. Exodus includes the extremely important answer from God when Moses asked Him His name: "I AM WHO I AM" (3:14).

4. The end of Genesis (death of Joseph) to the beginning of Exodus was a period of three hundred years.

5. In the New Testament are at least eight passages referencing Exodus: John 3:14–17, John 6:32, Acts 7:17–41, Romans 9:15, 1 Corinthians 10:1–13, 2 Corinthians 3:7–18, Hebrews 3:15–19, Hebrews 12:18–25.

6. Moses' birth is recorded in Exodus 2. His death is mentioned in Deuteronomy 34. He lived 120 years.

7. Exodus 1:5 says seventy-one Hebrews entered Egypt. When it was time for the Exodus itself, millions of Jews escaped Egypt.

8. The tabernacle God directed Moses to build in Exodus 26 is a copy modeled after one that exists in heaven (see Hebrews 8:5).

9. The title "Exodus" is taken from a Greek term that suggests "departure" or a "way out." Luke used this Greek term in 9:31 when he wrote, referring to Jesus, "They spoke about his departure." In 2 Peter 1:15, Peter wrote of Jesus' departure using the same word.

10. Throughout the Old Testament, one of the significant ways God reminds His people who He is by saying, "I am the LORD, who brought you up out of Egypt"— the Exodus story (see Leviticus 11:45; Deuteronomy 20:1; Judges 2:1; Judges 6:8; 1 Samuel 8:8, 10:18; 1 Kings 12:28; Psalm 81:10; Amos 2:10; Micah 6:4).

Who

Who Wrote It?

As with all five of the books of the Pentateuch, it is widely accepted that Moses is the author. One of the compelling reasons to accept Moses as the author of Exodus is the fact that

Jesus quoted him and connected him to verses in the book of Exodus. Here are some of them: Mark 7:10 (Exodus 20:12, 21:17); Luke 20:37 (Exodus 3:6); John 7:19. Also, Philip referred to Moses' authorship in John 1:45.

Who's in It?
Moses, the Pharaohs, Aaron, Miriam, the Israelites

What

In the book of Exodus, God leaves no doubt about who He is and what He can do. The things God accomplishes in these forty chapters sets the tone for the rest of the Old Testament and into the New for belief and faith of all who need a solid foundation of truth and greatness. By first wresting the Hebrews from the hands of the Pharaoh and rescuing them from the frightening armies of Egypt—and then leading the people back to the Promised Land—God shows that He is the King of redemption. Each of His miracles along the wilderness way, and even into the Promised Land as Israel reestablishes herself in the land, demonstrates the trustworthiness of His power. In addition, God reveals His presence with His covenant people—both in the wilderness and in the homeland. The tabernacle allowed the people to experience firsthand His presence with them.

When

The jury is still out on the exact dates of the Exodus. There are two possibilities: the fifteenth century BC or the thirteenth century BC. Some scholars use a dating process based on a passage in 1 Kings, which would mean 480 years had passed between the Exodus until the fourth year of the reign of King Solomon in 966 BC. That would put the Exodus at 1446 BC. However, there are some problems with this relating to dates of events in Egypt when the Hebrews lived there. The second possible date relates to archaeological evidence connected to the destruction of cities in the Promised Land (Jericho, for instance).

EXODUS

EXODUS

Where

It's clear where the Hebrews were as the book of Exodus begins (Egypt), and we know exactly where they were at the end of their wilderness wanderings: waiting to cross the Jordan and go into the land. But what about the forty years of meandering? Do we know that exact route? According to Bible scholar and expert on biblical geography John Beck, "The list of places is not a complete turn-by-turn list like we might use today to navigate toward a destination."[4] We know the Israelites did not take the shortest route, because God redirected them away from the dreaded Philistines (see Exodus 13:17). But the route they did take is open for debate. We know they made it down toward the southern tip of the Sinai Peninsula to Mount Sinai—and eventually back north toward Canaan.

Why

Clearly, God wants several things from His people. He wants us to trust Him even when we don't know the path ahead. He wants us to recognize who He is: the almighty God who can command seas to part, rocks to give up water, and breakfast to fall from heaven. And He wants a relationship with us. The forty-year journey, the convincing miracles, and the awe-inspiring presence of God in the tabernacle all underscore who God is and what He can do. How can we ever doubt this God? Well, Exodus was written to make it hard to doubt God, but as we keep reading in both the Old Testament and the New, and as we live our lives each day, we know that humans are pretty good at forgetting the lessons of the Exodus.

Wow!

- The story of the Exodus has been translated into film in *The Ten Commandments* (several versions), *The Prince of Egypt,* and the VeggieTales episode *Moe and the Big Exit.*
- In his song "Exodus," Jamaican reggae music legend Bob Marley referenced Moses and the Red Sea.

- It has been estimated that when Moses led the people out of Egypt, more than two million people embarked on one of the largest camping expeditions in history.
- Leon Uris' book *Exodus* details the Jews' return to Israel in 1948. Uris used the biblical Exodus for his themes.

Worth Remembering

- The descendants of Jacob numbered seventy in all; Joseph was already in Egypt (Exodus 1:5).
- There the angel of the LORD appeared to him in flames of fire from within a bush. Moses saw that though the bush was on fire it did not burn up (Exodus 3:2).
- God said to Moses, "I AM WHO I AM. This is what you are to say to the Israelites: 'I AM has sent me to you.'" (Exodus 3:14).
- "This," said the LORD, "is so that they may believe that the LORD, the God of their fathers—the God of Abraham, the God of Isaac and the God of Jacob—has appeared to you" (Exodus 4:5).
- Afterward Moses and Aaron went to Pharaoh and said, "This is what the LORD, the God of Israel, says: 'Let my people go, so that they may hold a festival to me in the wilderness'" (Exodus 5:1).
- "In days to come, when your son asks you, 'What does this mean?' say to him, 'With a mighty hand the LORD brought us out of Egypt, out of the land of slavery'" (Exodus 13:14).
- Then Moses and the Israelites sang this song to the LORD: "I will sing to the LORD, for he is highly exalted. Both horse and driver he has hurled into the sea" (Exodus 15:1).
- "Who among the gods is like you, LORD? Who is like you— majestic in holiness, awesome in glory, working wonders?" (Exodus 15:11).
- "Now if you obey me fully and keep my covenant, then out of all nations you will be my treasured possession. Although the whole earth is mine" (Exodus 19:5).

EXODUS

- When the people saw that Moses was so long in coming down from the mountain, they gathered around Aaron and said, "Come, make us gods who will go before us. As for this fellow Moses who brought us up out of Egypt, we don't know what has happened to him" (Exodus 32:1).
- When Moses came down from Mount Sinai with the two tablets of the covenant law in his hands, he was not aware that his face was radiant because he had spoken with the LORD (Exodus 34:29).

Wonders from the Past

- Archaeological excavations at Tell el-Dab'a have led to the discovery of many ancient buildings, including temples and monuments that may be the ones the Hebrew slaves constructed out of the bricks they made (see 5:7–19) in Pithom and Rameses (see 1:11).
- In Exodus 27:2, God gives Moses instructions for the construction of horned altars to be used for burnt offerings in the tabernacle. Several horned altars have been uncovered in archaeological digs in Israel.
- The hieroglyphic text of a stele found in Egypt mentions the name Israel in connection with a victory Egypt won over Israel in Palestine around 1230 BC. This is an indication that the Jews were living in the Promised Land at the time. (This would have been after the wanderings and after the crossing of the Jordan back into the land.)

LEVITICUS
Wilderness Wanderings: Laws and Regulations

Top Ten

1. In the book of Leviticus, the Israelites don't go anywhere. The book simply spells out God's laws

and standards for them. This book details 613 different laws.

2. Just to make sure the message gets through, Leviticus includes fifty-six instances in which the reader is told that God gave these standards and laws to Moses.

3. There is not much narrative in Leviticus, but we are told the story of Aaron's sons, Nadab and Abihu, who died because they "offered unauthorized fire before the LORD" (Leviticus 10:1).

4. The word *holy* appears in the book of Leviticus seventy-six times.

5. The word *atonement* appears forty-five times in Leviticus. This word means "the covering or pardoning of sin."

6. When Leviticus was translated into Greek for the Septuagint, the title of this book was *Leueitikon*, which means "related to the Levites."

7. The five key offerings spelled out in Leviticus are the burnt offerings, the cereal offerings, the peace offerings, the sin offerings, and the guilt offerings.

8. There are at least nineteen references to Leviticus in the New Testament. For instance: Leviticus 11:44 and 1 Peter 1:16: "Be holy, for I am holy." And Leviticus 17:7 and 1 Corinthians 10:20 both prohibit sacrificing to idols. Others: Leviticus 16:2, 12 and Hebrews 6:19; Leviticus 19:18 and Mark 12:31; Leviticus 24:19 and Matthew 5:38.

9. While we are not required today to obey the Levitical laws set forth in this book, we do learn an important truth as we read them: we should allow what God has told us in His Word is holy, clean, and honoring to Him to guide our thinking and actions. Just as the people of Israel in the days of Leviticus were to have a worldview that included God and His standards at the center, so should we. It's just that our standards are not dictated by the book of Leviticus but by the New

LEVITICUS

Testament and anything that carries over to the New from the Old.

10. The number 7 is important in Leviticus: the seventh day was the Sabbath; the seventh year was Sabbath year; the seventh Sabbath year (49 years) was the Year of Jubilee; and there were seven weeks between Passover and Pentecost. Passover lasted seven days.

Who

Who Wrote It?
This statement from Leviticus 1:1 appears about fifty-five times in the book: "The LORD called to Moses. . . ."

Who's in It?
Moses, Aaron, Nadab, Abihu, Ithamar, Eleazar

What

If you were to sign up to be an Old Testament priest, Leviticus would be a great book to use as your guide. It spells out the tasks the priests must perform and the sacrifices they must make. But since you are not an Old Testament priest, what is the book's value to you? Both the apostles Paul and Peter, writing in the New Testament, suggested that we can learn from such Old Testament teachings (see Romans 15:4, 1 Corinthians 10:11). Despite the fact that the sacrifices and ceremonies in the book of Leviticus don't apply to us today, we can learn from them about God's holiness and His high regard for strong biblical standards.

When

After the tabernacle was constructed according to the details given in the book of Exodus, the third book of the law—Leviticus—was begun. Now that there is a central place of worship, God begins to fill in the blanks with the laws and

LEVITICUS

regulations He wants the Israelites to follow. The time period that elapses during the giving of the Levitical standards is one month.

Where

The book of Leviticus takes place in the shadow of Mount Sinai. The central location for this literature is the newly constructed tabernacle.

Why

The people had lived for generation upon generation in the polytheistic land of Egypt, and now they were striking out on their own. The one true God would be guiding them, yet they did not know much about the standards and principles and worship practices He required. Thus, He had Moses record for them this book about how to worship Him and how to live according to His precepts. This was the beginning of the Jewish worship experience, which would take place for hundreds of years in Israel.

Wow!

Nineteenth-century missionary to India and Bible translator Dr. Samuel Kellogg considered the book of Leviticus the most important book in the Bible. Twentieth-century commentator J. Vernon McGee called it "one of the most important books of the Bible."

Worth Remembering

- "For the life of a creature is in the blood, and I have given it to you to make atonement for yourselves on the altar; it is the blood that makes atonement for one's life" (Leviticus 17:11).
- "Do not seek revenge or bear a grudge against anyone among your people, but love your neighbor as yourself. I am the LORD" (Leviticus 19:18).

LEVITICUS

- "You are to be holy to me because I, the LORD, am holy, and I have set you apart from the nations to be my own" (Leviticus 20:26).

Wonders from the Past

In 1970, the En-Gedi Scroll was discovered in Israel. The scroll contained passages from Leviticus 1. It was dated to the sixth century AD, making it the oldest fragment of the Pentateuch found since the Dead Sea Scrolls were discovered in the late 1940s. The scroll had been burned in a fire back in the sixth century, and it was unreadable when it was unearthed. However, new developments in digital imaging software allowed researchers to decipher it and see that it contained the first eight verses of Leviticus 1.

NUMBERS

Forty Years of Wilderness Travels

Top Ten

1. This book is called Numbers because it details two censuses that were taken and recorded.
2. Some would prefer that the book of Numbers be titled "Wilderness" or "In the Desert." The book's actual Hebrew title was *Bemidbar*, which means "In the Wilderness."
3. In the Septuagint, this book's Greek name is *Arithmoi*, which has the same root as "arithmetic."
4. The time covered in the book of Numbers is a little less than thirty-nine years.
5. One of the key elements of the book of Numbers is this statement: "the LORD spoke to Moses." This clause appears in the book eighty times.

6. The book of Numbers is a bit like your literature anthology back in high school. It contains a wide variety of genres: narratives, poems, songs, seemingly endless lists from two censuses, travel lists, letters, and some laws.

7. Does your pastor ever end a service with these words: "The LORD bless you and keep you; the LORD make his face to shine on upon you and be gracious to you"? That comes from Numbers 6:24–26. It was a blessing the Lord dictated to Aaron to "bless the sons of Aaron."

8. If you were to add up all the numbers from the census taken at Mount Sinai in chapter one of this book, you'd find that there were 603,550 males over the age of 20.

9. In the encampments of the Israelites, the tabernacle was in the middle, and the twelve tribes surrounded it: Naphtali, Asher, and Dan to the north, Judah, Issachar, and Zebulun to the east, Gad, Simeon, and Rueben to the south, and Ephraim, Manasseh, and Benjamin to the west.

10. Numbers contains the humorous story of Balaam, whose donkey sees an angel Balaam can't see—leading the donkey to turn around and have a few words with its owner (see Numbers 22:23–30).

Who

Who Wrote It?
As with the previous three books, it is widely assumed that Moses is the author of Numbers.

Who's in It?

• Moses; Miriam; Aaron; Korah and others who opposed Moses (chapter 16);

- Arad (king of Canaan), who tried to attack the Israelites (chapter 21); Balaam; Joshua; Caleb

What

This book begins with a census of "the whole Israelite community" (1:2) then details the journey of the people of Israel, beginning in the second year after their escape from Egypt. The narrative covers the next thirty-eight years and takes the people to the east side of the Jordan as they prepare to enter the Promised Land.

When

The events detailed in the book of Numbers begin two years after the Exodus began. The Israelites have made their way across the Red Sea, deep into the Sinai Peninsula, and to the foot of Mount Sinai. They have built the tabernacle, and they have received instructions from God about how He wants them to worship Him and live according to His standards. At this point, they have no idea that their journey to the Promised Land is about to take a forty-year detour.

Where

When the book begins, the Israelites are camped at the foot of Mount Sinai. In chapter 10, they leave that location and eventually travel to Kadesh-Barnea. Numbers 33:16–48 details all of the named locations where the Israelites camped after leaving Sinai. The place names given no longer exist, so we can't follow exactly where they camped along the way to the Jordan River. We know they went through the Desert of Sinai, the Desert of Paran, and the Desert of Zin, which indicate a south-to-north trek. After Kadesh Barnea, they traveled east to Edom, south to the tip of the Gulf of Aqaba, and north to the plains of Moab.

Why

In the book of Numbers, the Israelites are transported from Mount Sinai to the edge of the Promised Land. But it is not an easy journey, and the first generation of the people who escaped Egypt rejected the opportunity to enter the land of God's promise. Their struggles in the desert proved too much, and their complaints spelled their destruction. They did not trust God, who had proven to be faithful, so the older generation died off in the wilderness—leaving their children to be the ones to enter the Promised Land.

Wow!

- In his poem "And Did Those Feet in Ancient Time," nineteenth-century British poet William Blake paraphrased Numbers 11:29 this way: "Would to God that all the Lord's people were prophets."
- In the original *Star Trek* television series, Leonard Nimoy as Spock used a hand signal salute he said came from something he saw as a Jewish kid. As he recited a blessing found in Numbers 6:24–26, Nimoy recalled, the priest would make that signal of the two pairs of fingers separated. The signal represented the Hebrew letter Shin, which stands for El Shaddai.
- On the day before he was assassinated in 1968, Dr. Martin Luther King Jr. delivered a speech called "I've Been to the Mountain Top." In that speech, he referred to Numbers 27:12 when he said, "He's allowed me to go up to the mountain and I've looked over. And I've seen the Promised Land."

Worth Remembering

- "Take a census of the whole Israelite community by their clans and families, listing every man by name, one by one" (Numbers 1:2).
- And they called the whole community together on the first day of the second month. The people registered their ancestry by their clans and families, and the men

twenty years old or more were listed by name, one by one" (Numbers 1:18).

- "The LORD bless you and keep you" (Numbers 6:24).
- "God is not human, that he should lie, not a human being, that he should change his mind. Does he speak and then not act? Does he promise and not fulfill?" (Numbers 23:19).

Wonders from the Past

In the late 1970s, famed archaeologist Gabriel Barkay found a pair of amulets in a cave opposite the city of Jerusalem. These amulets contained a rolled-up sheet of silver. On that silver was inscribed a priestly benediction. It has been observed that this is the oldest extra-biblical document ever found containing biblical text. It predates the Dead Sea Scrolls. The quote is from Numbers 6:24–26: "The LORD bless you and keep you; the LORD make his face to shine upon you." It is also the oldest (seventeenth century BC) reference outside the Bible to YHWH (Yahweh).

DEUTERONOMY

The Law Revisited and Explained

Top Ten

1. The word *Deuteronomy* means "second law." The name of this book comes from the Greek Septuagint, which uses the term "second law" as the title (although it's not really a second law but a reiteration and expansion of the law). When the Latin Vulgate was translated from the Septuagint, the translators took "second law" and translated it as *Deuteronomium*.

2. The book of Deuteronomy is the second book in the Bible that records the Ten Commandments (Exodus 20:2-17 and Deuteronomy 5:6-21).

3. The book of Deuteronomy consists of three major speeches by elder statesman Moses (he is 120 years old at this time) to the Israelites who would soon be entering the Promised Land.

4. The word *command* or some form of the word appears ninety-nine times in the New International Version of Deuteronomy.

5. The New Testament has more than eighty direct or indirect references to verses in Deuteronomy.

6. Jesus quoted from Deuteronomy on ten occasions. Examples: when He refers to loving God and neighbor (Deuteronomy 6:5, Matthew 22:37–38); when He references the Ten Commandments (Deuteronomy 5:7–21, Matthew 19:18–19); when He addresses divorce (Deuteronomy 24:1–3, Matthew 5:31); when He refers to a standard for witnesses (Deuteronomy 19:15, Matthew 18:16); when Satan tempts him, He quotes Scripture (Deuteronomy 6:13; Matthew 4:4, 7).

7. In Deuteronomy 18:14–19, Moses prophetically points out that a prophet would one day come to the people. This is an Old Testament prophecy of the coming Messiah, Jesus.

8. There are two songs in the book of Deuteronomy. The first is "The Song of Moses" in chapter 32, and the second is "The Blessing of Moses" in chapter 33.

9. At the end of his speech just before his death, Moses climbed Mount Nebo (chapter 34), where he was allowed to see the Promised Land "only from a distance" (32:52). He couldn't enter the land because he disobeyed God by striking the rock at Meribah Kadesh instead of just talking to it to get water.

10. The death of Moses, at the age of 120, is recorded in Deuteronomy 34. Deuteronomy 34:6 says "no one knows where his grave is," but it was in a valley opposite Beth-Peor in Moab. According to

DEUTERONOMY

Deuteronomy 34:6, God himself buried Moses. The people mourned Moses' passing for thirty days.

Who

Who Wrote It?
Moses is addressing the second generation of Israelites after the exodus from Egypt. The first generation—with the exception of Moses, Joshua, and Caleb—has died off, so he is preparing the next generation for their move into the Promised Land.

Who's in It?
Moses, Joshua

What

The book of Deuteronomy contains Moses' three farewell messages to his people. One message centers on the history of the people (1:1-4:43). The second message reviews the laws of God (4-26). And the third message (27-30) is a review of the covenant God made with His chosen people. After Moses completes his sermons, leadership is transferred from Moses to Joshua (chapters 31-34). The book ends with a record of the death of Moses.

When

Early 1400s BC. The book covers about forty days, as the Israelites prepare to cross the Jordan River and enter the Promised Land.

Where

The Israelites are in the Plains of Moab—just east of the Jordan River. As was the case with Leviticus, there is no movement of the people throughout the book of Deuteronomy. The people are awaiting the time to cross over the river into the Promised Land. In order to get to this location, they had to defeat the Amorites, who refused to let them go through their land, and the kingdom of Og. This left the Israelites free to encamp east of the Jordan as they prepared to enter.

Why

Moses was preparing the people for their entrance into the Promised Land. The people gathered before him were the offspring of those who had escaped Egypt, and they were on the threshold of establishing a nation in the land God had promised them. Therefore, Moses wanted the people to understand how important it was to keep their covenant with God and to obey the standards He had given them. Because God loved them so much and provided for them, Moses expects the people to love and serve Him.

Worth Remembering

- "May the LORD, the God of your ancestors, increase you a thousand times and bless you as he has promised!" (Deuteronomy 1:11).
- "Sovereign LORD, you have begun to show to your servant your greatness and your strong hand. For what god is there in heaven or on earth who can do the deeds and mighty works you do?" (Deuteronomy 3:24).
- "Do not add to what I command you and do not subtract from it, but keep the commands of the LORD your God that I give you" (Deuteronomy 4:2).
- "Be careful not to forget the covenant of the LORD your God that he made with you; do not make for yourselves an idol in the form of anything the LORD your God has forbidden. For the LORD your God is a consuming fire, a jealous God" (Deuteronomy 4:23-24).
- "Walk in obedience to all that the LORD your God has commanded you, so that you may live and prosper and prolong your days in the land that you will possess" (Deuteronomy 5:33).

DEUTERONOMY

- "For you are a people holy to the LORD your God. The LORD your God has chosen you out of all the peoples on the face of the earth to be his people, his treasured possession" (Deuteronomy 7:6).
- "He is the one you praise; he is your God, who performed for you those great and awesome wonders you saw with your own eyes" (Deuteronomy 10:21).
- "Go to the Levitical priests and to the judge who is in office at that time. Inquire of them and they will give you the verdict. You must act according to the decisions they give you at the place the LORD will choose. Be careful to do everything they instruct you to do" (Deuteronomy 17:9-10).
- Since then, no prophet has risen in Israel like Moses, whom the LORD knew face to face, who did all those signs and wonders the LORD sent him to do in Egypt—to Pharaoh and to all his officials and to his whole land. For no one has ever shown the mighty power or performed the awesome deeds that Moses did in the sight of all Israel (Deuteronomy 34:10-12).

Wonders from the Past

- In Deuteronomy 29:23, Moses made historical reference to Sodom and Gomorrah. In the 1960s and 1970s, archaeologists discovered the ruins of cities in the location that fit the descriptions of the two cities. Upon excavation, they found evidence of a large, walled city that had been ruined by fire. A coating of ash covered the ruined city. One noted archaeologist, Dr. Bryant Wood, noted that it appeared that the fire had begun on the rooftops. In Randall Price's book *The Stones Cry*, Wood is quoted as saying, "The evidence would suggest that this site of Bab edh-Drha is the biblical city of Sodom."
- The Dead Sea Scrolls, which were discovered in the late 1940s at Qumran, include twenty-five fragments from Deuteronomy.

- In 2018, a new fragment of the Dead Sea Scrolls was discovered to have the writings of Deuteronomy on it. The fragment had been stored in a box since its discovery, and only because of recent advances in computer imaging has it been deciphered.

JOSHUA
New Leader; New Land of Promise

Top Ten

1. The book of Joshua transitions the Bible from the Pentateuch, or books of the Law, to the historical books.
2. The name Joshua means "Jehovah saves." Its equivalent in the New Testament is the name of Jesus himself, which means "Savior." In the King James Version, Joshua's name is rendered as "Jesus" in Acts 7:45 and Hebrews 4:8. The name Joshua in Hebrew is the same as "Jesus" in Greek, but the context calls for Joshua, not Jesus.
3. A whole new way of life awaits the Hebrew people on the other side of the Jordan River. Their ancestors had been slaves in Egypt; their parents had lived in tents as they spent forty years in the wilderness wanderings; now, they have the prospect of staying in one place, living in established cities, and dwelling in real houses.
4. Rahab, a prostitute who lived in Jericho, discovered faith in God, honored him, and ended up being mentioned in the genealogy of Jesus (see Matthew 1:5).
5. Under Joshua's leadership, the Hebrews built three important memorials or altars. The first was a twelve-stone memorial at the Jordan River. The second was an altar built on Mount Ebal that consisted

of unfinished stones, as directed by Moses (see Deuteronomy 27:1-8). The third was an altar built east of Jordan, not for sacrifices but as a witness for future generations (Joshua 22:28).

6. One of the Israelites' key tasks in the book of Joshua is to annihilate the Canaanites. This doesn't sound like a very neighborly thing to do, but it is essential, for the Canaanites are bent on destroying God's people. They are pagan worshipers of false gods, and if they are left alone they will overwhelm the Israelites. They are a people God's prophet Noah has already cursed (Genesis 9:25), and they face God's judgment for their immorality and rejection of Him.

7. It is going to take two major military campaigns to conquer the land. There will be a southern campaign (Joshua 9:1-10:43) and a northern campaign (11:1-15).

8. Another interesting development is the dividing of the land into sections for each of the tribes of Israel to occupy (13:1-21:45). The Levites did not get a territory; instead, they were given cities in which to dwell.

9. An important meeting took place at Shechem after Joshua had given a farewell to the Jewish leaders. He had summoned the leaders of the tribes to meet with him there, and after reviewing with them their history together, he challenged them: "Choose for yourselves this day whom you will serve" (24:15). They responded: "We will serve the LORD our God and obey him" (24:24).

10. Shortly after that, Joshua died at the age of 110, and he was buried in Ephraim.

Who

Who Wrote It?

Most conservative scholars hold that Joshua wrote the book that bears his name. There are approximately fourteen references to the expression "to this day" in Joshua. This seems to indicate that the writing of the book took place in the lifetime of the author—even though it could have been years later. If Joshua wrote the book, an editor or scribe or someone else would have had to add Joshua 24:28–33, which records Joshua's death.

Who's in It?
Joshua, Caleb, Rahab, Achan, Phinehas, Eleazar

What
Finally, after forty years in the wilderness, the Israelites are allowed to enter the land promised to Abraham and his offspring so long ago. A miraculous crossing of the flooded Jordan River gives them access to the land, but it is going to take much effort to settle it, make it their own, and distribute the population throughout the country. As the people take on this task, they must have the courage God spoke to Joshua about (1:6–9), and they must learn that obedience to God's directions is still the key to accomplishing what He wants them to do. It is a happy prospect for these hundreds of thousands of people that it is now possible for them to stop traveling, settle down, and establish themselves in towns and villages throughout the land.

When
The events of Joshua began toward the end of the 1400s BC and continued for about the next twenty-five years.

Where
Joshua begins where Deuteronomy left off. The people are on the east side of the Jordan River, waiting for the command to enter the land they had been promised. When the time comes for them to cross, it is in the spring of the year and the river is flooded. Bible scholar and geography expert Dr. John Beck suggests that the river could have been ten to twelve feet deep and a mile wide at the time of crossing. Once the people cross into Canaan, they then have to conquer it through a series

JOSHUA

of battles. As they do, the twelve tribes of Israel scattered throughout the land.

Why

It wasn't easy, but God's promise to Abraham was finally fulfilled. This land had been promised to Abraham's offspring, and now, hundreds of years later, the people are home. It took a four-hundred-year exile, a forty-year desert excursion, and a number of hard-fought battles, but the twelve tribes now have a place to call their own—except the Levites, for whom "the LORD is their inheritance" (Deuteronomy 18:2). The book of Joshua details the fulfilment of the great covenant God made with Abraham (Genesis 12:7).

Wow!

- In the early fourteenth century poem *Divine Comedy*, Italian poet Dante Alighieri refers to Joshua as a "warrior of faith."
- In 1987, the Irish rock group U2 released an album titled "The Joshua Tree," which is full of biblical imagery.

Worth Remembering

- "No one will be able to stand against you all the days of your life. As I was with Moses, so I will be with you; I will never leave you nor forsake you" (Joshua 1:5).
- "Be strong and very courageous. Be careful to obey all the law my servant Moses gave you; do not turn from it to the right or to the left, that you may be successful wherever you go" (Joshua 1:7).
- "Keep this Book of the Law always on your lips; meditate on it day and night, so that you may be careful to do everything written in it. Then you will be prosperous and successful" (Joshua 1:8).

JOSHUA

- "Have I not commanded you? Be strong and courageous. Do not be afraid; do not be discouraged, for the LORD your God will be with you wherever you go" (Joshua 1:9).
- "Just as we fully obeyed Moses, so we will obey you. Only may the LORD your God be with you as he was with Moses" (Joshua 1:17).
- But Joshua spared Rahab the prostitute, with her family and all who belonged to her, because she hid the men Joshua had sent as spies to Jericho—and she lives among the Israelites to this day (Joshua 6:25).
- "But if serving the LORD seems undesirable to you, then choose for yourselves this day whom you will serve, whether the gods your ancestors served beyond the Euphrates, or the gods of the Amorites, in whose land you are living. But as for me and my household, we will serve the LORD" (Joshua 24:15).

Wonders from the Past

- Archaeologists have discovered the city of Jericho, the first city the Israelites attacked and conquered upon entering the Promised Land—and its location is accurate regarding it being the first city they would need to conquer after crossing the Jordan.
- While examining the region of Mount Ebal, archaeologist Adam Zertal discovered an unusual mound at the top of the location. After years of work on the site, he concluded that it was Joshua's altar described in Joshua 8:30–31.
- In Joshua 11:11, we read that Joshua "burned Hazor itself." Archaeological digs at the site of Hazor showed that it was indeed burned in approximately 1400 BC.

JUDGES

JUDGES
A New Era under the Judges

Top Ten

1. Women play a key role in the book of Judges. One of them was Deborah, the only woman among the twelve judges of Israel listed in this book.

2. Another key woman in this book was Jael, whose bravery helped Israel defeat the Canaanites. After Sisera, the leader of the Canaanite army, fled a battle in which his soldiers were defeated, he sought refuge in Jael's tent. After he fell asleep, she drove a stake through his head. Not a pretty sight, but remember that it was a matter of self-protection for the Israelites to defeat the Canaanites.

3. After Joshua died, there was a void in governance for Israel. No one was established as the top official, and the twelve tribes were operating without central leadership. This might have worked if the people had kept their promise at Shechem to obey God, but they couldn't keep their minds focused on Him and off the false promises of idolatry. Therefore, anarchy began to reign, and something had to be done.

4. The twelve judges were Othniel, Ehud, Shamgar, Deborah, Gideon, Tola, Jair, Jephthah, Ibzan, Elon, Abdon, and Samson.

5. Judges were in charge in Israel for around 350 years. The longest-serving judge was Ehud, who led for eighty years.

6. The story of Deborah's defeat of Sisera's army—with help from her somewhat reluctant sidekick Barak (see 4:8) and from Jael—is told in a song in Judges 5: "The Song of Deborah."

7. Another of the key judges during this time period was Gideon, who was threshing wheat one day when an angel of the Lord dropped in on him and said, "The LORD is with you, mighty warrior" (6:12). Gideon then went on to lead a small army (300 soldiers) in a defeat of the Midianites (7:15-25).

8. In Numbers 6, we read of the Nazarites, who made a vow of separation. Included in this vow were things such as abstaining from wine and not getting a haircut. In Judges 13, we read about an angel appearing to an Israelite woman. He told her she would have a son and that he should take the Nazarite vow. This was Samson, who famously had long hair. He was the final judge of Israel in this book, and he met his downfall by his association with Delilah.

9. As we can see in Judges 19–21, the era of the Judges was disastrous morally, as "everyone did as he saw fit" (21:25).

Who

Who Wrote It?
One possible writer for the book of Judges is Samuel the prophet, who has been traditionally credited with its composition. However, there is no historical evidence to support that contention.

Who Is in It?
Othniel, Ehud, Shamgar, Deborah, Gideon, Abimelech, Jephthah, Samson, Delilah

What
Under the leadership of Joshua, the Israelites had conquered the Promised Land and established themselves, with ancestral tribes settling into their own territories. Also under the leadership of Joshua, and the direction of God himself, an

entire generation grew old in this new land. After Joshua died, however, things changed.

After Caleb led Israel to a preliminary victory, the Israelites began to lose their edge, beginning in Judges 1:19, which says, "they were unable to drive the people from the plains." Over and over, they failed to do as they were commanded, and that was to rid the region of pagan people: "The Benjamites failed to drive out the Jebusites," (vs. 21); "Manasseh did not drive out the people of Beth Shan," (vs. 27). Little by little, the people began to accept the ways of the Canaanites, including their pagan religious practices. Judges 3:5–6 explains, "The Israelites lived among the Canaanites, Hittites, Amorites, Perizzites, Hivites, and Jebusites. They took their daughters in marriage and gave their daughters to their sons, and served their gods." A pattern developed during this era. The people would disobey God's standards and adopt the idolatrous practices of surrounding people groups. God would bring judgment on the people through enemy nations, and then He would give them a judge to deliver them and lead them to repentance. Then the cycle would start all over.

When

It has been estimated that the judges had jurisdiction over Israel between approximately 1350 until 1050 BC.

Where

The events portrayed in the book of Judges took place throughout the Promised Land. When the book begins, Israel controlled large sections of the land from the southern part of the Dead Sea north to the southern edge of the Jezreel Valley. They also controlled the area west and northwest of the Sea of Galilee, plus land east of the Jordan. However, the geographical problem areas would be the coastal land on the Mediterranean Sea, where cities such as Gezer and Aijalon were not captured (see Judges 1:29, 35), and the Jezreel Valley, where Beth Shan and Megiddo were also not captured (1:27). The failure to subjugate these cities led to the influence of people who worshiped Baal and other false deities.

Why

God kept His promise to the Israelites when He made sure they were able to settle in the Land of Promise. The Israelites, though, did not reciprocate and keep their end of the bargain. Therefore, the book of Judges demonstrates the results of disobedience and turning away from God. It paints a picture of what happens when people of God fail to trust Him and instead turn to idols. Yet God always proves faithful, and He sends the people deliverers who guide them back to the truth. Unfortunately, as Israel continued to do throughout its Old Testament history, it soon turned away from its godly roots and repeated a cycle of disobedience. God showed himself to be merciful, and the Israelites showed themselves to be human.

Wow!

The story of Samson has been retold or referred to in various ways over the years, including in John Milton's "Samson Agonistes," in *Quatrain,* in Benjamin Franklin's *Poor Richard's Almanac*, and even in a song by the Grateful Dead called "Samson and Delilah." There are hundreds of references to the story of Samson and Delilah in poems, art, novels, movies, and songs throughout cultural history.

Worth Remembering

- When the angel of the LORD appeared to Gideon, he said, "The LORD is with you, mighty warrior" (Judges 6:12).
- Gideon said to God, "If you will save Israel by my hand as you have promised—look, I will place a wool fleece on the threshing floor. If there is dew only on the fleece and all the ground is dry, then I will know that you will save Israel by my hand, as you said" (Judges 6:36-37).

- The three companies blew the trumpets and smashed the jars. Grasping the torches in their left hands and holding in their right hands the trumpets they were to blow, they shouted, "A sword for the LORD and for Gideon!" While each man held his position around the camp, all the Midianites ran, crying out as they fled (Judges 7:20-21).
- In those days Israel had no king; everyone did as they saw fit (Judges 21:25).

Wonders from the Past

- An object called the Merneptah Stele, which was made in the land of Egypt, mentions the name Israel, making it the earliest mention of the Hebrews outside the Bible. The stele mentions a battle in which the Egyptians defeated Israel. While this battle is not detailed in Scripture, the mention of the battle, which occurred in 1230 BC, verifies that the Israelites lived in the Promised Land during this time. This battle took place during the time of the judges. The stele was discovered at Thebes, Egypt in 1896.
- Archaeologists who have examined the ruins of cities in Israel have found that beginning in around 1200 BC, there was a change in buildings and pottery. Those changes indicate that a less-advanced culture was replacing one that was more advanced. Charles Fensham says this: "The break is thus obvious and points to seminomadic groups in process of settling down. This evidence is clearly to be connected with the invading Israelite tribes."[5] This quote, from the *International Standard Bible Encyclopedia*, indicates that researchers see the Israelites, who had not developed to a higher level culturally because they had been moving around so much, were supplanting the more advanced Canaanite peoples. This corresponds with the Israelites' conquest of the land.

RUTH
Faithful Ruth Joins the Lineage of Jesus

Top Ten

1. Ruth would become the great grandmother of Israel's King David.
2. Moabites were noted as being a pagan people, yet this story reveals that a Moabite woman was grafted into the family line of Jesus himself.
3. The term "guardian-redeemer" appears nine times in the New International Version of the book of Ruth—always in reference to Boaz. This was a relative who had means and who could be depended upon by other family members in a time of need.
4. Ruth pictures for us what redemption looks like. She rejected her old pagan way and stood strong for her faith by forsaking the old and openly accepting God's love for her and giving Him control over her life. She shined in an era of darkness (the Judges era).
5. The name of Boaz, who can be seen as a type of Christ, meant "strength."
6. Contrasting with the horrific final chapters of Judges, this benign, peaceful love story that follows provides the reader with hope and joy before heading into the complicated stories of Hebrew monarchies.
7. In the Hebrew version of the Old Testament, this book appears after the book of Proverbs. You will notice that Ruth is referred to as a "woman of noble character" (3:11), an appellation that is repeated in Proverbs 31.
8. The chivalrous behavior of Boaz toward Ruth as she visited him in the night is a model for all men as they consider how to treat women (Ruth 3:1-9).

RUTH

9. Take note that the setting for this all-important story in Israel's history is Bethlehem, which plays an integral part in God's story.
10. Ruth's story is a picture of God's grace. According to Deuteronomy 23:3, "a Moabite . . . shall not enter into the assembly of the LORD." God's grace overrides the law—especially when God's plan is in view.

Who

Who Wrote It?
Tradition gives the nod to Samuel for the little book.

Who's in It?
Elimelech, Ruth, Naomi, Orpah, Boaz

What

Who doesn't like this story? It has drama (a family must move across the river in order to get food). It has tragedy (Naomi loses her husband and her sons to death). We don't know the details about these three deaths—perhaps they occur in battle, perhaps they are due to disease, or maybe they are the results of an accident. But we can only imagine the heartbreak and sadness that must accompany these three women. Naomi and Ruth have no means of support as they arrive in Bethlehem, and they must depend on the kindness of others. But God has gone before to set things up for them, and the surprising outcome becomes a flashpoint of joy in the midst of a dark time in Israel's history.

When

Naomi and her family had stayed for ten years in Moab, and we don't know how long they stayed in Bethlehem on their return. We do know that this event took place during the time of the Judges, which was between 1350 and 1050 BC.

Where

As noted above, the story starts in Bethlehem, moves to Moab, and concludes back in Bethlehem.

Why

Naomi and her husband Elimelech have migrated out of the Promised Land, moving from Bethlehem to Moab because of a food shortage. In Moab, they do not find life easy. Naomi loses three family members: her husband and her two sons. There is no peace in Moab. Yet on her return to Israel with her two widowed daughters-in-law, she finds peace. And Ruth finds Boaz. It's a picture of the comfort found in trusting God and staying in fellowship and unity with Him.

Wow!

One of nineteenth-century English Romantic poet John Keats' greatest poems is "Ode to a Nightingale." This poem contains this reference to Ruth: "Perhaps the self-same song that found a path/ Through the sad heart of Ruth, when, sick for home/ She stood in tears amid the alien corn."

Worth Remembering

- When Naomi heard in Moab that the LORD had come to the aid of his people by providing food for them, she and her daughters-in-law prepared to return home from there (Ruth 1:6).
- But Ruth replied, "Don't urge me to leave you or to turn back from you. Where you go I will go, and where you stay I will stay. Your people will be my people and your God my God" (Ruth 1:16).
- So the two women went on until they came to Bethlehem. When they arrived in Bethlehem, the whole town was stirred because of them, and the women exclaimed, "Can this be Naomi?" (Ruth 1:19).

RUTH

- "When he lies down, note the place where he is lying. Then go and uncover his feet and lie down. He will tell you what to do" (Ruth 3:4).
- "I have also acquired Ruth the Moabite, Mahlon's widow, as my wife, in order to maintain the name of the dead with his property, so that his name will not disappear from among his family or from his hometown. Today you are witnesses!" (Ruth 4:10).
- The women said to Naomi: "Praise be to the LORD, who this day has not left you without a guardian-redeemer. May he become famous throughout Israel!" (Ruth 4:14).

Wonders from the Past

In Hebron is a tomb referred to as the tomb of Ruth. Some believe Ruth's grandson Jesse is buried there as well.

1 SAMUEL

Israel Asks for a King

Top Ten

1. The name Samuel means "the name of God."
2. First and Second Samuel were at one time joined as one book. In the Septuagint (earliest Greek translation of Hebrew Scriptures), they were divided into two parts and were referred to as "The First and Second Book of Kingdoms."
3. Samuel was one of seven people in the Bible God calls by name (the other six are Abraham, Jacob, Moses, Martha, Simon, and Saul).
4. Samuel had long hair (1 Samuel 1:11).
5. Samuel was the last judge of Israel.

6. Samuel was the first prophet of Israel during this post-Moses era. As such, he was God's choice to anoint the first two kings: Saul and David.
7. Samuel represents the transition of Israel from a country led by judges to one led by a king.
8. A number of interesting events take place in 1 Samuel:
   a. Samuel's mother releases him to serve the priest.
   b. The Philistines capture the Ark of the Covenant, but it is eventually brought back to Israel.
   c. Israel asks God for a king, and He relents.
   d. Saul, who looks like a king, is anointed as the first monarch of Israel. After he fails, David, who was anointed when he was just a shepherd boy, replaces him.
9. After a great victory over the Philistines, Samuel offered a sacrifice to God in front of his people. Then he "took a stone and set it up" as a memorial. He named it Ebenezer, and he said, "Thus far the LORD has helped us" (7:12). The location of this monument, Mizpah, was north of Samuel's birthplace in Ramah.
10. Samuel was a priest, a prophet, and a judge.

Who

Who Wrote It?
While Samuel has been credited with writing 1 and 2 Samuel, he could not have done so, as his death is recorded in 1 Samuel 25:1. Other candidates for penman of this book and 2 Samuel are Gad and Nathan (see 1 Chronicles 29:29).

Who's in It?
Hannah, Elkanah, Peninnah, Eli, Hophni, Phinehas, Samuel, Dagon, Abinadab, Joel, Abijah, Kish, Saul, David

1 SAMUEL

What

This book marked the end of the theocracy—when God was the head of the land—and the beginning of the monarchy, when a human king would lead the nation. Samuel became the last of the judges of Israel, but the people wanted a king, so Samuel anointed tall, good-looking Saul for that position. Saul and the next anointed king, David, had a rocky relationship because of Saul's jealousy of the young king-in-waiting. Eventually, Saul's monarchy went from good to bad to worse—and he eventually killed himself instead of facing defeat on the battlefield.

When

Samuel was written somewhere around 1000 BC. Saul was king of Israel from 1051 to 1011, and David was king from 1011 until 971.

Where

The action eventually moves to Jerusalem after David becomes king and makes it Israel's capital city. Before that, the events of 1 Samuel take place in various locations.

Why

The purpose of the books of Samuel is to reveal Israel's transition period from judges to kings. While telling that story, the book arrives in chapter 16 at the central character of Israel's story: David.

Wow!

- The story of the battle between David and Goliath has spawned hundreds of comparisons—in sports, in politics, in almost every field. Examples: In the late 1960s, Ford beat Ferrari in three straight Le Mans races. In 1934–40, Finland outbattled Russia in a war, though outnumbered by a four-to-one ratio. In 1980, the U.S. hockey team beat the Soviet Union in the Winter Olympics in a match between grizzled vets (the Soviets) and untested college players (the Americans).

1 SAMUEL

- Some of the greatest sculptures of all time were depictions of David (by Donatello, Michelangelo, and Bernini).
- In 1876, Samuel Tilden ran for president against Rutherford B. Hayes. Tilden began using the phrase "The Lord called Samuel," from 1 Samuel 3:4, as his campaign slogan.

Worth Remembering

- "There is no one holy like the LORD; there is no one besides you; there is no Rock like our God" (1 Samuel 2:2).
- So Samuel said to all the Israelites, "If you are returning to the LORD with all your hearts, then rid yourselves of the foreign gods and the Ashtoreths and commit yourselves to the LORD and serve him only, and he will deliver you out of the hand of the Philistines" (1 Samuel 7:3).
- Samuel summoned the people of Israel to the LORD at Mizpah and said to them, "This is what the LORD, the God of Israel, says: 'I brought Israel up out of Egypt, and I delivered you from the power of Egypt and all the kingdoms that oppressed you.' But you have now rejected your God, who saves you out of all your disasters and calamities. And you have said, 'No, appoint a king over us.' So now present yourselves before the LORD by your tribes and clans" (1 Samuel 10:17–19).
- "If you fear the LORD and serve and obey him and do not rebel against his commands, and if both you and the king who reigns over you follow the LORD your God—good!" (1 Samuel 12:14)
- "Do not be afraid," Samuel replied. "You have done all this evil; yet do not turn away from the LORD, but serve the LORD with all your heart" (1 Samuel 12:20).
- But Samuel replied: "Does the LORD delight in burnt offerings and sacrifices as much as in obeying the LORD? To obey is better than sacrifice, and to heed is better than the fat of rams" (1 Samuel 15:22).

1 SAMUEL

- "All those gathered here will know that it is not by sword or spear that the LORD saves; for the battle is the LORD's, and he will give all of you into our hands" (1 Samuel 17:47).
- David was greatly distressed because the men were talking of stoning him; each one was bitter in spirit because of his sons and daughters. But David found strength in the LORD his God (1 Samuel 30:6).

Wonders from the Past

- In 2015, a team of archaeologists found what they believe are the city gates to Gath, the city of Goliath. Two inscriptions at the site include names similar to the name Goliath.
- Three archaeological discoveries have revealed inscriptions with the name of David on them: the Tel Dan Stele, the Mesha Inscription, and an Egyptian inscription that refers to a place in the Negev called "the heights of David." More information can be found in the article "53 People in the Bible Confirmed Archaeologically" at biblicalarchaeology.org.

2 SAMUEL

The Story of King David

Top Ten

1. Second Samuel is in many ways a biography of David as an adult. As we read about David, we see how Jerusalem became the capital of the kingdom and what the Davidic Covenant is all about.
2. At the beginning of 2 Samuel, Israel is without a king. Saul had taken his own life on the battlefield, making way for David, whom Samuel had anointed, to ascend to the throne of Israel.

3. David's poetic prowess is shown in his lament for Saul in 2 Samuel 1:19–27.

4. David was made the new king of Israel at Hebron. He was thirty years old at the time.

5. Forces loyal to the late king, Saul, put together a contingent of soldiers to go up against the new king, David. David's forces won, ensuring his control over the whole land.

6. The city of Jerusalem was under the control of the Jebusites when David became king. It is apparent that David attacked Jerusalem by means of a water tunnel, routing the Jebusites and establishing Jerusalem as the City of David. This took place around 1000 BC.

7. One of David's key goals was bringing the Ark of the Covenant to Jerusalem. As it was being taken there, it was mishandled and a man named Uzzah died. This angered King David. The ark remained at the home of Obed-Edom for three months before it was finally taken to Jerusalem (6:1–15).

8. The Lord makes a covenant with David, promising to build a house (meaning a royal dynasty that will last forever) and a kingdom forever (see 2 Samuel 7). After hearing this covenant, David worships God in humility.

9. David's rule unifies Israel, and all goes well—until David sins grievously with Bathsheba (see 11–12:25).

10. Things turn against David after his sin. He faces a coup by his son Absalom, degradation by other family members, and a rebellion by the ten tribes located in the northern part of Israel.

Who

Who Wrote It?

While we don't know who wrote 1 and 2 Samuel, we do know some of the writer's sources. In 2 Samuel 1:18, we read of a document called the Book of Jashar. Also, 1 Chronicles 27:24

mentions the annals of King David, and in 1 Chronicles 29:29, the author mentions the records of Gad, Nathan, and Samuel.

Who's in It?
David, Abigail, Abner, Joab, Amnon, Absalom, Adonijah, Michal, Uzzah, Obed-Edom, Nathan, Bathsheba

What

Because 1 and 2 Samuel were originally recorded as one scroll, it is logical that the story that ends with the conclusion of 1 Samuel continues into 2 Samuel. Second Samuel records the pertinent events of David's forty-year reign over Israel. Also supremely important to the overall story of the Bible is the Davidic Covenant, which we read about in 2 Samuel. We see David as both a benevolent and wise leader who leads in completing Israel's takeover of the Promised Land, and as a major sinner in the episode with Bathsheba and Uriah. Before the Bathsheba incident, David's reign was mostly smooth sailing; afterward, his kingdom was fraught with difficulties.

When

After Saul's death around 1010 BC, David ruled for forty years—from 1011–971.

Where

At the beginning of David's reign, Israel's capital was Hebron, which is south and west of Jerusalem. He reigned at Hebron for seven and a half years. David picked a challenging target when he set his sights on Jerusalem for the capital. Neither the tribes of Judah nor the tribes of Benjamin had been able to wrest it from the Jebusites. But David figured out a way to beat the Jebusites and take Jerusalem. The kingdom of Israel under David stretched from Beersheba in the south to Dan in the north.

Why

Perhaps it is best to see the book of 2 Samuel in light of two very different ideas. First, David showed the wisdom of waiting on the Lord and trusting Him. He didn't rush into becoming king after Saul died. When he was declared king of Judah (chapter 2), he launched a civil war that eventually led to his becoming king of Israel as well (chapter 5). He was patient in taking the crown for which he had been anointed so long before. Second, David found out the truth of this statement: "Be sure your sin will find you out" (Numbers 32:23). David was the king, but he was not above the disastrous consequences of his sin: great trouble brought on his family for years to follow.

Wow!

- William Faulkner's novel *Absalom! Absalom!* incorporated the conflict between David and Absalom as the basis for his Civil War father-son tale.
- Madeleine L'Engle used the story of David and his wives as the basis for her book *Certain Women*. L'Engle's most famous work was *A Wrinkle in Time*.

Worth Remembering

- "When your days are over and you rest with your ancestors, I will raise up your offspring to succeed you, your own flesh and blood, and I will establish his kingdom. He is the one who will build a house for my Name, and I will establish the throne of his kingdom forever" (2 Samuel 7:12–13).
- "How great you are, Sovereign LORD! There is no one like you, and there is no God but you, as we have heard with our own ears" (2 Samuel 7:22).
- "You, LORD, are my lamp; the LORD turns my darkness into light" (2 Samuel 22:29).

- "As for God, his way is perfect: The LORD'S word is flawless; he shields all who take refuge in him" (2 Samuel 22:31).
- "For who is God besides the LORD? And who is the Rock except our God?" (2 Samuel 22:32).

Wonders from the Past

- Archaeologists have discovered the water tunnels David probably used to get into the city of Jerusalem to take it from the Jebusites. The tunnels have been studied for well over 100 years.
- Archaeologists in Dan, in the far northern regions of Israel, unearthed physical evidence of David's existence as king. A stone stele was discovered that includes the words "the house of David."

1 KINGS
Solomon Reigns in Israel

Top Ten

1. Just as was true of 1 and 2 Samuel, 1 and 2 Kings at one time joined as one book of the Bible.
2. In 1 Kings, we will see the kingdom divided into two parts: Israel, the Northern Kingdom, and Judah, the Southern Kingdom.
3. As 1 Kings begins, one of David's sons, Adonijah, attempts to take the throne as king. Problem was, David had already promised the throne to Solomon. The prophet Nathan and David's wife Bathsheba confronted David about this—and the king quickly anointed Solomon, ending Adonijah's attempt to be king.

4. One of the most famous scenes in 1 Kings is Solomon's ruling regarding the two women who both claimed to be a child's mother (see 3:16-28).
5. The wisdom of Solomon, as described in 4:29–34, is legendary.
6. One of the most monumental events recorded in 1 Kings is the construction of Solomon's temple. David proposed building the temple during his reign, but God declared that Solomon would be the one to do it.
7. In addition, Solomon built a magnificent palace, which took thirteen years to construct.
8. The Queen of Sheba, who had heard about Solomon's wealth, dropped in for a visit with the Hebrew king.
9. After the death of Solomon at the end of his forty-year reign in Israel (11:41-43), the kingdom was divided. The rest of 1 Kings recounts the records of a number of kings who followed Solomon.
10. First Kings introduces readers to two of Israel's greatest prophets: Elijah and Elisha.

Who

Who Wrote It?
There is no byline for 1 Kings; no one is sure who wrote it. One possible candidate is Jeremiah. It was probably written in the mid-500s BC. It has been speculated that the audience for the book we call Kings was the people of Israel who had been sent into exile. It gave them an explanation for what happened: that the exile came about because of the people's disobedience. They could see through this story what a magnificent temple and nation Solomon had built—only to see it fall apart because they failed to do what God told them.

Who's in It?
Adonijah, Nathan, David, Bathsheba, Solomon, Hiram (king of Tyre), Huram (skilled craftsman for the temple), Queen of

1 KINGS

Sheba, Jeroboam (king of Israel), Rehoboam (king of Judah), Abijah (king of Judah), Asa* (king of Judah), Nabab (king of Israel), Baasha (king of Israel), Elah (king of Israel), Zimri (king of Israel), Omri (king of Israel), Ahab (king of Israel), Elijah, Elisha, Naboth, Jehoshaphat* (king of Judah), Jehoram (king of Judah), Ahaziah (king of Judah)

Good kings of Judah

What

As 1 Kings begins, Israel's second king, David, is elderly and bedridden. David's fourth son, Adonijah, nearly took the throne as the third king, but, fortunately for Solomon, Nathan and Solomon's mother Bathsheba got wind of Adonijah's attempt to nab the crown. They marched into David's bedroom and made sure Solomon became the monarch. The book then follows Solomon's reign, his construction projects, his wisdom, his administrative prowess, and, finally, his death. The rest of the of the book details how the kingdom of Israel split into two lands—Israel and Judah—and recounts the lives of the kings who followed Solomon. It is a fascinating look at a key portion of Israel's history.

When

The events of 1 Kings took place between 970 and 586 BC, which ties into the idea of the exiles reading a history of their people—explaining what happened to Judah and Israel before the people were dispersed (Northern Kingdom) and carried off into exile (Southern Kingdom). This record, which the exiles in Babylon may have read while in that foreign land, would have reminded them why they were in the situation they were in. God was powerful and loving, yet He could no longer tolerate the disobedience they read about in these two books of the kings.

Where

The main events of 1 Kings happened in the vicinity of Jerusalem. The temple, however, was not built inside the City of David. It was constructed on a hill north of the city called Mount Moriah. Also, geography played a part in the visit of the Queen of Sheba. She traveled from Egypt to Jerusalem to see what the fuss over Solomon was all about. In addition, Solomon carried out trade with far-flung nations—expanding the reach of Israel. Jeroboam also changed history with his geographical decision. He opened up centers for the false worship of golden calves in Dan and Bethel so the people of the Northern Kingdom would not have to worship at Jerusalem.

Why

In 1 Kings, we get the picture of what happens when kings obey God's laws . . . and what happens when they disobey—and how either decision carries down to the citizens. This will be a pattern to watch all the way through to the Babylonian Captivity. Solomon was by no means perfect, but he established a great nation with a strong reputation in the region. He asked for and received wisdom, which led to much good happening in the country. However, the book of Kings explains that many of the kings who followed Solomon did evil in God's eyes. The pattern of disobedience begins with the kings of 1 Kings. (For instance, 1 Kings 15:3 tells us, "[Abijah] committed all the sins his father had done before him.") We know of Jeroboam's revolt against the right kind of worship (1 Kings 12), and we see the actions of Ahab, who killed a good man (Naboth) just to get his vineyards. The prophets Elijah and Elisha did all they could to counter the evil of the monarchs.

Wow!

- In the 1950 movie *King Solomon's Mines* (and the 1985 remake), adventurer Allan Quartermain sets out to find the legendary diamond mines of King Solomon. The movie was based on a novel by H. Rider Haggard.
- In the same vein, researchers have long believed that Solomon had mines for diamonds or gold or other highly

1 KINGS

valuable materials—and some have been searching for those mines in various regions in the Middle East and Africa.

- In Herman Melville's novel *Moby Dick*, a mysterious man named Elijah gives Ishmael a warning to beware of Captain Ahab. This seems to be an allusion to the biblical story of Elijah warning King Ahab (1 Kings 18:16-19).

Worth Remembering

- Now Adonijah, whose mother was Haggith, put himself forward and said, "I will be king." So he got chariots and horses ready, with fifty men to run ahead of him. (His father had never rebuked him by asking, "Why do you behave as you do?" He was also very handsome and was born next after Absalom.) (1 Kings 1:5-6).
- Then Nathan asked Bathsheba, Solomon's mother, "Have you not heard that Adonijah, the son of Haggith, has become king, and our lord David knows nothing about it?" (1 Kings 1:11).
- "Observe what the LORD your God requires: Walk in obedience to him, and keep his decrees and commands, his laws and regulations, as written in the Law of Moses. Do this so that you may prosper in all you do and wherever you go" (1 Kings 2:3).
- In building the temple, only blocks dressed at the quarry were used, and no hammer, chisel or any other iron tool was heard at the temple site while it was being built (1 Kings 6:7).
- When the priests withdrew from the Holy Place, the cloud filled the temple of the LORD (1 Kings 8:10).
- Now Elijah the Tishbite, from Tishbe in Gilead, said to Ahab, "As the LORD, the God of Israel, lives, whom I serve, there will be neither dew nor rain in the next few years except at my word" (1 Kings 17:1).

- "Now summon the people from all over Israel to meet me on Mount Carmel. And bring the four hundred and fifty prophets of Baal and the four hundred prophets of Asherah, who eat at Jezebel's table" (1 Kings 18:19).

Wonders from the Past

- First Kings says that Solomon built cities outside of Jerusalem (9:15). Recent archaeologic digs at Hazor, Megiddo, and Gezer have revealed buildings that could have housed Solomon's horses and chariots, as mentioned in 10:26, 28. Each of these locations has gates similar to the ones Solomon had built at his palace. Archaeologists surmise that Solomon's men built those three cities, just as Scripture indicates.
- The city of Megiddo (as mentioned above) was one of the key cities Solomon rebuilt or refortified. Later, Ahab also had Megiddo strengthened (1 Kings 22:39 mentions Ahab's work, which archaeologists have concluded included Megiddo). Among the things Ahab had done there was to dig a deep water shaft and a long water tunnel. The shaft can still be seen at Tel Megiddo in the Jezreel Valley of Israel. Megiddo is a key biblical archaeological research area in the country.

2 KINGS

Two Kingdoms: Divided and Conquered

Top Ten

1. As noted earlier, the division of the book of Kings into two parts was arbitrary. The writers of the Septuagint divided the scroll into two sections because it was simply more convenient to have two scrolls instead of one.

2. In 2 Kings, we are introduced to twenty-eight different kings—the final dozen kings of Israel (Northern Kingdom) and the final sixteen kings of Judah (Southern Kingdom). *The kings of Israel*: Ahaziah, Joram, Jehu, Jehoahaz, Jehoash, Jeroboam II, Zechariah, Shallum, Menahem, Pekahiah, Pekah, Hoshea. *The kings of Judah*: Jehoram, Ahaziah, Athaliah, Joash, Amaziah, Azariah, Jotham, Ahaz, Hezekiah, Manasseh, Amon, Josiah, Jehoahaz, Jehoiakim, Jehoiachin, Zedekiah.

3. All twelve kings of Israel are noted as being evil. They all followed the idolatrous ways of King Jeroboam, who set up two places to worship golden calves—one at Bethel and one at Dan (see 1 Kings 12:28-30).

4. Of the kings of Judah mentioned in 2 Kings, seven were considered good: Jehoshaphat, Joash, Amaziah, Azariah, Jotham, Hezekiah, and Josiah.

5. One of the most fascinating images in 2 Kings is the depiction of Elijah being taken to heaven in what appeared to be a chariot of fire (see 2 Kings 2).

6. Four miracles performed through Elisha are recorded in 2 Kings 4: he poured oil endlessly from a poor woman's pots; he raised the Shunammite woman's son from the dead; he used flour to make a poisonous pot of stew safe to eat; he fed a hundred people with a small portion of bread.

7. Among the most interesting stories in 2 Kings is the account of Namaan, who was healed of leprosy by washing in the Jordan River.

8. One of the most endearing stories in 2 Kings is the discovery of the Book of the Law during a repair of the temple. King Josiah led the people of Judah in a revival that came as a result of this discovery and the subsequent reading of the law.

9. The last king of the Northern Kingdom of Israel was the evil Hoshea. Even though the prophets Micah, Hosea,

and Isaiah tried to warn Israel, the people refused to repent—and thus they fell to the marauding Assyrians.

10. The story of Judah's captivity at the hands of the Babylonians is also recorded in 2 Kings. Chapter 25 gives the account of the Babylonian siege of Jerusalem. King Zedekiah tried to escape, but he was captured and blinded by the Babylonians. The people of Judah were then led to captivity in Babylon.

Who

Who Wrote It?

As with 1 Kings, there is no byline for 2 Kings, so no one is sure who wrote it. One possible candidate is the prophet Jeremiah. It was probably written in the mid-500s BC. It has been speculated that the audience for book we call Kings was the people of Israel who had been sent into exile. It gave them an explanation for what happened: that the exile came about because of their disobedience. They could see through this story what a magnificent temple and nation Solomon had built—and how it fell apart because they had failed to do what God told them.

Who's in It?

Jehoshaphat (king of Judah), Ahaziah (king of Judah), Elijah, Elisha, Joram (king of Israel), Mesha (king of Moab), Naaman, Jehoram (king of Judah), Ahaziah (king of Judah), Jehu (king of Israel), Athaliah (ruler of Judah), Joash (king of Judah), Jehoahaz (king of Israel), Jehoash (king of Israel), Amaziah (king of Judah), Jeroboam II (king of Israel), Azariah (king of Judah), Zechariah (king of Israel), Shallum (king of Israel), Menahem (king of Israel), Pekahiah (king of Israel), Pekah (king of Israel), Jotham (king of Judah), Ahaz (king of Judah), Hoshea (last king of Israel), Hezekiah (king of Judah), Sennacherib (king of Assyria), Manasseh (king of Judah), Anon (king of Judah), Josiah (king of Judah), Jehoahaz (king of Judah), Jehoiakim (king of

2 KINGS

Judah), Jehoiachin (king of Judah), Zedekiah (king of Judah), Nebuchanezzar (king of Babylon)

What

As might be expected, this book is about kings—lots of them: twenty-eight in all. Interspersed with the stories of the kings of both the Northern Kingdom and the Southern Kingdom are accounts of others, such as Elijah, Elisha, and Naaman. What we see happening in 2 Kings is the demise of the great kingdom God had provided for His people. He had taken them through the wilderness and then allowed them to establish themselves throughout the land. All the tribes (except the Levites) were given land, and prosperity was theirs. But little by little, the whole thing came crashing down because of corrupt leaders and equally corrupt followers. From the grand kingdoms of David and Solomon to the disastrous endings of Zedekiah and Hoshea, we see this great people crash into destruction and captivity.

When

The time period for the records of the last twenty-eight kings of Israel/Judah is about 250 years (850–586 BC). The Northern Kingdom lasts about 130 years—until Assyria carries off the people and the ten tribes of Israel are dispersed. The Southern Kingdom lasts those 130 years and another 120 or so before Babylon takes the people into captivity.

Where

The events that take place in 2 Kings are a cartographer's dream. These things happen throughout the Promised Land. We have both kingdoms operating with their three religious capitals: Jerusalem for Judah and Dan (in the north) and Bethel (in the south) for Israel. Also, if you were to follow the exploits of Elijah and Elisha, you would also need a map. In 2 Kings 2 alone, they travel from Gilgal to Bethel to Jericho to the Jordan River. And just east of the Jordan, Elijah goes to heaven in his fiery chariot. Then Elisha goes north to Shunem, where he raises a boy from

2 KINGS

the dead. Then back to Gilgal. The final events of the two kingdoms in 2 Kings come as the result of attacks from Assyria to the north and Babylon to the northeast.

Why

As with 1 Kings, this book details—probably for the returning captives from Babylon—the history of the kingdom from Solomon through the two invasions of the land. Again, we can assume that the record was meant to remind the people why judgment had fallen on them—the idolatry, the acceptance of the religions of other people groups, and the disobedience of the kings and their subjects. In the middle of all that, there were hints at righteousness (Elijah and Elisha, as well as the good kings of Judah). The record was clear: righteousness is rewarded and disobedience leads to destruction.

Wow!

- Probably the most famous allusion to 2 Kings in recent popular culture is the title of the movie *Chariots of Fire*, which tells the story of Scottish sprinter Eric Liddell. Also, in his poem "Jerusalem," poet William Blake included the line "Bring me my Chariot of fire," which became part of a British hymn. The references came from 2 Kings 2:11 and 6:17.
- William Golding's classic novel *Lord of the Flies* gets its title from the term "Beelzebub" or "Baal-Zebub" (2 Kings 1:2-3), a deity the Philistines worshiped. In the book, the Lord of the Flies was the head of a slain pig.
- English poet Lord Byron's poem "The Destruction of Sennacherib" is based on 2 Kings 18–19, which tells of Assyria's capture of Jerusalem.

Worth Remembering

- But the angel of the LORD said to Elijah the Tishbite, "Go up and meet the messengers of the king of Samaria and

2 KINGS

ask them, 'Is it because there is no God in Israel that you are going off to consult Baal-Zebub, the god of Ekron?'" (2 Kings 1:3).

- Elijah answered the captain, "If I am a man of God, may fire come down from heaven and consume you and your fifty men!" Then fire fell from heaven and consumed the captain and his men (2 Kings 1:10).
- When the LORD was about to take Elijah up to heaven in a whirlwind, Elijah and Elisha were on their way from Gilgal (2 Kings 2:1).
- Elijah took his cloak, rolled it up and struck the water with it. The water divided to the right and to the left, and the two of them crossed over on dry ground (2 Kings 2:8).
- As they were walking along and talking together, suddenly a chariot of fire and horses of fire appeared and separated the two of them, and Elijah went up to heaven in a whirlwind. Elisha saw this and cried out, "My father! My father! The chariots and horsemen of Israel!" And Elisha saw him no more. Then he took hold of his garment and tore it in two (2 Kings 2:11–12).
- When all the jars were full, she said to her son, "Bring me another one." But he replied, "There is not a jar left." Then the oil stopped flowing (2 Kings 4:6).
- When Elisha reached the house, there was the boy lying dead on his couch. He went in, shut the door on the two of them and prayed to the LORD (2 Kings 4:32–33).
- Now Naaman was commander of the army of the king of Aram. He was a great man in the sight of his master and highly regarded, because through him the LORD had given victory to Aram. He was a valiant soldier, but he had leprosy (2 Kings 5:1).
- Now Elisha had been suffering from the illness from which he died. Jehoash king of Israel went down to see him and wept over him. "My father! My father!" he cried. "The chariots and horsemen of Israel!" (2 Kings 13:14).

2 KINGS

- So the LORD was very angry with Israel and removed them from his presence. Only the tribe of Judah was left (2 Kings 17:18).

Wonders from the Past

- In 1868, missionary Frederick Augustus Klein discovered the Mesha Stele, sometimes called the Moabite Stone, in Jordan. The stele has a carved inscription that tells a story that parallels one told in 2 Kings 3:4–8. This stone contains the earliest reference outside the Bible to the Hebrew God Yahweh.
- In 2 Kings 8:7–15, we read the story of how Hazael arose to the throne of Syria. Or we could read an inscription from Shalmaneser III, king of Assyria. His words are found on the Black Obelisk of Shalmaneser III, which was discovered in 1846 in what is now Iraq. It now resides in the British Museum in London.
- In the mid-nineteenth century, the Tiglath-Pileser III inscriptions were unearthed in northern Iraq. Among the inscriptions is a reference to what 2 Kings 17:3 describes: tributes by Hoshea, the evil king of Israel, paid to the king of Assyria.

1 CHRONICLES
David's Reign Revisited

Top Ten

1. The title of the book of Chronicles (again, divided into two books, although written as one) comes from the Vulgate (Latin) version of the Old Testament: *Liber Chronicorum*.
2. First Chronicles 6:15 indicates that this book was written after the Babylonian Exile.

3. The first nine chapters of 1 Chronicles is a fascinating list of names—from Adam all the way to Azel.

4. Think of what it means that at this late date in Old Testament-era Jewish history (about 400 BC), there is a record of families from Adam to that day. Not all people and families are included, but the ones listed were real people—many mentioned in other Scripture passages—and careful records were kept of them. This book is a personal, historically accurate record.

5. The basic story of 1 Chronicles is nearly the same as the one presented in 2 Samuel, so you might notice a bit of a repeat as you read 1 Chronicles.

6. One of the differences between 2 Samuel and 1 Chronicles is that the person (or persons) who wrote 1 Chronicles did not include the sordid stories of the kings of Israel, all of whom were considered evil in God's eyes. Also, there is no retelling of David's sin with Bathsheba or Solomon's problem of having foreign wives.

7. The writer of 1 Chronicles gave short shrift to Saul—not even calling him the king. First Chronicles 10:13–14 presents a bleak picture of Saul.

8. First Chronicles 16 includes multiple references to passages in the book of Psalms: Psalm 96, Psalm 105, and Psalm 106.

9. One of the strangest stories in 1 Chronicles is David's ill-begotten idea of taking a census of the people. Clearly, this was not God's plan (see 1 Chronicles 21:1), and one of David's key leaders, Joab, thought it was a dumb idea. But Joab did as he was told, traveling from Dan in the north to Beersheba in the south to count up more than a million sword-handling men. David was punished for carrying through on this wasteful idea.

10. First Chronicles 22–29 gives information that is not repeated from an earlier book of the Bible. It shows David's intense involvement in the upcoming temple, even though he cannot build it.

Who

Who wrote it?
Ezra is sometimes mentioned as a possible writer of the
Chronicles. However, because of the emphasis on the priestly
roles of the people, others suggest that a Levite could have
written it.

Who's in It?
First Chronicles includes an extensive genealogy. In it you'll see
lots of familiar names: Adam, Noah, Ham, Nimrod, Abraham,
Isaac, Reuben and his brothers, Caleb, Saul, David, Solomon—
and on it goes.

What

This is another retelling of the history of Israel for the returning
Hebrews after their time in Babylon came to a close. This
shortened version of the history emphasizes a more positive
approach. Thus, some of the bad stories and people are not
rehashed. First Chronicles emphasizes temple worship, which
might be an encouragement for the returning people to
reestablish their worship in Jerusalem. Also, this book reminds
the people of the Davidic Covenant, which could also encourage
them by reminding them of God's promises.

When

The genealogies take readers all the way back to Adam and moves
them into the time period of King David. The book ends with
the death of David after his forty-year reign. Therefore, the actual
time period for the book from chapters 10 through 29 is from
1050 to 971 BC.

Where

Technically, the beginning location is the garden of Eden, and the
narrative moves through all the places the people of the genealogies
lived and to Jerusalem, where David established his throne.

Why

Upon returning home, the Babylonian captives need encouragement. They can see it in their genealogies, in the positive influence of David, and in the excitement about the new temple that is to be constructed in the next installment of this narrative. The people have returned to a land where the walls of their capital had been torn down and the temple destroyed. As they saw their city reconstructed, they needed to see that God's hand would be on them as it was on David and that His promises would still hold true for them. They needed a reminder of how God was to be worshiped.

Wow!

One of the most successful books in Christian publishing was *The Prayer of Jabez*, which took an obscure prayer from 1 Chronicles 4:10 and turned it into a bestseller. According to published reports, more than ten million copies of *The Prayer of Jabez* were sold, putting it in the top five of Christian bestsellers of all time (the Bible not included).

Worth Remembering

- All Israel came together to David at Hebron and said, "We are your own flesh and blood. In the past, even while Saul was king, you were the one who led Israel on their military campaigns. And the LORD your God said to you, 'You will shepherd my people Israel, and you will become their ruler'" (1 Chronicles 11:1–2).
- Let the trees of the forest sing, let them sing for joy before the LORD, for he comes to judge the earth (1 Chronicles 16:33).
- "I will be his father, and he will be my son. I will never take my love away from him, as I took it away from your predecessor. I will set him over my house and my kingdom forever; his throne will be established forever" (1 Chronicles 17:13–14).

- David said to Gad, "I am in deep distress. Let me fall into the hands of the LORD, for his mercy is very great; but do not let me fall into human hands" (1 Chronicles 21:13).
- "Yours, LORD, is the greatness and the power and the glory and the majesty and the splendor, for everything in heaven and earth is yours. Yours, LORD, is the kingdom; you are exalted as head over all" (1 Chronicles 29:11).

Wonders from the Past

In the 1980s, a stepped-stone structure was discovered at an archaeological site near the City of David. It may have been the original wall of the oldest part of Jerusalem—perhaps built by the Jebusites, whom David conquered to turn the city into the Hebrew capital.

2 CHRONICLES

From the Heights of Solomon's Reign to the Fall of Jerusalem

Top Ten

1. The book of 2 Chronicles parallels 1 and 2 Kings.
2. Second Chronicles reviews the history of Judah but does not mention the Northern Kingdom.
3. As the book begins, Solomon goes to the tabernacle located in Gibeon in order to worship. This was the building he was going to replace with the new temple. At the tabernacle, he offered a thousand burnt offerings.
4. Later on the night Solomon offered the thousand burnt offerings, God told him to ask for whatever he wanted. He asked for wisdom, which God granted him in abundance.
5. The workforce enlisted to build the temple included seventy thousand carriers of building materials,

eighty thousand stone cutters, and thirty-six hundred foremen.

6. The location of the temple was full of history: it was constructed on Mount Moriah, where Abraham took Isaac to sacrifice him (see Genesis 22:1–19), and it was the location of the threshing floor David had acquired (see 2 Samuel 24:18–25).

7. One interesting fact mentioned in 2 Chronicles 5:10 is that the only item in the Ark of the Covenant was Moses' tablets from Mount Sinai. At one time, the ark contained a jar of manna and Aaron's rod that budded, but for some reason, those latter two items had been removed.

8. Beyond the entrance of the ark and its transferal to the Holy Place, an even more wondrous event followed. After 120 priests played their trumpets and singers sang in unison in praise to God, the temple was "filled with a cloud." It was the glory of the Lord (see 5:12–14). That had to be a *Wow!* moment for all of Judah.

9. Another magnificent spectacle had to be the visit to Jerusalem of the Queen of Sheba. Solomon put on a grand welcome for her, so grand that "she was overwhelmed" (9:4). And we can guess the citizens of Jerusalem were a bit swept away as well.

10. About a hundred years later, during the reign of Joash, the temple needed repairs. Joash collected funds throughout the land and hired workmen to restore the temple to its splendor of a hundred years earlier.

Who

Who wrote it?
Ezra is sometimes mentioned as a possible writer of the Chronicles. Because of the emphasis on the priestly roles of the people, others suggest that a Levite could have written it.

Who's in It?

Solomon, Asa (king of Judah), Jehoshaphat (king of Judah), Joash (king of Judah), Hezekiah (king of Judah), Josiah (king of Judah)

What

The narrative of 2 Chronicles details some key events in the life of King Solomon, including his request for wisdom and his leadership in building the temple. We see the spectacle of the visit by the Queen of Sheba, and then we read of Solomon's death after his forty-year reign. The book then turns to the stories of several other kings of Judah—stories we also read in 1 and 2 Kings. At the conclusion of the book, the story of the fall of Jerusalem at the hands of Nebuchadnezzar is told, as well as the edict from Cyrus that allowed the Jews to return home seventy years later.

When

Solomon became king in 971 BC. The Babylonian Captivity began in 586, and the return came seventy years later.

Where

Because 2 Chronicles tells the stories of various kings of Judah, most of the book takes place in Jerusalem. There was a battle with the king of Egypt during Rehoboam's reign, and Jehoshaphat did battle in Moab and Ammon during his time as king. Plus, the people were carried off to Babylon after Nebuchadnezzar sacked Jerusalem in 586.

Why

The second section of the Chronicles scrolls, which we call 2 Chronicles, reminds us of the pattern that so famously marks not only the people of Israel but so many of us today. The book begins on a high note, with true devotion to God as Solomon strives to build a temple that honors God. Then we see a decline from honoring God in chapters 10 through 23—which leads to a departure from the Lord. Finally, the sad story of the Babylonian Exile results. The book again reminds its audience to stay true to God and not waver.

Wow!

Of all the images presented in 2 Chronicles, the one that has attracted the most attention is the arrival of the Queen of Sheba to Jerusalem to see Solomon. From medieval times to more modern days, it has been a popular scene for artists. The scene is represented in a twelfth-century stained glass representation in Canterbury Cathedral. Also, in the Nuremberg Bible of 1483 is artwork called *The Queen of Sheba visits Solomon with a view of Jerusalem*.

Worth Remembering

- Now David had brought up the ark of God from Kiriath Jearim to the place he had prepared for it, because he had pitched a tent for it in Jerusalem (2 Chronicles 1:4).
- God said to Solomon, "Since this is your heart's desire and you have not asked for wealth, possessions or honor, nor for the death of your enemies, and since you have not asked for a long life but for wisdom and knowledge to govern my people over whom I have made you king" (2 Chronicles 1:11).
- King Solomon and the entire assembly of Israel that had gathered about him were before the ark, sacrificing so many sheep and cattle that they could not be recorded or counted (2 Chronicles 5:6).
- There was nothing in the ark except the two tablets that Moses had placed in it at Horeb, where the LORD made a covenant with the Israelites after they came out of Egypt (2 Chronicles 5:10).
- "My father David had it in his heart to build a temple for the Name of the LORD, the God of Israel" (2 Chronicles 6:7).
- On the eighth day they held an assembly, for they had celebrated the dedication of the altar for seven days and the festival for seven days more (2 Chronicles 7:9).

- When Solomon had finished the temple of the LORD and the royal palace, and had succeeded in carrying out all he had in mind to do in the temple of the LORD and in his own palace (2 Chronicles 7:11).
- "If my people, who are called by my name, will humble themselves and pray and seek my face and turn from their wicked ways, then I will hear from heaven, and I will forgive their sin and will heal their land" (2 Chronicles 7:14).
- King Solomon gave the queen of Sheba all she desired and asked for; he gave her more than she had brought to him. Then she left and returned with her retinue to her own country (2 Chronicles 9:12).
- "If you return to the LORD, then your fellow Israelites and your children will be shown compassion by their captors and will return to this land, for the LORD your God is gracious and compassionate. He will not turn his face from you if you return to him" (2 Chronicles 30:9).

Wonders from the Past

- A relief was found in the 1800s that tells the stories of some conquests of Sennacherib of Assyria. Among the recorded stories is the explanation of an attack on the city of Lachish, a battle described in 2 Chronicles 32.
- Hezekiah's tunnel (see 32:3–4, 30) has been found. It was constructed to transport water into the city.

EZRA
The Exiles Return, Rebuild, and Reestablish Worship

Top Ten

1. The book of Ezra was originally part of Ezra-Nehemiah, which was one book.

EZRA

2. Not all Old Testament books appear chronologically, but 2 Chronicles and Ezra continue their narrative in historical order.
3. The book tells us that both Ezra and Zerubbabel were responsible for leading groups of Jewish people out of captivity in Babylon and back into Judea.
4. Historically, Esther's story fits into the book of Ezra, between chapters 6 and 7.
5. Ezra told the Jewish men they would have to divorce their wives from foreign lands.
6. As a part of restoring the Jewish people to their land, Ezra reinstituted important religious festivals.
7. Parts of the book of Ezra were discovered in the Dead Sea scrolls.
8. Although the book of Malachi is hundreds of pages after Ezra in most Bibles, the two were contemporaries.
9. As a scribe, one of Ezra's jobs would have been to meticulously copy down Scripture.
10. The name Ezra means "help" in Hebrew.

Who

Who Wrote It

The consensus is that the author of Ezra is Ezra himself. If that is true, the book was written no later than 420 BC. Ezra was a priest. Ezra's great grandfather was Hilkiah, the priest under Josiah's reign who was cleaning out a storeroom in the temple when he found the lost Book of the Law (see 2 Kings 22). That discovery initiated major revival in the land.

Who's in It

Cyrus (king of Persia), Zerubbabel, a list of all the exiles who returned to Jerusalem with Zerubbabel, Jeshua, Xerxes and Artaxerxes, Haggai and Zechariah (prophets), King Darius, Ezra, a list of the exiles who returned to Jerusalem with Ezra

What

The remnant has returned from captivity in Babylon to Jerusalem. However, there will be no return to the glory days of David and Solomon. The presence of other powers in the region are making that a certainty. However, the people need to return to their worship in the temple and they need to rebuild their city walls to provide security. Ezra is pivotal in the return of the people and in the rebuilding of key structures in Jerusalem.

When

Cyrus made his proclamation allowing the Hebrews to return to Jerusalem in 538 BC. Zerubbabel took a contingent back to Israel the following year. It was not until 458 that Ezra left Babylon for his return with another group of returnees.

Where

The book of Ezra begins in Babylon at the end of the captivity of the Israelites in that land. It is under new leadership—Cyrus— when the book begins. The scene shifts to Jerusalem upon Zerubbabel's return. The list of those who returned with him is found in Ezra 2. In Jerusalem, the people build an altar and begin rebuilding the temple. Because of some letters that pass back and forth between Jerusalem and Babylon, the scene shifts between the two. In chapter seven, Ezra and his group return to Jerusalem. The list of people who returned with Ezra is found in Ezra 8. The remainder of the book takes place in Jerusalem.

Why

The nation of Israel cannot simply disappear. A large portion of it did because of the Assyrian invasion and the dispersion of the ten tribes of the Northern Kingdom. But Israel needs to remain viable because from it will come the Messiah. The Southern Kingdom has suffered greatly, and not all of the people who went into captivity in Babylon will return (some died; some chose to stay in Babylon). But the people must maintain an identity for God's plan of salvation to be carried out. This is

EZRA

the beginning of the new preparation for the Messiah. Worship must begin again the Jewish way (thus the rebuilding of the temple is essential).

Wow!

- Confucius lived at about the same time as Ezra.
- In his book *Antiquities of the Jews*, the first-century Jewish historian Josephus wrote of Ezra. He contended that when Ezra died, he was buried in Jerusalem. Others hold that Ezra returned to Babylon and died there. There is a grave in Babylon tradition says is Ezra's.

Worth Remembering

- In the first year of Cyrus king of Persia, in order to fulfill the word of the LORD spoken by Jeremiah, the LORD moved the heart of Cyrus king of Persia to make a proclamation throughout his realm and also to put it in writing (Ezra 1:1).
- "This is what Cyrus king of Persia says: 'The LORD, the God of heaven, has given me all the kingdoms of the earth and he has appointed me to build a temple for him at Jerusalem in Judah'" (Ezra 1:2).
- Moreover, King Cyrus brought out the articles belonging to the temple of the LORD, which Nebuchadnezzar had carried away from Jerusalem and had placed in the temple of his god (Ezra 1:7).
- In all, there were 5,400 articles of gold and of silver. Sheshbazzar brought all these along with the exiles when they came up from Babylon to Jerusalem (Ezra 1:11).
- Ezra arrived in Jerusalem in the fifth month of the seventh year of the king (Ezra 7:8).
- For Ezra had devoted himself to the study and observance of the Law of the LORD, and to teaching its decrees and laws in Israel (Ezra 7:10).

Wonders from the Past

The Cyrus Cylinder, which was discovered in 1879 in Babylon, gives an account of Persian King Cyrus' defeat of the Babylonians. But it also includes an edict very much like the one recorded in Ezra 1, allowing the Jews to return home. The Cylinder now resides in the British Museum in London.

NEHEMIAH

A Cupbearer Returns to Rebuild the Wall

Top Ten

1. The book of Nehemiah was originally part of a combined scroll connected to the book of Ezra. The two books were divided somewhere around the fourteenth century AD.
2. The reestablishment of Israel as a nation continues. The earlier returnees to Jerusalem had rebuilt the temple (completed in 516 BC), but something important remains to be reconstructed: the wall.
3. Not everyone returned to Israel from the Babylonian Captivity. One of the people still there decades later is Nehemiah.
4. Another Jewish person who is possibly still in Babylon is the Jewish queen of the land: Esther.
5. Nehemiah will lead the third wave of Hebrews back to their homeland.
6. As with Cyrus at the beginning of Ezra, Artaxerxes at the beginning of Nehemiah looked kindly on the expatriate Jewish people. Two secular leaders took extraordinary action to assist the Jews. This in itself seems like more than an act of benevolence but an act of God himself.

7. One of the auxiliary lessons that can be learned from the book of Nehemiah—in addition to the importance of the reestablishment of the Jews to their homeland—is the consummate skill of Nehemiah in administration. He is a model of excellent leadership.

8. Another key element of Nehemiah's success—and one we can all learn from—is his dependence on prayer during his times of crisis.

9. Even though the books of Nehemiah and Malachi are hundreds of pages apart in Scripture, the two men were contemporaries. It seems that the problems Nehemiah faced were the same ones Malachi addressed in the book that bears his name.

10. Have you ever been asked to show some important papers but couldn't find them? Then you can relate to the unfortunate folks in Nehemiah 7:64–65. They were asked to come up with family records in order to prove their ancestry, but they just couldn't find them.

Who

Who Wrote It
The first seven chapters of Nehemiah are written in the first person, so we can deduce that this autobiographical information came from Nehemiah himself. Many scholars believe Ezra compiled the book of Nehemiah, using Nehemiah's notes and other sources.

Who's in It
Nehemiah, Hanani, Artaxerxes, Sanballat, Tobiah, all the people who repaired the wall (chapter 3), Gesham the Arab (opposed the wall), Ezra

What

It's been nearly a hundred years since the Jewish people returned to Jerusalem. Some lived in the old capital, and some lived in villages in the region. However, even this long after the return from Babylon, the city was still vulnerable to outside attacks because the walls had not been rebuilt after their destruction at the hands of Nebuchadnezzar and his army in 586. Thus, the key event of the book is to rebuild the walls—and Nehemiah is the man to lead that project. Also, there has to be another reconstruction—a spiritual reconstruction of the nation that had been so devastated. This will be the combined work of Ezra and Nehemiah.

When

In 445 BC, Nehemiah received some visitors from Jerusalem, and they told him about the sorry state of his homeland. This is the beginning of the book of Nehemiah. After Nehemiah returned to Jerusalem with his group of repatriated Jews, they rebuilt the wall. Ezra stood before the people and read the Book of the Law. The people celebrated hearing God's Word, and they reinstituted the Feast of Tabernacles. They also confessed their sins (chapter 9). Later, Nehemiah returned to Babylon for 26 years (433–407 BC) before returning as a local governor. At the end of the book, the people had returned to their disobedient ways. The end of the book of Nehemiah marks the end of the history of the Old Testament age.

Where

The story begins in Babylon with a brokenhearted Nehemiah. It shifts to Jerusalem, where the rebuilding of the wall brings hope to the people. They are excited about their faith after Ezra reads the Bible to them—and they reinstitute some of the traditional Jewish worship customs. The nation of Israel seems to be back on track, at least temporarily. However, the people return to their sinful ways, and again Nehemiah seems brokenhearted when he says of the people, "They defiled the priestly office and the covenant of the priesthood and of the Levites" (13:29).

Why

As was the case with the book of Ezra, it is essential for the people to reestablish the kingdom of Israel. There must be a Jewish

NEHEMIAH

people from which the Messiah will come. Thus, Nehemiah is doing God's work by taking more people back home and by building a security barrier (the wall) and helping to reboot the needed worship among the people. Now that this has been accomplished, the recorded Old Testament era closes and the wait for the Messiah begins.

Wow!

- A song based on the rebuilt wall in Jerusalem is called "Twelve Gates to the City." It was written by Rev. Gary Davis and has been covered by Bob Dylan, James Taylor, Carly Simon, Judy Collins, and others.
- In a book commenting on famous painters such as Rembrandt, British romantic era writer Samuel Taylor Coleridge wondered why Rembrandt or some other painter had never captured Nehemiah's nighttime ride around Jerusalem (Nehemiah 2:11-16) on canvas.

Worth Remembering

- They said to me, "Those who survived the exile and are back in the province are in great trouble and disgrace. The wall of Jerusalem is broken down, and its gates have been burned with fire" (Nehemiah 1:3).
- When I heard these things, I sat down and wept. For some days I mourned and fasted and prayed before the God of heaven (Nehemiah 1:4).
- The king said to me, "What is it you want?" Then I prayed to the God of heaven (Nehemiah 2:4).
- I also told them about the gracious hand of my God on me and what the king had said to me. They replied, "Let us start rebuilding." So they began this good work (Nehemiah 2:18).
- So we rebuilt the wall till all of it reached half its height, for the people worked with all their heart (Nehemiah 4:6).

- But we prayed to our God and posted a guard day and night to meet this threat (Nehemiah 4:9).
- All the people came together as one in the square before the Water Gate. They told Ezra the teacher of the Law to bring out the Book of the Law of Moses, which the LORD had commanded for Israel (Nehemiah 8:1).
- Then Nehemiah the governor, Ezra the priest and teacher of the Law, and the Levites who were instructing the people said to them all, "This day is holy to the LORD your God. Do not mourn or weep." For all the people had been weeping as they listened to the words of the Law (Nehemiah 8:9).

Wonders from the Past

In 2007 archaeologist Eilat Mazar identified remnants of the rebuilt wall of Nehemiah's day. This portion of the wall, which was located outside the Dung Gate (3:14) and faced the Mount of Olives, was dated to the time period (2,500 years ago) through pottery fragments found with it. Remnants of the Broad Wall, the Valley Gate, and Water Gate have also been found.

ESTHER

A Surprise Jewish Queen Saves Her People

Top Ten

1. The incidents described in the book of Esther fit in the chronology of the book of Ezra, between chapters six and seven. The events take place about thirty years before the events of Nehemiah begin. Both the book of Esther and the first chapter of Nehemiah take place in Babylon (then controlled by Persia).
2. A major Jewish special day was created to commemorate the events of Esther's day—especially

ESTHER

her courage in saving the Jewish nation from being killed off. The day, which is celebrated in Jewish homes in mid-March, is called the Feast of Purim.

3. You could call Esther by the name Myrtle, which is the meaning of her Hebrew name.
4. Or you could call her Star, for that is the meaning of her Persian name: Esther.
5. Esther was of the tribe of Benjamin.
6. Before Esther went before King Ahasuerus when he was looking for a replacement for his banished queen, she underwent a year-long beauty makeover.
7. After Esther became queen, she reigned for thirteen years.
8. The name of God is not mentioned in the book of Esther. Also, Esther is not quoted anywhere in the New Testament.
9. The entire plan of God for the salvation of sinners depended on Esther's rescue of her people. If the king had carried through on his determination to exterminate the Jews, the line leading to Jesus would have been permanently broken.
10. Two books of the Bible are named after women: Ruth and Esther.

Who

Wrote it?
It is not clear who wrote this book. Some say it was Ezra, while others suggest Mordecai. And still others say it was scribes of the synagogue. Because the book has so many details about Persian life, some believe that the writer used official state documents as a source. For instance, there are 187 references to the title of the king of Persia.

Who is in it?
King Ahasuerus, Queen Vashti, Esther and her Uncle Mordecai, Haman

What

The amazing story in the book of Esther was set in motion when the king's wife, Vashti, refused to parade her beauty in front of her drunken husband and "the people and nobles" (1:11). An irate King Ahasuerus disowned Vashti and sought another queen. His search for a new queen led him to Esther, a Jewish orphan girl, and she became the new queen. Later, the king's right-hand man Haman tricked Ahasuerus into proclaiming an edict condemning all Jews to death. It was only when Esther bravely entered the king's presence and asked him to reverse his decree that the Jewish people were saved from annihilation.

When

The story of Esther takes place between the years of 464 BC and 435 BC.

Where

This story took place in the capital city of Susa, where the King of Persia lived, while some of the Israelites were still exiled in the land. Susa was located in what is present-day Iran, near its western border. The Jewish people in this book had chosen not to return to Jerusalem when others went back under the leadership of Zerubbabel and Ezra. Some would later return with Nehemiah. Esther herself would have been considered an exile, since she was Jewish.

Why

The book of Esther demonstrates God's commitment to work behind the scenes to protect His people and to preserve His plan. The circumstances in this book are anything but ordinary, and disaster seems imminent—yet in the end God's purposes and plans move forward. For an exiled Jew such as Esther to become queen of Persia seems outrageous. For her people to be threatened with annihilation by an incontrovertible law seemingly made the demise of the Jews a certainty. For the queen

ESTHER

to address the king as Esther did without losing her head was not expected. And for the king to not only agree to save the Jews but also make a way for it to work when everyone knew the laws of the Medes and Persians could be broken is truly miraculous. God's name is not mentioned, but His hand is clearly evident.

Wow!

- In a speech before a joint session of the U.S. Congress in 2015, Israeli Prime Minister Benjamin Netanyahu referred to the book of Esther and Esther's role in saving the Jewish people. "Queen Esther . . . gave for the Jewish people the right to defend themselves against their enemies," he said.
- The VeggieTales version of the Esther story is a bit different and less dangerous—for instance, Haman isn't hanged but will be tickled forever—but it still gives kids the general idea of what Esther did.

Worth Remembering

- This is what happened during the time of Xerxes, the Xerxes who ruled over 127 provinces stretching from India to Cush (Esther 1:1).
- "For if you remain silent at this time, relief and deliverance for the Jews will arise from another place, but you and your father's family will perish. And who knows but that you have come to royal position for such a time as this?" (Esther 4:14).
- The king's edict granted the Jews in every city the right to assemble and protect themselves; to destroy, kill and annihilate the armed men of any nationality or province who might attack them and their women and children (Esther 8:11).

ESTHER

Wonders from the Past

- In 1852, archaeologists discovered the city of Susa, which was a winter residence for the king. One of the artifacts found was an inscription by Artaxerxes II that said, in part, "My ancestor Darius built this palace."
- The name of Mordecai (Marduka) was found in Persia on a cuneiform tablet from the era and area in which he lived and served the court of Persia.

JOB
A Godly Man's Suffering

Top Ten

1. The book of Job, in the order of the books of the canon of Scripture, changes the biblical narrative from history to poetry and wisdom literature.
2. The book of Job is both poetry and wisdom. Its subject matter is primarily about suffering and how people of faith handle it.
3. Job is the central character of this book. Similar to Noah in the flood narrative, he is depicted as a man of high morals, godliness, and righteousness.
4. One of the key questions Job addresses is one of the heart. It is a pleading that comes so readily from those for whom life is hard: why do crummy things happen to people who are trying to live right? If you haven't asked that question, wait a while. It will come up when trouble strikes.
5. While Job is most notably considered a book about suffering, it contains the second-most frequent references to creation and other such events—second only to Genesis. Job 38:31 says, "Can you bind the chains

of Pleiades? Can you loosen Orion's belt?" Science tells us that Pleiades is a cluster of stars that travel together through the universe (thus, "the chains"). Science has discovered that the stars forming Orion's belt are moving away from each other (thus, "belt loosened").

6. Another scientific item mentioned is the hydrologic cycle (Job 36:27-28).
7. God himself appears in the book—both at the beginning and at the end.
8. Satan also appears in the book, when he converses with God in chapter 1.
9. One of the key elements of the book is the interaction between Job and his friends Eliphaz, Bildad, Zophar, and Elihu.
10. Proof that Job was a real person and not a mythical character is found in two passages of Scripture: Ezekiel 14:14 and James 5:11, both of which mention him with other historical people.

Who

Who Wrote It
No one knows conclusively who recorded the events found in the book of Job. Some believe that Job himself penned it (see Job 19:23-34), while others hold that Moses discovered the document and served as something of its editor. Another theory is that Elihu, one of Job's friends, wrote it.

Who's in It?
Job, God, Satan, Eliphaz, Bildad, Zophar, Elihu

What

The book begins with tragedy and ends in triumph. In the middle, we see the friends of Job—a righteous man who has lost everything—counseling him about how he should view his misfortune. He never finds out why tragedy visited him (how true this is in our lives!), but after he receives an eye-opening visit from God himself, he comes to terms with God's sovereignty.

When

As with the author, the time period for this book of the Bible is unknown. Some scholars believe this was the first book of the Bible ever written. According to Job 42:16, Job lived upwards of 200 years, which could be an indication of when he lived.

Where

This account took place in the land of Uz (1:1), which is near Midian, where Moses lived for forty years.

Why

We have the advantage of looking at the whole picture, so it is easy for us to criticize Job's friends for their responses to Job's suffering. They seem to be saying more than they know about Job's situation—sometimes wrongly placing blame and putting too much burden on Job. But in reality, we make the same mistakes in our times of trouble today. We cannot see the whole picture, so we question God and wonder why an all-powerful God does not simply make sure nothing bad happens to us. When we start to do that, we need to take the little walk with Him and listen as He shows us the big picture—that He is in charge, that He has much more power than we have, and that we need to trust Him to do what is right.

Wow!

- Two great writers turned the Job story into plays: Neil Simon wrote *God's Favorite*, and Archibald MacLeish wrote *J. B.* Both set Job-like stories in modern times.
- Montag, a character in Ray Bradbury's *Fahrenheit 451*, refers to the book of Job.

JOB

Worth Remembering

- In the land of Uz there lived a man whose name was Job. This man was blameless and upright; he feared God and shunned evil (Job 1:1).
- The LORD said to Satan, "Very well, then, everything he has is in your power, but on the man himself do not lay a finger." Then Satan went out from the presence of the LORD (Job 1:12).
- At this, Job got up and tore his robe and shaved his head. Then he fell to the ground in worship (Job 1:20).
- His wife said to him, "Are you still maintaining your integrity? Curse God and die!" He replied, "You are talking like a foolish woman. Shall we accept good from God, and not trouble?" In all this, Job did not sin in what he said (Job 2:9–10).
- "What strength do I have, that I should still hope? What prospects, that I should be patient?" (Job 6:11).
- "To God belong wisdom and power; counsel and understanding are his" (Job 12:13).
- "Will the one who contends with the Almighty correct him? Let him who accuses God answer him!" (Job 40:2).
- "I know that you can do all things; no purpose of yours can be thwarted. . . . My ears had heard of you but now my eyes have seen you. Therefore I despise myself and repent in dust and ashes" (Job 42:2, 5–6).

Wonders from the Past

- Job's conversation with God unveiled a series of scientific elements, including:
- Job 38:16: "springs of the sea." In 2003, Andrew Fisher, professor of earth and planetary sciences at the University of California Santa Cruz, discovered that seawater sinks into the seafloor's crust then rises through vents many miles away.[6]

JOB

- Job 38:31: "Can you bind the cluster of Pleiades, or loose the belt of Orion?" Scientists have concluded that the stars of the constellation Pleiades are gravitationally bound together.
- Job 40:15–19: "Look at Behemoth . . . What strength it has in its loins, what power in the muscles of its belly! Its tail sways like a cedar." Some see this as a description of a dinosaur called the Apatosaurus.
- Job 9:8: "[God] alone stretches out the heavens." Sounds a bit like an expanding universe.

PSALMS
The Songbook of the Bible

Top Ten

1. The text of the book of Psalms was written over a span of about 1,000 years.
2. Psalms has the most chapters (150) of any other Bible book.
3. The book of Psalms is quoted 116 times in the New Testament.
4. Some of the psalms (25, 34, and 37, for example) were written as acrostic Hebrew poems. This means that the first letter of each line begins with a successive letter of the Hebrew alphabet. (Think of an English poem beginning with a for the first line, b for the second line, and so forth.)
5. The oldest psalm, scholars have deduced, is Psalm 90. Moses wrote this psalm *before* he rescued the people of God from Egypt.
6. The word *praise* appears in the New International Version of the book of Psalms 211 times.

7. Nearly half of the Old Testament quotes in the New Testament come the book of Psalms.

8. Of Jesus' seven statements from the cross, two of them were quotes from the Psalms (22:1, Matthew 27:46; 31:5, Luke 23:46).

9. Here is a list of musical instruments used in worship in the Psalms: harp, lyre, trumpet, cornet, organ, timbrel, cymbals.

10. At least eleven Psalms (2, 8, 16, 22, 45, 69, 72, 89, 110, 118, and 132) are considered messianic, meaning they include prophetic references to the coming Messiah: Jesus.

Who

Who Wrote It?
Unlike most books of the Bible, the book of Psalms has multiple writers. The rundown of writers goes like this: David, 73 psalms; Asaph, 12; sons of Korah, 12. Other possible writers include Hezekiah, Solomon, Moses, Heman, Ethan, Ezra, and Jeremiah. Fifty of the psalms are considered anonymous.

What

The variety in the book of Psalms is one of its most fascinating components. The collection was compiled over a very long period of time and written by many different people, which accounts for its variety. For instance, there are lament psalms—both corporate and individual—in which writers make complaints to God. Also, there are corporate and individual thanksgiving psalms. Many of the psalms are considered praise songs—psalms in which the people of God sent songs of glory and adoration to Him. And there are what are called pilgrimage psalms, songs the Israelites sang on their way to worship.

When

The book of Psalms covers a time period from the days of Moses (c. 1400 BC) to the post-exilic days of Ezra and Nehemiah (c. 400 BC).

Why

For most people, the book of Psalms is intensely personal. That makes sense because of what these 150 inspired chapters do for us. On the one hand, they encourage us and instruct us in how to praise and pray to God and how to meditate on Him and respond to His provisions for us. On the other hand, they allow us to complain a little bit. The lament psalms show us that it is okay to take our concerns and difficulties to God—and without cleaning them up to make them look all scrubbed and right. These psalms show us that He takes us as we are—gripes and all—and always shows us that at the end of our complaints is His promise of protection and hope. We can go to God with the same boldness as the lament writers and know that He listens, cares, and provides.

Wow!

- Composer Igor Stravinsky wrote a symphony based on three psalms: 38, 40, and 150. Penned in the 1930s, it is called *Symphony of Psalms*.
- In his 2004 song "Jesus Walks," Kanye West quotes Psalm 23: "I walk through the valley of death."
- When President George W. Bush addressed the nation following the terrorist attacks on September 11, 2001, he quoted from Psalm 23 when he said, "And I pray they will be comforted by a Power greater than any of us, spoken through the ages in Psalm 23: 'Even though I walk through the valley of the shadow of death, I fear no evil for you are with me.'"
- On the tombstone of famed rocket scientist Wernher Von Braun is this verse reference: Psalm 19:1. That verse says, "The heavens declare the glory of God."

Worth Remembering

- Blessed is the one who does not walk in step with the wicked or stand in the way that sinners take or sit in the company of mockers, but whose delight is in the law of the LORD, and who meditates on his law day and night. That person is like a tree planted by streams of water, which yields its fruit in season and whose leaf does not wither—whatever they do prospers (Psalm 1:1–3).

- I will give thanks to you, LORD, with all my heart; I will tell of all your wonderful deeds (Psalm 9:1).
- I keep my eyes always on the LORD. With him at my right hand, I will not be shaken (Psalm 16:8).
- The heavens declare the glory of God; the skies proclaim the work of his hands (Psalm 19:1).
- The LORD is my shepherd, I lack nothing (Psalm 23:1).
- The LORD is my light and my salvation—whom shall I fear? The LORD is the stronghold of my life—of whom shall I be afraid? (Psalm 27:1).
- LORD my God, I called to you for help, and you healed me (Psalm 30:2).
- Taste and see that the LORD is good; blessed is the one who takes refuge in him (Psalm 34:8).
- The LORD is close to the brokenhearted and saves those who are crushed in spirit (Psalm 34:18).
- God is our refuge and strength, an ever-present help in trouble (Psalm 46:1).
- Have mercy on me, O God, according to your unfailing love; according to your great compassion blot out my transgressions. Wash away all my iniquity and cleanse me from my sin (Psalm 51:1–2).
- Cast your cares on the LORD and he will sustain you; he will never let the righteous be shaken (Psalm 55:22).
- Shout for joy to the LORD, all the earth. Worship the LORD with gladness; come before him with joyful songs. Know that the LORD is God. It is he who made us, and we are his; we are his people, the sheep of his pasture (Psalm 100:1–3).
- Praise the LORD, my soul; all my inmost being, praise his holy name (Psalm 103:1).

- Children are a heritage from the LORD, offspring a reward from him. Like arrows in the hands of a warrior are children born in one's youth. Blessed is the man whose quiver is full of them. They will not be put to shame when they contend with their opponents in court (Psalm 127:3–5).
- Your eyes saw my unformed body; all the days ordained for me were written in your book before one of them came to be (Psalm 139:16).
- He heals the brokenhearted and binds up their wounds (Psalm 147:3).

Wonders from the Past

The Dead Sea Scrolls, which were discovered in the Qumran region of Israel, include more manuscripts from book of Psalms than from any other Bible book. Fifty-one psalms were found in the Dead Sea Scrolls.

PROVERBS
Selected Sayings of the Wise

Top Ten

1. The Bible's wisdom literature consists of these five books: Job, Psalms, Proverbs, Ecclesiastes, and Song of Songs.
2. While eight hundred of Solomon's wise sayings are recorded in the book of Proverbs, the writer of 1 Kings wrote that Solomon wrote three thousand proverbs and more than a thousand songs (see 1 Kings 4:32).
3. Solomon had much to say about wisdom because he requested wisdom (see 1 Kings 3:9–12).
4. The New Testament quotes from Proverbs just eight times.

5. Most cultures have pithy, wise sayings with which people pass on information to others. We can learn from such short aphorisms as "A bird in the hand is worth two in the bush" because they are easy to remember and helpful in their advice. In a small sense, that is what the biblical proverbs are. They are godly, wise sayings that are applicable to life.

6. A biblical proverb is based on underlying theological truths: 1. God is the arranger of our world and our society, and He has revealed His desires for us through the Bible; and 2. If our hearts are right, we will want to live according to God's standards and will follow God's wisdom. Proverbs 1:2–4 explains: "for gaining wisdom and instruction; for understanding words of insight; for receiving instruction to prudent behavior; doing what is right and just and fair; for giving prudence to those who are simple, knowledge and discretion to the young."

7. One way to understand the book of Proverbs is to realize that the sayings presented are accurate and true under usual circumstances, but they are not universally true. It's the difference between "You shall have no other gods before me," (Exodus 20:3), which is a universal, incontrovertible truth, and "a generous person will prosper" (Proverbs 11:25), which is a general truth that reminds us the importance of generosity but does not guarantee that every generous person will get rich.

8. Solomon probably borrowed some of his proverbs from surrounding cultures (see Ecclesiastes 12:9), for they were known to have existed in places like Egypt and Mesopotamia. Plus, he penned many of his own. When it was time to compile the book of Proverbs, the Holy Spirit would have guided whoever put it together to include only ones that reflected God's wisdom.

9. The book of Proverbs tells about knowing wisdom, but it also informs us about foolishness: the simple

fool (1:22), the hard fool (1:7), the arrogant fool (14:3). There are several "checklists for fools" in the book.

10. This book gives us Spirit-inspired advice on a variety of subjects, including sexual immorality, fools vs. wise people, parenting, the tongue, friends, and families.

Who

Who Wrote It?

The main writer of the book of Proverbs is King Solomon. Others who contributed to the book were Hezekiah, who compiled proverbs he discovered (Proverbs 25:1); Agur, who is credited for writing Proverbs 30; and Lemuel, who is given credit for Proverbs 31.

What

The book of Proverbs is a compilation of pithy sayings that tell us how to be wise and how to avoid being a fool, a scoffer, or a simple person. This collection of profound adages, compiled from a wide variety of sources, reflects practical information about how to live under God's rule and by His standards. While it is important to consider context when reading the Bible, Proverbs is a bit different because the wisdom is often doled out one or two verses at a time—and one wise saying may not be related to the next. For instance, in Proverbs 20 is a warning about alcoholic beverages in verse 1, followed immediately in verse 2 with advice about handling a king's wrath. The two ideas seem disconnected, but both are valuable. The key to understanding the book may be Proverbs 1:7, which says, "The fear of the LORD is the beginning of knowledge, but fools despise wisdom and instruction."

When

Solomon lived in the tenth century BC, and Hezekiah reigned from 715 to 686 BC, so clearly the proverbs were collected over

PROVERBS

a long period of time. We do not know when these sayings were finally compiled into one document.

Where

While the bulk of the proverbs were compiled in and around Jerusalem, they also came from a wide variety of sources—even from as far away as Egypt.

Why

Clearly, the purpose of the book of Proverbs is to promote wisdom and godly character in its readers. One who intends to please God can use these sayings as guides for making right choices. While there is a certain randomness to the presentation in the book, there is always the theme of learning to practice wisdom in the pursuit of godly living.

Wow!

- The title and lyrics of Canadian rapper k-os' song "Steel Sharpens Steel" are a paraphrase of Proverbs 27:17: "As iron sharpens iron, so one person sharpens another."
- British writer T.E. Lawrence took the title for his book *The Seven Pillars of Wisdom* from Proverbs 9:1.

Worth Remembering

- The fear of the LORD is the beginning of knowledge, but fools despise wisdom and instruction (Proverbs 1:7).
- For the LORD gives wisdom; from his mouth come knowledge and understanding (Proverbs 2:6).
- Trust in the LORD with all your heart and lean not on your own understanding; in all your ways submit to him, and he will make your paths straight (Proverbs 3:5-6).
- Blessed are those who find wisdom, those who gain understanding, for she is more profitable than silver and yields better returns than gold (Proverbs 3:13-14).

PROVERBS

- A little sleep, a little slumber, a little folding of the hands to rest—and poverty will come on you like a thief and scarcity like an armed man (Proverbs 6:10–11).
- There is a way that appears to be right, but in the end it leads to death (Proverbs 14:12).
- The name of the LORD is a fortified tower; the righteous run to it and are safe (Proverbs 18:10).
- Whoever pursues righteousness and love finds life, prosperity and honor (Proverbs 21:21).
- Start children off on the way they should go, and even when they are old they will not turn from it (Proverbs 22:6).
- Let someone else praise you, and not your own mouth; an outsider, and not your own lips (Proverbs 27:2).
- "Every word of God is flawless; he is a shield to those who take refuge in him" (Proverbs 30:5).
- A wife of noble character who can find? She is worth far more than rubies (Proverbs 31:10).

ECCLESIASTES

The Meaning of Life with and without God

Top Ten

1. Ecclesiastes requires a careful reading, for the author presents some ideas that seem to contradict the rest of the Bible. But in reality, he is presenting the perspective of the ungodly, so we know how others think. An example: "money is the answer for everything" (10:19).
2. The desperation that marks much of the book of Ecclesiastes is highlighted by the fact that the word *meaningless* appears thirty-eight times.

ECCLESIASTES

3. By contrast, God is mentioned forty times as the writer works through his teaching on meaninglessness.

4. A secondary title given to this book is "The Preacher." This is derived from the Septuagint, in which the book was titled *Koheleth*, which means a person who addresses an assembly of people.

5. The word *Ecclesiastes* is a Latin translation of the Hebrew word *Koheleth*.

6. The book of Ecclesiastes clearly depicts the many avenues much of society takes in an effort to make life meaningful. People try pleasure, hard work, and riches, but they often find, as the writer explains, emptiness at the end of the effort. While that sounds pessimistic, the book ends in optimism and hope.

7. In the book of Proverbs, the writers present expected norms for the godly. In Ecclesiastes, the writer paints a picture of the results of not following those norms : meaninglessness.

8. The writer of Ecclesiastes uses the Hebrew word *Elohim* (meaning creator) every time he refers to God. He never uses the word *Jehovah*, which we would translate "Lord."

9. Ecclesiastes takes a careful reading and an understanding of what the writer is ultimately trying to accomplish. It would be unbiblical to read verses such as Ecclesiastes 3:16–22 and consider that passage as teaching a biblical truth.

10. It has been said that the Jewish sages (who were around from about 250 BC to AD 625), "wished to hide the book of Ecclesiastes," fearing it would negatively influence those who read it.

Who

The traditionally accepted writer of Ecclesiastes is Solomon. Some verses that indicate Solomon was the penman are 1:1

("The words of the Teacher, son of David, king in Jerusalem") and 2:4–9, which is clearly a description of Solomon's kingdom.

What

It would not be wise to read the book of Ecclesiastes as one would read the Proverbs. Whereas the aphorisms in the Proverbs can, for the most part, be read one at a time and taken from their verse moorings without damaging the meaning, Ecclesiastes cannot be read as a series of unrelated truisms. The context is all-important.

When

If Solomon wrote this book, it would have to have been written before 930 BC.

Where

Again, assuming that the writer is Solomon, one can assume that it was written in the city of Jerusalem during his reign as Israel's third king.

Why

This book is an up-close-and-personal look at people as they really are. We can see many people in our day who live outside of a God-context—as if He does not exist. The results of that kind of living and thinking are shown in Solomon's oft-used word *meaningless*. Humans, by shutting out the light of God on their lives, live "under the sun" in perpetual darkness. No book of the Bible shows this more than Ecclesiastes. The ending is a warning to all who live that way: "Fear God and keep his commandments, for this is the duty of all mankind."

Wow!

- Singer/songwriter Pete Seeger took the lyrics of the Byrds' huge 1965 hit song "Turn! Turn! Turn!" from Ecclesiastes 3.

ECCLESIASTES

- *A Time to Kill*, the first of John Grisham's bestselling novels, also took its title from Ecclesiastes 3.
- Famed author Ernest Hemingway also dipped into Ecclesiastes for a title: *The Sun Also Rises*, from Ecclesiastes 1:3–5.

Worth Remembering

- "Meaningless! Meaningless!" says the Teacher. "Utterly meaningless! Everything is meaningless" (Ecclesiastes 1:2).
- There is a time for everything, and a season for every activity under the heavens (Ecclesiastes 3:1).
- No one can fathom what God has done from beginning to end (Ecclesiastes 3:11).
- The quiet words of the wise are more to be heeded than the shouts of a ruler of fools (Ecclesiastes 9:17).
- Ship your grain across the sea; after many days you may receive a return (Ecclesiastes 11:1).
- Remember your Creator in the days of your youth, before the days of trouble come and the years approach when you will say, "I find no pleasure in them" (Ecclesiastes 12:1).
- Now all has been heard; here is the conclusion of the matter: Fear God and keep his commandments, for this is the duty of all mankind (Ecclesiastes 12:13).

SONG OF SONGS
The Delights of Love

Top Ten

1. Song of Songs is one of the two Bible books that don't mention the name of God.
2. This is unlike any other book of the Bible in its straightforward portrayal of the love relationship between a man and a woman.

3. Song of Songs is the only book in the Bible that consists of a single poem.

4. The book contains a number of interesting figures of speech to describe the love relationship between a man and a woman. For example: "Your love is more delightful than wine" (1:2), "your eyes are doves" (1:15), "my beloved is like a gazelle" (2:9), and, surprisingly, "your hair is like a flock of goats" (4:1).

5. Song of Solomon mentions more than twenty plant species and more than a dozen animals.

6. There is some geography in this book as well: Chapter 1: Jerusalem, Kedar, En Gedi. Chapter 2: Sharon, Jerusalem. Chapter 3: Jerusalem (Zion), Lebanon. Chapter 4: Mount Gilead, Lebanon, Amana, Hermon. Chapter 5: Jerusalem, Lebanon. Chapter 6: Tirzah, Gilead, Shulam. Chapter 7: Heshbon, Bath-Rabbim, Damascus, Mount Carmel. Chapter 8: Jerusalem, Baal Hamon.

7. In some Bibles, this book is called *Song of Solomon*; in others, it is *Song of Songs*. *Song of Songs* is the Hebrew title of the book; in addition, the writer calls it that in verse one of chapter one. Some title the book with a nod to Solomon, for many scholars have concluded that Israel's third monarch wrote it.

8. The book is also called *Canticles*, its title in the Latin Vulgate.

9. If you ever run out of compliments for the girl of your dreams, turn to Song of Songs 7 and then refer to her nose as being "like the tower of Lebanon" and see how that turns out.

10. Nobody knows where Shulem was located. Some believe it is synonymous with Shunem. That would make the Shulemite woman (the object of the writer's affection) a resident of a village north of the Jezreel Valley and south of Mount Gilboa. Another theory

is that she was the daughter of a Pharaoh. No matter where she was from, Solomon was quite taken with her.

Who

Who Wrote It?
The first verse of this book starts: "Solomon's Song of Songs." That is a good indication that the wise man himself penned this book.

Who's in It?
The Shulamite woman, a chorus, Solomon

What

Is this book simply about the romantic relationship between a man and a woman, or is it an allegory for our relationship with God? Some have suggested that it is the actual love story between Solomon and a woman. Others see it as an allegory for the union between Christ and the church—or between Christ and an individual He is working to win to faith.

When

Solomon lived in the 900s BC, which puts Song of Solomon's completion date during the same time period the first temple was constructed.

Where

As mentioned above, the book has plenty of geographic references, which could apply if it is an actual depiction of a love story. In other words, some see the Song of Songs as an allegory and that the characters are representatives of something else—for instance, the bridegroom is Christ and the bride is the church. Or it could be seen as a true love story between two real people. If that is the case, the geographic references are places related to those real people.

Why

This is one of the key questions relating to this book and its unique subject matter in the canon of Scripture. Some say it is wisdom literature that gives the reader information about how a man and woman are to properly live and love in a spousal relationship. It has been suggested that the book was intended for use in wedding ceremonies. As mentioned, some also believe it is an allegory for the love relationship between God and His people.

Wow!

- Longtime Detroit Tigers baseball play-by-play announcer Ernie Harwell (1918–2010) used Song of Songs 2:11–12 to begin his first broadcast every spring: "Lo! The winter is past; the rain is over and gone. The flowers appear on the earth; the time of the singing of birds is come, and the voice of the turtle is heard in our land."
- Johann Sebastian Bach wrote a cantata using images and words from Song of Songs.
- The American musical group mewithoutYou used a Song of Songs reference (2:15) for the title of its album *Catch for Us the Foxes*.
- The Song of Songs was used for readings and a sermon at the 2018 royal wedding of the Duke and Duchess of Sussex.

Worth Remembering

- I am a rose of Sharon, a lily of the valleys (Song of Songs 2:1).
- Let him lead me to the banquet hall, and let his banner over me be love (Song of Songs 2:4).
- I am my beloved's and my beloved is mine; he browses among the lilies (Song of Songs 6:3).
- How beautiful you are and how pleasing, my love, with your delights! (Song of Songs 7:6).

Wonders from the Past

While some suggest that Song of Songs was written after the exile, archaeological evidence is clear that Solomon was king during the tenth century BC. Discoveries at Hazor, Megiddo, and Gezer verify that Solomon was the common denominator between those places and construction in Jerusalem. Also, those who study literature of that era suggest that the poetry of Solomon matches what was common in those days.

ISAIAH
The Prophet of the Messiah

Top Ten

1. Isaiah is a transitional book in Scripture in that it moves us away from wisdom literature and lands us squarely in the section called the prophets. This section will take us to the end of the Old Testament canon.
2. It was the task of the prophets (those who have books of the Bible named after them) to persuade the people to return to God and to obey His law. Some prophets did not write books (Samuel, Elijah, Elisha, and Micaiah, for example).
3. To put the book of Isaiah in its proper chronological order in Scripture, it would fit into the final years of the divided kingdom era. Isaiah wasn't the first of the book-writing prophets, even though he's the first in order in the canon.
4. According to John 12:41, Isaiah had the grand privilege of seeing "Jesus' glory" and of speaking about Him. That would have happened seven hundred years before Jesus' incarnation!

5. Isaiah is quoted in the New Testament more times (eighty-five) than any other Old Testament prophet, though some passages are quoted more than once. In total, sixty-one separate Isaiah passages are referenced in the New Testament.

6. Because Isaiah lived toward the end of Israel's history (before Assyria scattered the tribes), he was witness to the Assyrian's attack and disbursement of the people in the late 700s BC.

7. Assyria was stopped at the gates of Jerusalem, though, and it was as a result of Isaiah's prayer. Isaiah asked for God's help, and He intervened to prevent Sennacherib from overrunning the Holy City.

8. As we have already seen in the Old Testament history books, there is a pattern—one the prophets try their best to break. The prophets warn the people that they have disobeyed God and need to turn toward Him. The people do not repent, and the prophet warns them of judgment. The judgment comes, but at the end there is always the hope of a glorious future. Then the pattern repeats.

9. The book of Isaiah is not the first go-around biblically for its namesake. He appeared in 2 Kings 19 and 20, and his name is bandied about in 2 Chronicles 26 and 32.

10. In Isaiah 7–9, the prophet gives a prophecy with both current and future implications. While the near prophecy concerns King Ahaz, the future prophecy is about the coming Immanuel (see 7:14, 9:6–7).

Who

Who Wrote It?
The writer of this book, Isaiah, began his work as a prophet toward the end the reign of Uzziah, one of Judah's good kings. Uzziah was Judah's leader from approximately 792 until 740 BC. Isaiah was the son of Amoz—who some believe was the son

of Joash, another king of Judah. His wife was a prophetess, and they had two sons. Isaiah prophesied during the reigns of Uzziah, Jotham, Ahaz, and Hezekiah (see 1:1).

Who's in It?
Ahaz, Hezekiah, Immanuel, Sennacherib, Uzziah, and Adrammelech and Sharezer (sons of Sennacherib, king of Assyria).

What

Judgment is coming, but there is hope. That is the bad news-good news message of Isaiah's prophecy. He kicks off this long prophetic book with a word of judgment on the kingdoms of Judah and Israel because of their disregard for the covenant God has made with them, accentuated by their idol worship. But in the midst of judgment comes word of something hopeful—a branch, a child, the prospect of a mighty counselor. We now know that Isaiah was speaking of the coming Messiah, Jesus. Yet his contemporaries' rejection of God is still on the prophet's mind, so he speaks of God's judgment on many surrounding areas. Isaiah acts heroically in helping to stop Assyria from destroying Jerusalem before he writes further about the coming Messiah. At the end of his writing, Isaiah exhorts his readers to live righteously. It is a long, complicated book, but its goal is to persuade the people to trust God, worship Him the right way, and live according to His standards—while anticipating the coming Messiah.

When

Isaiah gives us the historical time parameters for his book in the first verse of his prophecy. He mentions the four kings during whose reign he spoke for God to the nations. Uzziah died in 740 BC (Isaiah referred to his death in 6:1), and the last of the four kings mentioned in Isaiah 1:1 was Hezekiah, who reigned from 716 to 687.

ISAIAH

Where

It appears that Isaiah spent most of his time in Jerusalem.

Why

The book of Isaiah can be seen as a bridge between the Old Covenant and the New. While Isaiah addresses his contemporaries—warning them of judgment—he also projects into the future a coming answer to the problem of sin: the Messiah.

Wow!

- The Christian metal band Stryper based its name on Isaiah 53:5: "with his stripes we are healed" (KJV).
- Musician/songwriter Bob Dylan's song "All Along the Watchtower" has Isaiah 21:5–9 as its basis.
- Michelangelo painted a portrait of Isaiah among his seven Old Testament prophets on the ceiling of the Sistine Chapel in the Vatican.
- The following presidents of the United States referenced Isaiah's mention of beating "swords into plowshares" (2:4): Dwight Eisenhower in his famous military-industrial complex speech in 1961; Richard Nixon, who had family Bibles open to the passage in both of his oath-taking ceremonies; Jimmy Carter, in a speech about the 1979 Egypt-Israel peace accord; and Ronald Reagan, addressing the United Nations in 1986.

Worth Remembering

- "Come now, let us settle the matter," says the LORD. "Though your sins are like scarlet, they shall be as white as snow; though they are red as crimson, they shall be like wool. If you are willing and obedient, you will eat the good things of the land" (Isaiah 1:18–19).

ISAIAH

- Then I heard the voice of the Lord saying, "Whom shall I send? And who will go for us?" And I said, "Here am I. Send me!" (Isaiah 6:8).
- The people walking in darkness have seen a great light; on those living in the land of deep darkness a light has dawned (Isaiah 9:2).
- For to us a child is born, to us a son is given, and the government will be on his shoulders. And he will be called Wonderful Counselor, Mighty God, Everlasting Father, Prince of Peace (Isaiah 9:6).
- They will neither harm nor destroy on all my holy mountain, for the earth will be filled with the knowledge of the LORD as the waters cover the sea (Isaiah 11:9).
- "Surely God is my salvation; I will trust and not be afraid. The LORD, the LORD himself, is my strength and my defense; he has become my salvation" (Isaiah 12:2).
- They raise their voices, they shout for joy; from the west they acclaim the LORD's majesty. Therefore in the east give glory to the LORD; exalt the name of the LORD, the God of Israel, in the islands of the sea. From the ends of the earth we hear singing: "Glory to the Righteous One." But I said, "I waste away, I waste away! Woe to me! The treacherous betray! With treachery the treacherous betray!" (Isaiah 24:14–16).
- He will swallow up death forever. The Sovereign LORD will wipe away the tears from all faces; he will remove his people's disgrace from all the earth. The LORD has spoken (Isaiah 25:8).
- But those who hope in the LORD will renew their strength. They will soar on wings like eagles; they will run and not grow weary, they will walk and not be faint (Isaiah 40:31).
- "So do not fear, for I am with you; do not be dismayed, for I am your God. I will strengthen you and help you; I will uphold you with my righteous right hand" (Isaiah 41:10).
- "For I am the LORD your God who takes hold of your right hand and says to you, Do not fear; I will help you" (Isaiah 41:13).
- "When you pass through the waters, I will be with you; and when you pass through the rivers, they will not sweep

over you. When you walk through the fire, you will not be burned; the flames will not set you ablaze" (Isaiah 43:2).

- "I will go before you and will level the mountains; I will break down gates of bronze and cut through bars of iron" (Isaiah 45:2).
- "See, I have engraved you on the palms of my hands; your walls are ever before me" (Isaiah 49:16).
- But he was pierced for our transgressions, he was crushed for our iniquities; the punishment that brought us peace was on him, and by his wounds we are healed (Isaiah 53:5).

Wonders from the Past

- In 2018, archaeologists associated with Eilat Mazar were digging in an area called the Ophel at the foot of the southern wall of the Temple Mount. They found what appears to be a bulla (used to press a seal) that contains the name Isaiah. This could be the first archaeological proof of Isaiah's existence.
- Isaiah 22:10 says of Hezekiah, "You counted the buildings in Jerusalem and tore down houses to strengthen the wall." Exploring the Jewish Quarter of Jerusalem, Nahum Avigad discovered a large wall that was built on top of houses, similar to what the verse describes. It would have been built between 715 and 686 BC.

JEREMIAH
The Heroic Prophet

Top Ten

1. In his book *A Nation in Crisis*, pastor and author Ray Stedman called Jeremiah the "most heroic of all the prophets" because of what he faced during his long

JEREMIAH

years of trying to persuade the people to repent and return to God.

2. At approximately 33,000 words, the book of Jeremiah is the longest in the Bible.

3. Jeremiah is often referred to as the weeping prophet because of the many passages in his book in which he complains through his tears about the persecution he faced (which was considerable).

4. To put the times of Jeremiah in proper biblical, historical perspective, you would read it alongside 2 Kings 22:1–25, 2 Kings 30, and 2 Chronicles 34:1–36:21.

5. The events of the book of Jeremiah are not all presented in chronological order.

6. Other biblical prophets who lived during the time of Jeremiah were Ezekiel, Daniel, Habakkuk, Zephaniah, Nahum, and Obadiah.

7. God forbade Jeremiah to get married because the times were so horrible it would have been a bad time to raise a family (16:1–4).

8. The last great hope for Judah was Josiah, who was king when God called Jeremiah to be a prophet. Josiah instituted reforms in an attempt to steer Judah in the right direction. He was killed at Megiddo, and no other king after him was considered good in God's eyes.

9. In Jeremiah 25:11, the prophet explains in his plea to the people that Nebuchadnezzar will take them into captivity, and he tells them the exact length of time of the captivity: seventy years.

10. In Jeremiah 33:15–16, he delivers an even more astounding prophecy, foretelling the coming of "a righteous Branch," who is the Messiah.

Who

Who Wrote It?
The writer, Jeremiah, was the son of a priest named Hilkiah, who was from a town outside of Jerusalem called Anathoth.

Jeremiah was so young when God called him, he protested, "I am a child" (Jeremiah 1:6 KJV). Jeremiah also wrote the book of Lamentations.

Who's in It?
Potter, Pashur, Zedekiah, Shallum, Jehoiakim, Jehoiachin, Nebuchadnezzar, Hananiah, Shemaiah, Hanamel, Baruch, Jehukal, Gedaliah, Ebed-Melech

What

In a nutshell, this book is about desolation, destruction, and depravity. There is no way to clean this up and make it shine. God calls Jeremiah (probably during or just after his teen years) to proclaim His news to a nation that can't seem to keep its eyes away from idols and other useless distractions. So Jeremiah does it. He tells his people to repent, to turn to God. He dedicates himself totally to this thankless task, forsaking even marriage in order to stay focused on his message. Yet even when he promises the people something new (chapters 30-33), they and their kings reject his message. He even tells them about the coming captivity if they don't turn things around. It is the sad story of a faithful man and a completely unfaithful kingdom.

When

The events in the book of Jeremiah span about forty years—from 627 BC to 586 BC. The kings who reigned during this time were Josiah, Jehoahaz, Jehoiakim, Jehoiachin, and Zedekiah. Of this bunch, only Josiah was considered a good king.

Where

For the most part, the action of the book of Jeremiah takes place in Jerusalem, where God had sent the prophet (see Jeremiah 2:2). In chapter 43, after the fall of Jerusalem, a remnant goes to Egypt and takes Jeremiah with them.

JEREMIAH

Why

The pattern continues. Judah disobeys God, and He sends a messenger to warn them of destruction for their disobedience. Sometimes they make efforts to reform (see Josiah), and then they return to their old ways and face judgment. The only difference this time is that Judah makes no effort under Jeremiah's warnings to turn back to God. The only hopefulness found in Jeremiah is in chapters thirty through thirty-three, when he speaks of the coming new covenant. After that, it's back to more doom and gloom. Jeremiah does his job, but no one listens—and then Nebuchadnezzar shows up and Jerusalem falls. Jeremiah's faithfulness in spite of having no success reminds us that it is our job to be faithful and entrust the results to God.

Wow!

- Artists such as Michelangelo, Rembrandt, and Donatello rendered Jeremiah as dark, melancholy, and depressed, which is easy to understand given content of the books (Jeremiah and Lamentations) he wrote.
- In 1942, composer Leonard Bernstein premiered a symphony titled *Jeremiah*. The three movements of the piece are "Prophecy," "Profanation," and "Lamentation."

Worth Remembering

- "Do not be afraid of them, for I am with you and will rescue you," declares the LORD (Jeremiah 1:8).
- Hear the word of the LORD, you descendants of Jacob, all you clans of Israel (Jeremiah 2:4).
- "They make ready their tongue like a bow, to shoot lies; it is not by truth that they triumph in the land. They go from one sin to another; they do not acknowledge me," declares the LORD (Jeremiah 9:3).

JEREMIAH

- But the LORD is the true God; he is the living God, the eternal King. When he is angry, the earth trembles; the nations cannot endure his wrath (Jeremiah 10:10).
- When your words came, I ate them; they were my joy and my heart's delight, for I bear your name, LORD God Almighty (Jeremiah 15:16).
- "Cursed is the one who trusts in man, who draws strength from mere flesh and whose heart turns away from the LORD" (Jeremiah 17:5).
- The heart is deceitful above all things and beyond cure. Who can understand it? (Jeremiah 17:9).
- "For I know the plans I have for you," declares the LORD, "plans to prosper you and not to harm you, plans to give you hope and a future" (Jeremiah 29:11).
- "You will seek me and find me when you seek me with all your heart" (Jeremiah 29:13).
- "The days are coming," declares the LORD, "when I will make a new covenant with the people of Israel and with the people of Judah" (Jeremiah 31:31).
- "Call to me and I will answer you and tell you great and unsearchable things you do not know" (Jeremiah 33:3).

Wonders from the Past

- Clay tablets discovered in the ruins of Babylon mention that Jehoiachin, the king of Judah, was treated well in Babylon. Jeremiah 52:31–34 says the new king of Babylon "spoke kindly to him and gave him a seat of honor." The clay tablets say he was given provisions for his family and was cared for well.
- In Jeremiah 40, the record states that Gedaliah was appointed as a governor of Judah. In 1935, a series of documents called "the Lachish Letters" were found in Jerusalem—left over from the Babylon's siege of Jerusalem. In the letters was this: "Belonging to Gedaliah, the one who is over the house."

JEREMIAH

- Over the years, archaeologists have recovered a number of seals, or bullas, bearing the names of several people mentioned in the book of Jeremiah: Seraiah (51:59-64), Baruch (32:12), Gemariah (36:10).

LAMENTATIONS
Sorrow over Jerusalem's Downfall

Top Ten

1. The structure of Lamentations is poetic in nature.
2. The first four chapters of Lamentations each make up a new poem and a new theme.
3. If you were to read the chapters in Hebrew, you would see that the writer begins with the first letter of the alphabet (Aleph) and then uses subsequent letters in order to lead off each subsequent verse.
4. In chapter one, which describes the destruction of Jerusalem, the writer uses personification. For example: "Bitterly she weeps at night, tears upon her cheeks" (vs. 2), as if the city could feel pain.
5. In chapter two, the reader senses God's anger toward Jerusalem. She had been warned, but now judgment has fallen—and we can see God's wrath: "Without pity, the Lord has swallowed up all the dwellings of Jacob" (vs. 2).
6. In chapter three, the writer's sadness and sorrow continues, but for the first time, there is hope, which he expresses in verse 22: "Because of the LORD's great love we are not consumed."
7. In chapter four, the scene returns to Jerusalem and its destruction—sacred gems are strewn about, children beg for food, famine abounds. Hope of the end of the exile appears near the end.

8. At the end, the writer offers a prayer to the Lord, asking for restoration.
9. In the Hebrew Bible, the book of Lamentations was not placed after Jeremiah but alongside Song of Songs, Ruth, Ecclesiastes, and Esther.
10. Nearly 600 years after Jeremiah penned this book, Jesus would also cry over Jerusalem (see Matthew 23:37–39, Luke 19:41–44).

Who

While some scholars are not certain who wrote Lamentations, it is widely accepted in both the Jewish and Christian traditions that Jeremiah wrote down these laments. The Septuagint lists Jeremiah as the author.

What

This short book follows the book of Jeremiah, in which the prophet continually tries to warn the people of Jerusalem about the consequences of their sin against God. But because they don't listen, destruction falls. Thus, Lamentations mourns that destruction. It is a detailing of all that was lost through the disobedience of God's people.

When

The destruction mourned in this book took place in approximately 586 BC; therefore, this book had to have been written soon after that date. The temple would be rebuilt and the wall repaired seventy years later—so the writing had to take place in the years between.

Where

The laments are centered on the City of David, Jerusalem.

Why

If the book of Jeremiah seems clouded in sadness because of the prophet's failure to turn the people of Judah from their evil ways, the book of Lamentations is enveloped in a nighttime of sorrow. You can read it in the first few verses, as Jeremiah weeps over the destruction of his beloved Jerusalem. Pity drips from each verse, beginning with "how deserted lies the city, once so full of people" (vs. 1). Even "the roads to Zion mourn" (vs. 4) as the entire region lies immersed in destruction. The temple itself has been violated in unthinkable ways: "the enemy laid hands on all her treasures; she saw pagan nations enter her sanctuary" (vs. 10). And on goes the lament, through chapter two and into chapter three. Then, finally, in chapter 3 there is hope: "Yet this I call to mind and therefore I have hope" (vs. 21). Although he returns to his recitation of sorrows at the end, the prose rises back to hope with "You, LORD, reign forever . . . Restore us!" (5:19, 21). The book can't let us forget the destruction, but it also reminds us of future hope—a message for all time.

Wow!

In modern-day Jerusalem, a scroll of Lamentations is opened and read in synagogues on Tisha B'Av, a special day that commemorates the destruction of the temple in c. 586 BC.

Worth Remembering

- How deserted lies the city, once so full of people! How like a widow is she, who once was great among the nations! She who was queen among the provinces has now become a slave (Lamentations 1:1).
- The roads to Zion mourn, for no one comes to her appointed festivals. All her gateways are desolate, her priests groan, her young women grieve, and she is in bitter anguish (Lamentations 1:4).
- He has made my skin and my flesh grow old and has broken my bones (Lamentations 3:4).
- I became the laughingstock of all my people; they mock me in song all day long (Lamentations 3:14).

- Yet this I call to mind and therefore I have hope (Lamentations 3:21).
- Because of the LORD's great love we are not consumed, for his compassions never fail. They are new every morning; great is your faithfulness (Lamentations 3:22–23).
- I say to myself, "The LORD is my portion; therefore I will wait for him" (Lamentations 3:24).
- The LORD is good to those whose hope is in him, to the one who seeks him (Lamentations 3:25).
- You came near when I called you, and you said, "Do not fear" (Lamentations 3:57).

EZEKIEL
The Coming and Going of God's Presence

Top Ten

1. The name Ezekiel means "he whom God strengthens."
2. The prophet Ezekiel tells about the departure of God's glory from the temple in Jerusalem.
3. Ezekiel prophesies that God will send the Holy Spirit to His people (36:24-27).
4. The book of Ezekiel contains a series of bizarre visions and events the prophet uses to symbolize the message God has given him.
5. Right away in chapter one, Ezekiel receives a vision of the glory of God on a throne. It has four wheels and is encompassed by four creatures—each with four faces and four wings.
6. Later, Ezekiel tells about building a clay representation of Jerusalem, and he then lies down next to it for an extended period of time. This represented the siege of Jerusalem under the hand of Nebuchadnezzar (chapter 4).

7. Another time, Ezekiel shaved his hair and beard and divided the clipped hair into three parts to symbolize the fate of the people of Jerusalem (chapter 5).

8. Ezekiel's prophecies extend beyond the time of Jerusalem's struggles and have implications for the future in the New Jerusalem (chapter 48).

9. Ezekiel speaks of a fourth temple that will be built in the city of Jerusalem (40-48). There is a third temple to be built on the site of the first and second, but it will be destroyed (plans are currently under way in Jerusalem for that building).

10. One of the enduring mysteries from the often-unusual elements of Ezekiel's prophecies is the presentation of Gog and Magog. Throughout history, people have speculated about who Gog is and what country he represents. The two names reappear in the book of Revelation. No one has been able to pinpoint exactly who Gog and Magog might be in future events.

Bonus Facts

11. The book of Ezekiel tells of a theophany, which is an appearance of God to a human. You can read about this in Ezekiel 1.

12. The phrase "I am the LORD" appears in the book of Ezekiel more than fifty times. For instance, Ezekiel 39:28: "Then they will know that I am the LORD their God, for though I sent them into exile among the nations, I will gather them to their own land, not leaving any behind."

Who

Who Wrote It?

Imagine the life and experiences of Ezekiel. Like Jeremiah, Ezekiel was a priest. Like Daniel, he was taken captive and moved from Judah to Babylon. While in Babylon during the forced captivity, he sensed God's call to become a prophet. His record of what he prophesied to the people in captivity began when he was thirty years old (Ezekiel 1:1), and he seems to be living in the country, not in the city as Daniel did. According to Ezekiel 24, Ezekiel's wife died before the captivity began but after the siege of Jerusalem had begun (1-2, 15-18).

Who's in It?
Ezekiel, Pelatiah, Jaazaniah, Nebuchadnezzar, Pharaoh

What

As an eyewitness to the destruction of Jerusalem, Ezekiel is the perfect prophet to talk to the Jewish people about both the glory and presence of God. Ezekiel is in Jerusalem when he sees the glory of God in a spectacular vision—symbolizing the soon departure of that glory from the temple. God shows Ezekiel the actions that will cause the glory to depart the temple (chapter 8). And in chapter 10, the departure is depicted. Two chapters later, Ezekiel performs a skit to show the people what is in store for them. He packs up a suitcase (or whatever they used to transport their possessions back then) and escapes the city through a hole he has to dig through the wall. Jeremiah and Ezekiel, in their own ways, have told the people of their fate if they don't repent. After the captivity begins, Ezekiel also pronounces judgment on neighboring countries Ammon, Tyre, Egypt, and others. The remainder of the book looks ahead to the coming hope God will bring through His plan of redemption—extending all the way to the New Jerusalem.

When

Ezekiel was a contemporary of the prophet Jeremiah. He lived and prophesied at the time of the Babylonian attacks on Jerusalem in 597 and 586 BC. Ezekiel was taken to Babylon in the 597 AD invasion and capture of the Jewish people.

EZEKIEL

Where

Ezekiel began his story in Jerusalem, but he continued to prophesy after he was taken captive and transported to Babylon.

Why

Like the people of Israel 2,500 years ago, we need the continual reiteration of Ezekiel in his book: "I am the LORD." The people back then rebelled and faced communal judgment by being swept into Babylon. Today, each individual must recognize the need for God's presence and must understand that life has value only in recognizing the Lordship of the Savior. Israel being taken into captivity can be seen as a warning to us to repent or face judgment. The glory of God's presence can then be ours in the future glorious kingdom Ezekiel describes at the end of his prophecy.

Wow!

- English poet William Blake (1757-1827) was fascinated with Ezekiel's images. He created a painting called *The Whirlwind,* in which he portrayed Ezekiel's vision of a cherubim in Ezekiel 1. He also referred to Ezekiel in his book *Marriage of Heaven and Hell.*
- At least one writer has noted that in his blockbuster movie *Close Encounters of the Third Kind,* Steven Spielberg based some of his images of the flying saucer on images in Ezekiel's descriptions.

Worth Remembering

- Like the appearance of a rainbow in the clouds on a rainy day, so was the radiance around him. This was the appearance of the likeness of the glory of the LORD. When I saw it, I fell facedown, and I heard the voice of one speaking (Ezekiel 1:28).

- He then said to me: "Son of man, go now to the people of Israel and speak my words to them" (Ezekiel 3:4).
- Then the Spirit lifted me up, and I heard behind me a loud rumbling sound as the glory of the LORD rose from the place where it was standing (Ezekiel 3:12).
- "Yet in her wickedness she has rebelled against my laws and decrees more than the nations and countries around her. She has rejected my laws and has not followed my decrees" (Ezekiel 5:6).
- "For everyone belongs to me, the parent as well as the child—both alike belong to me. The one who sins is the one who will die" (Ezekiel 18:4).
- "The one who sins is the one who will die. The child will not share the guilt of the parent, nor will the parent share the guilt of the child. The righteousness of the righteous will be credited to them, and the wickedness of the wicked will be charged against them" (Ezekiel 18:20).
- "Do I take any pleasure in the death of the wicked? declares the Sovereign LORD. Rather, am I not pleased when they turn from their ways and live?" (Ezekiel 18:23).
- "I will carry out great vengeance on them and punish them in my wrath. Then they will know that I am the LORD, when I take vengeance on them" (Ezekiel 25:17).
- "I will give you a new heart and put a new spirit in you; I will remove from you your heart of stone and give you a heart of flesh" (Ezekiel 36:26).
- The hand of the LORD was on me, and he brought me out by the Spirit of the LORD and set me in the middle of a valley; it was full of bones (Ezekiel 37:1).

Wonders from the Past

- The traditional tomb of Ezekiel is in Iraq, and it is a place Muslims who live there revere. Most Jewish Iraqis left the country between the 1930s and 1950s, but the traditional site of the tomb is still valued.

EZEKIEL

- In Ezekiel 26, the prophet pronounced coming disaster for the city of Tyre at the hands of Nebuchadnezzar of Babylon. The siege Ezekiel prophesied came true, and later Alexander the Great attacked the city. Historical and archaeological records confirm both of these attacks.

DANIEL
Beyond the Lions' Den

Top Ten

1. Daniel was a teenager, perhaps fifteen or sixteen years old, when he was taken into captivity and transported to Babylon.
2. Ezekiel mentions someone named Daniel three times in his book, but many scholars believe it was another Daniel, not the one who wrote this book.
3. Through Daniel's eyes, we see the entire sweep of the seventy years of captivity.
4. In Scripture, not a negative word is said about anything Daniel said or did in his life. Think through other Bible characters, and you'll realize how rare this is.
5. Daniel was around eighty years old when he was tossed in the lions' den for praying to God.
6. Daniel's Babylonian name was Belteshazzar (see Daniel 1:7).
7. Daniel's work was mostly secular—he was as an administrator. He was not a prophet or a priest by profession, but he was indeed a prophet in the sense that he foretold things (Jesus called him a prophet in Matthew 24:15). However, he was not a warner of the people like Jeremiah and Ezekiel were.
8. Dreams and visions play important roles in this book.

9. Daniel must have been a language expert. This book was written in two separate languages: Hebrew (1:1-2:4; 8:1-12:13) and Aramaic (2:5-7:28). Aramaic was the Babylonian tongue.
10. Babylon (where Daniel was taken) was a magnificent city. Some of its features: a splendid main entrance called the Ishtar Gate; an avenue that led from palaces to temples; the Hanging Gardens; and Etemenanki, a grand ziggurat.

Who

Who Wrote It?
Daniel's authorship is affirmed in Daniel 9:2 and 10:2, and in Matthew 24:15.

Who's in It?
Nebuchadnezzar, Ashpenaz, Hananiah (Shadrach), Mishael (Meshach), Azariah (Abednego), Aroich (commander of the king's guard), King Belshazzar, King Darius, Gabriel (angel), King Cyrus

What

Babylon was a powerful empire—powerful enough to send an army 900 miles to subdue Jerusalem and surrounding Judah and transport thousands of people back home. It had built a magnificent city and had established its kingdom all the way from Egypt north to Assyria, west to the Mediterranean, and east to the Persian Gulf. Its strength was great and its kings were powerful. But they were no match for God, as Daniel's book shows. From Daniel's diet being better than theirs, to Daniel's dream interpretations being far superior than the king's wisest men's guesses, to Nebuchadnezzar's inability to kill three young men who wouldn't bow to him—God demonstrated His dominance in Daniel's book. Then, at just the time God had promised, the captivity ended. Daniel's grand prophecies at the

DANIEL

end of the book show that God has sovereignty over the leaders of great nations, then and into the future. The book of Daniel leaves no doubt about God's power over even the strongest world leaders.

When

The events of Daniel began in 605 BC (1:1) and extend through 537 BC, which was during the reign of Persian king Cyrus. The prophets Ezekiel, Habakkuk, Zephaniah, and Jeremiah were all contemporaries of Daniel.

Where

After being taken into Babylon, Daniel remained there throughout the seventy years of captivity and beyond. So the entire book of Daniel (after 1:2) takes place in Babylon, where Daniel rose to a high administrative position in the government.

Why

One of the key themes of the book of Daniel is the value of faithfulness, which the prophet and his friends display clearly. They stuck to their standards regarding the king's food, they refused to bow to a human king (at the risk of their very lives), and Daniel continued his devotion to God in prayer despite a law forbidding it. These examples challenge all of us. Another reason the book is so valuable is that it shows us, through God's instruction and teaching through Daniel, that in the big picture, God is faithful. He has a plan for humankind, and in Daniel's prophecies, we see that it will lead to a Savior and a great culmination of God's glory.

Wow!

- In his song "Survivors," iconic Jamaican singer Bob Marley equated Daniel in the lions' den to the situation black Africans faced when they became slaves: "Like Daniel out of the lions' den, Survivors, survivors."

- In his book *Novum Organum,* which espoused a different way to think about logic, Francis Bacon (1561-1626) used Daniel 12:4 as a tag line in his title: "Many will travel and knowledge will be increased."

Worth Remembering

- But Daniel resolved not to defile himself with the royal food and wine, and he asked the chief official for permission not to defile himself this way. Now God had caused the official to show favor and compassion to Daniel (Daniel 1:8-9).
- During the night the mystery was revealed to Daniel in a vision. Then Daniel praised the God of heaven (Daniel 2:19).
- "Praise be to the name of God for ever and ever; wisdom and power are his" (Daniel 2:20).
- "There is a God in heaven who reveals mysteries. He has shown King Nebuchadnezzar what will happen in days to come" (Daniel 2:28).
- Then the king placed Daniel in a high position and lavished many gifts on him. He made him ruler over the entire province of Babylon and placed him in charge of all its wise men (Daniel 2:48).
- At the end of that time, I, Nebuchadnezzar, raised my eyes toward heaven, and my sanity was restored. Then I praised the Most High; I honored and glorified him who lives forever. His dominion is an eternal dominion; his kingdom endures from generation to generation (Daniel 4:34).
- I prayed to the LORD my God and confessed: "Lord, the great and awesome God, who keeps his covenant of love with those who love him and keep his commandments, we have sinned and done wrong. We have been wicked and have rebelled; we have turned away from your commands and laws" (Daniel 9:4-5).

DANIEL

- "Those who are wise will shine like the brightness of the heavens, and those who lead many to righteousness, like the stars for ever and ever" (Daniel 12:3).

Wonders from the Past

In 1854, the historical existence of Belshazzar of Babylon was confirmed when an archaeologist discovered the Nabonidus Cylinder from Ur. It included this quote: "Belshazzar, the eldest son, my offspring."

HOSEA
A Shocking Story

Top Ten

1. Hide the children. This is a story one would not expect to find in the Bible. It involves God's specific instructions to Hosea to take an action most would find repulsive.
2. God's first command to Hosea, His prophet, was to "Go, marry a promiscuous woman" (1:2).
3. The book of Hosea consists of both poetry and prose.
4. Hosea is called a minor prophet, but not because his message was less important than the messages of people like Jeremiah. The word *minor* in this context suggests that we have less quantity of prophecies from Hosea than we do from those considered major prophets.
5. There is no mention of Hosea anywhere else in the Bible.
6. Hosea is the only Old Testament prophet from the Northern Kingdom (Israel).
7. Of the twelve minor prophets in the Old Testament, Hosea is listed first in the canon of Scripture.

8. Hosea sometimes refers to Israel as "Ephraim." This is because Ephraim was the largest tribe and became symbolic of the land.

9. Hosea 8:5 ("Samaria, throw out your calf-idol!") is a direct contradiction of the actions of Jeroboam I, the first king of the Northern Kingdom. Jeroboam had placed golden calves at Dan and Bethel to encourage people to worship there and not in Jerusalem (the worship center for the Southern Kingdom of Judah).

10. According to Hosea 13:1, the people of Israel added another grievous error to their pattern of worship of the golden calf obeisance when they began practicing Baal worship as well.

Who

Who Wrote It?
Hosea is the writer here. He introduces himself in Hosea 1:1 as the son of Beeri. Some traditions consider Beeri a prophet and hold that he uttered the words of Isaiah 8:19–20, and others believe he is Beerah of 1 Chronicles 5:6. Both of these ideas are pure speculation. Hosea's name means "salvation" or "God's salvation." He was a contemporary of Jonah and Amos, who both prophesied in the eighth century BC. Hosea prophesied in the Northern Kingdom (Israel), which he sometimes refers to as Ephraim. Jeroboam II was king during Hosea's time.

Who's in It?
Hosea, Gomer (Hosea's wife), Jezreel (Hosea and Gomer's first son), Lo-Ruhamah (their daughter), Lo-Ammi (their second son)

What

This is a jarring book because of its content. It is about a longtime prophet of God who is commanded to live in a way that seems contrary to what we would expect Him to ask of one of His people. God asked Hosea to illustrate the unfaithfulness of Israel by marrying an unfaithful woman named Gomer. Hosea and Gomer had three children, each of whom was given a name heavy in symbolism but clearly not a name any child would want to carry: Jezreel ("God sows"), Lo-Ruhamah ("not pitied"), and Lo-Ammi ("Not my people"). God was showing the people of the rebellious nation of Israel that He desired them to return to His good graces.

When

Hosea prophesied to the northern kingdom of Israel during the second half of the eighth century (from about 750 BC until the fall of Israel in 722). He lived during the reigns of four kings of Judah (Uzziah, Jotham, Ahaz, and Hezekiah) and the reign of one king of Israel (Jeroboam II). The backstory of Hosea's time period can be found in 2 Kings 15:1–18:2.Historian and archaeologist Philip J. King wrote, "Hosea's prophetic career may have extended over three decades, from the last years of Jeroboam II [786–747] to the fall of Samaria [721]. He seems to have had firsthand information of the Syro-Israelite war in 735–734."[7]

Where

During the time of Hosea, both the Northern Kingdom and Southern Kingdom (Judah and Israel, respectively) were in operation. The nation of Israel had been divided this way for about 200 years, since the days of Solomon.

Why

God used the seemingly outlandish situation Hosea found himself in as an illustration to Israel of the people's unfaithfulness to Him. In chapter 2, we see God telling the people of Israel that He would continue loving them, even though they had sinned. Similarly, Hosea was to continue loving his unfaithful wife.

Wow!

The 2012 movie *Amazing Love: The Story of Hosea* joins a modern-day church youth group setting with the Hosea story. The lead actor in the movie is Sean Astin.

Worth Remembering

- When the LORD began to speak through Hosea, the LORD said to him, "Go, marry a promiscuous woman and have children with her, for like an adulterous wife this land is guilty of unfaithfulness to the LORD" (Hosea 1:2).
- Hear the word of the LORD, you Israelites, because the LORD has a charge to bring against you who live in the land: "There is no faithfulness, no love, no acknowledgment of God in the land" (Hosea 4:1).
- "Because you have rejected knowledge, I also reject you as my priests; because you have ignored the law of your God, I also will ignore your children" (Hosea 4:6).
- "For I desire mercy, not sacrifice, and acknowledgment of God rather than burnt offerings" (Hosea 6:6).
- "Sow righteousness for yourselves, reap the fruit of unfailing love, and break up your unplowed ground; for it is time to seek the LORD, until he comes and showers his righteousness on you" (Hosea 10:12).
- "When Israel was a child, I loved him, and out of Egypt I called my son" (Hosea 11:1).
- Who is wise? Let them realize these things. Who is discerning? Let them understand. The ways of the LORD are right; the righteous walk in them, but the rebellious stumble in them (Hosea 14:9).

Wonders from the Past

King Uzziah was a contemporary of Hosea. When he died, he was interred "in a cemetery that belonged to the kings" (2 Chronicles 26:23). A stone burial plaque with his name on it has been discovered on the Mount of Olives. It reads, "Here the bones of Uzziah, King of Judah, were brought. Do not open."[8]

JOEL
Watch Out for Locusts!

Top Ten

1. Joel's name means "Yahweh is God."
2. Other than the one who wrote the book of Joel, there are twelve other Joels mentioned in the Bible.
3. Because Joel references the temple, some have suggested that he was a priest as well as a prophet.
4. Joel used such literary devices as personification (1:6, 1:10, 2:21, 3:19) and simile (1:8, 15; 2:2-4; and chapters 5, 7, 9).
5. Some historians believe Joel was one of the earliest prophets. As a prophet in the early days of the reign of King Joash, he may have known Elijah and Elisha.
6. Joel uses the term "The Day of the LORD" several times (1:15; 2:1, 11, 28, 31; 3:14, 18). This phrase can be seen to mean more than one thing, depending on the context—from an outpouring of God's wrath (2:1-2) to a bestowal of God's blessing (3:9-21).
7. The locusts in the first chapter are literal, but the locusts in the second chapter represent an invading army.
8. Peter quotes Joel 2:28–32 during his sermon on the Day of Pentecost (Acts 2:16-21). Key verse: "Everyone who calls on the name of the LORD will be saved" (Joel 2:32; see Acts 2:21).
9. Amos quoted from Joel in Amos 1:2 and Amos 9:13.

10. The historic background for the book of Joel is apparently based on events of 2 Kings 11–12 and 2 Chronicles 24–25.

Who

Who Wrote It?
Joel has a short name and an even shorter biography. Scripture doesn't tell us where Joel was from or even when he lived. All we know about him is that "the word of the LORD came to [him]" (Joel 1:1) and that he was the son of Pethuel. Clearly, who he was pales in importance to the message he presented.

Who's in It?
No individuals are named in the book of Joel, but he refers to elders and priests. He also references Judah, Jerusalem, Tyre and Sidon, and the Greeks.

What

The message of Joel can be explained with two descriptions: he delivered a strong message of judgment to Judah, and he promised that the Holy Spirit of God would someday come to dwell with believers (this would be fulfilled in the book of Acts in the New Testament). In his warning to Judah in chapters one and two, Joel describes a great invasion of locusts.

When

A mystery surrounds the book of Joel, and that is this question: when was it written? Unlike Amos (the book that follows Joel in the canon of Scripture), there are no historical markers to pinpoint the events of the book. Some suggest that Joel was one of the earliest writing prophets.

Where

The city of Zion is well represented in the book of Joel. It is mentioned in 2:1, 15, 23, 32; 3:16, 17, 21. This has nothing

JOEL

to do with where Joel was when he wrote the book, but it does speak to the importance of the city. He also mentions Judah. He mentioned the Valley of Jehoshaphat as a key place where nations will gather for judgment (3:2, 12). Although we cannot say with certainty where this will be, biblical geography scholar John A. Beck suggests it is at the Kidron Valley, outside Jerusalem.

Why

Joel offers hope after judgment. The locusts will come and cause destruction, but there will later come a time of restoration that includes the blessing of God's Spirit upon the people (2:18–32).

Wow!

- Michelangelo painted his conception of the prophet Joel as part of his work displayed on the ceiling of the Sistine Chapel in Rome. The painting shows Joel seated and looking at a scroll. It was painted in the early 1500s.
- Tradition holds that Joel was buried in Gush Halav, which is located in northern Israel.

Worth Remembering

- What the locust swarm has left the great locusts have eaten; what the great locusts have left the young locusts have eaten; what the young locusts have left other locusts have eaten (Joel 1:4).
- Blow the trumpet in Zion; sound the alarm on my holy hill. Let all who live in the land tremble, for the day of the LORD is coming. It is close at hand—a day of darkness and gloom, a day of clouds and blackness. Like dawn spreading across the mountains a large and mighty army comes, such as never was in ancient times nor ever will be in ages to come. Before them fire devours, behind them a flame blazes.

Before them the land is like the garden of Eden, behind them, a desert waste—nothing escapes them (Joel 2:1–3).

- Rend your heart and not your garments. Return to the LORD your God, for he is gracious and compassionate, slow to anger and abounding in love, and he relents from sending calamity (Joel 2:13).

- "Then you will know that I am in Israel, that I am the LORD your God, and that there is no other; never again will my people be shamed. And afterward, I will pour out my Spirit on all people. Your sons and daughters will prophesy, your old men will dream dreams, your young men will see visions. Even on my servants, both men and women, I will pour out my Spirit in those days. I will show wonders in the heavens and on the earth, blood and fire and billows of smoke. The sun will be turned to darkness and the moon to blood before the coming of the great and dreadful day of the LORD. And everyone who calls on the name of the LORD will be saved; for on Mount Zion and in Jerusalem there will be deliverance, as the LORD has said, even among the survivors whom the LORD calls" (Joel 2:27–32).

Wonders from the Past

The prophecy regarding Tyre (Ezekiel 29:18–20) has a partial mention in Joel 3:6. The question "What have you against me, Tyre and Sidon?" may refer to the fact that Tyre had sold Israelites as slaves. Ezekiel prophesied of Tyre's demise, which would come later—especially during the time of Alexander the Great.

AMOS
An Intense Warning for Israel

Top Ten

1. Amos was unlike every other prophet in that he was a man of the earth—a shepherd and keeper of fig trees (7:14).

2. Amos mentions both an earthquake and an eclipse—and both natural phenomena have been identified historically.
3. Amos was a bit harsh with some of his descriptions, even referring to the women of Bashan as "cows" (4:1).
4. The prophecy of Amos is relentless—without any ray of hope until he gets to verse 11 of the last chapter, where he finally speaks of restoration.
5. Amos' name means "burden."
6. While Amos was from a Judean town (Tekoa), his prophecies were aimed at the Northern Kingdom of Israel.
7. The historical background for the book of Amos is found in 2 Kings 14:23–15:7 and in 2 Chronicles 26.
8. The time of Amos was also the era of the prophet Joel, who prophesied in the Southern Kingdom, and Hosea, who was in the Northern Kingdom.
9. Amos is quoted directly twice in the New Testament (Acts 7:42–43 and Acts 15:16–17) and is alluded to many times (example: Matthew 11:21–22 refers to Amos 9:11–12).
10. The times in which Amos prophesied were typified by luxurious living and oppression of the poor (see Amos 2:4–8, 3:10, 5:7, 8:4).

Who

Who Wrote It?
Have you ever met a tell-it-like-it-is farmer who has strong opinions about everything from the government to the way people treat each other? If you have, you'll recognize Amos—an eighth-century BC man of the land. Amos kept and bred sheep, and he tended some sycamore-fig trees in the town of Tekoa, south of Jerusalem. But he was also a prophet of God, and his task was to address the prosperous Northern Kingdom of Israel and tell the people that they needed to repent.

AMOS

Who's in It?
Uzziah (king of Judah), Jehoash (king of Israel), Israel and
its neighbors (Damascus, Gaza, Tyre, Edom, Ammon, Moab,
Judah), Amaziah (priest of Bethel)

What

Amos prophesied during the reigns of Judah's king Uzziah and
Israel's king Jeroboam I. Prosperity was found throughout the
land, and the rich people kept getting richer—at the expense of
the poor. Also, especially in the Northern Kingdom, idol worship
had replaced worship of the one true Jehovah-God.

When

The first verse of Amos mentions a historical event that helps
pinpoint when the events of the book take place. It mentions
an earthquake, which is thought to have occurred in 750 BC.[9]
Archaeological evidence for the earthquake includes debris in at
least six locations in the region. Amos referred to damage from
the earthquake four times in his book. This historic event helps
date the book to the mid-eighth century.

Where

About ten miles south of Jerusalem is the town of Tekoa. It is
mentioned a few other times in the Bible, including the account
of when the people of Israel returned to Jerusalem to rebuild the
wall and received help from a contingent from Tekoa (Nehemiah
3:5). Also, as mentioned in 2 Samuel 14, a wise woman from
Tekoa talked with King David in an attempt to get him and his
son Absalom to reconcile. Amos appears to have prophesied in
both Bethel (chapter 7) and Samaria (chapter 4).

Why

Amos' task as a prophet of God was to get the people of the
Northern Kingdom of Israel to repent. He let them know that
they faced judgment because they had broken their covenant
with God.

AMOS

Wow!

- In Dr. Martin Luther King Jr.'s 1963 "I Have a Dream" speech, he alluded to Amos 5:24 when he said, "we will not be satisfied until justice rolls down like waters and righteousness like a mighty stream."
- Bernie Sanders, while running for president in 2016, also referenced Amos 5:24.

Worth Remembering

- Do two walk together unless they have agreed to do so? (Amos 3:3).
- Surely the Sovereign LORD does nothing without revealing his plan to his servants the prophets (Amos 3:7).
- This is what the LORD says to Israel: "Seek me and live" (Amos 5:4).
- Seek good, not evil, that you may live. Then the LORD God Almighty will be with you, just as you say he is (Amos 5:14).
- But let justice roll on like a river, righteousness like a never-failing stream! (Amos 5:24).
- And the LORD asked me, "What do you see, Amos?" "A plumb line," I replied. Then the Lord said, "Look, I am setting a plumb line among my people Israel; I will spare them no longer" (Amos 7:8).

Wonders from the Past

- Amos' mention of an earthquake (1:2) corresponds to Zechariah's mention of it in Zechariah 14:5. Archaeologists believe they have found the ruins of that earthquake. Its epicenter was north of the Sea of Galilee.
- Amos mentions "garments taken in pledge" (2:8). This refers to the practice of giving a garment to someone owed money—as security. But the debtor had the right to get the garment back. An ostracon (a piece of pottery with writing

AMOS

on it) archaeologists found, dating to the seventh century BC, mentions this practice, just as Amos described it.

OBADIAH
Judgment on Edom

Top Ten

1. One of the shortest books in the Bible, Obadiah has only twenty-one verses.
2. Obadiah's name means "servant of the Lord." Other than that, and what he said in his twenty-one verses, we know nothing about him.
3. In Amos 9:12, the prophet mentions Edom—an enemy of Israel. Some suggest that this mention is a reason the book of Obadiah appears next in the canon of Scripture.
4. Edom includes Petra, the amazing city carved from stone. In Obadiah 1:3–4, the prophet mentions that the people "live in the clefts of the rocks and make your home on the heights."
5. Do you think the name Obadiah is a bit rare? There are twelve different people in the Old Testament who shared the name.
6. Obadiah 1:1–4 is nearly identical to Jeremiah 49:14–16, and Obadiah 1:5–8 is very similar to Jeremiah 49:9. Apparently, Obadiah borrowed from Jeremiah—since Obadiah most likely prophesied after Jeremiah.
7. Among the people Edom resisted, other than Moses and the children of Israel (see "Where" below), were the monarchs Saul, Jehoshaphat, and Jehoram.
8. After the Edomites were forced out of the land, they eventually resettled and became the Idumeans, and from their group came Herod the Great—who eventually sought to kill Jesus.

9. Obadiah said of the Edomites: "You will be destroyed forever" (vs. 10). They were erased from history in about AD 70.
10. Obadiah uses the term "day of the LORD" in relation to God's judgment on Edom.

Who

Who Wrote It?
Obadiah is the author of the book that bears his name. There are several other Obadiahs in Scripture (see 1 Kings 18:3-16; 1 Chronicles 3:21, 7:3, 8:38).

Who Is in it?
The land of Edom, Esau (the Edomites were descendants of Esau), Jacob (Israel)

What

In the tradition of a true prophet, Obadiah had bad news. Most biblical prophets testify about Judah or Israel. In this book, however, the object of the prophecy is Edom. Because she was so prideful and full of sin, the country is about to be destroyed.

When

Obadiah prophesied against Edom shortly after the Babylonian invasion. He was a contemporary of the prophet Jeremiah.

Where

Edom was south and west of Judah—on the east side of the Jordan River. As the people of Israel were completing their exodus from Egypt to the Promised Land, they asked Edom for permission to cross its territory to get to the Jordan. Edom refused, and from then on there was animosity between Israel and Edom. Later, Edom teamed up with Judah to fend off some attackers, but when Babylon invaded Judah in 586 BC, Edom sided with Babylon.

Why

Edom received this prophecy from Obadiah because the people had turned on their ancestors and supported Babylon in the 586 BC invasion of Judah.

Wow!

- Esau and his descendants founded the Old Testament kingdom of Edom. Even the name Edom, which means "red" and suggests the color of much of the land, derives from its association with Esau, who had red hair (see Genesis 25:25).
- The land of Petra has been the setting for many movies, including *Indiana Jones and the Last Crusade.*
- The mythical search for the Holy Grail took place inside Al Khazneh, an elaborate temple in Petra known as The Treasury.

Worth Remembering

- "You should not gloat over your brother in the day of his misfortune, nor rejoice over the people of Judah in the day of their destruction, nor boast so much in the day of their trouble" (Obadiah 1:12).
- "You should not wait at the crossroads to cut down their fugitives, nor hand over their survivors in the day of their trouble" (Obadiah 1:14).
- "The day of the LORD is near for all nations. As you have done, it will be done to you; your deeds will return upon your own head" (Obadiah 1:15).

Wonders from the Past

What was once the land of Petra was covered in the debris of history for thousands of years—until archaeologists rediscovered it in the nineteenth century.

JONAH
Proclaiming Salvation Reluctantly

Top Ten

1. Jonah's name means *dove*.
2. Historians have discovered a number of events that may relate to the time of Jonah's visit to Nineveh, including a solar eclipse that appeared in the city in 763 BC and two plagues that hit there within a ten-year period (765–755).
3. Among the Old Testament prophets, only Jonah finds himself in a situation where he is called on to serve in a gentile kingdom (Assyria).
4. Jonah is mentioned in 2 Kings 14:25. He apparently proclaimed a prophecy not recorded in the book that bears his name.
5. Jonah is mentioned seven times in the New Testament. The context of a historical Jonah being used as a sign or a type of Jesus Christ helps prove that the Jonah story is a true event and not an allegory. Matthew 12:40 is especially strong: "Just as Jonah was three days and three nights in the belly of a sea monster, so will the Son of Man be three days and three nights in the heart of the earth" (Matthew 12:40 NASB).
6. Clearly, Jonah is an aberration as a prophet because he did exactly what the prophets spoke against: disobeying God and His directives. Yet God turned him into perhaps the greatest evangelist ever as his message caused an entire city to turn to God.
7. Lest we be too hard on Jonah for going 2,500 miles in the other direction from where God had sent him, we need to recognize the danger of going to Nineveh. The city of Nineveh was in Assyria, and the Assyrians

JONAH

didn't have the best reputation. They were known for their ruthlessness in their attacks of neighboring places. They were idolaters, bowing to Dagon, the fish god. None of this justifies disobedience, but when we think about scary things we've been asked to do, it's easier to see why Jonah felt intimidated.

8. To many people, the most memorable fact from Jonah is the sea creature that swallowed up the prophet. What was it? The Hebrew words *gadowl dag* simply mean "great fish." We may wonder whether this is a made-up story, but then we would have to deal with Jesus himself (see Matthew 12:40, reference above). Surely the One who created fish knows how to make one big enough to house a man for three days.

9. Of all the Old Testament prophets, only Jonah saw his ministry take place on land that was neither Judah nor Israel.

10. God seemed to express pity and affection for the animals of Nineveh (Jonah 3:8 and 4:6-10).

Who

Who Wrote It?
No one is quite sure whether or not Jonah wrote the book himself, but tradition strongly suggests that he was its author. One element that suggests that Jonah wrote the book was that he was mentioned to be the son of Amittai—both in 2 King 14:25 and in Jonah 1:1. Jonah was from Gath Hepher, which is in lower Galilee. This fact makes this statement from the Pharisees in John 7:52 false: "Look into it, and you will find that a prophet does not come out of Galilee."

What

Nineveh, the capital of Assyria, was a city of several hundred thousand people (120,000, according to Jonah 4:11), and its wickedness had come to the Lord's attention (Jonah 1:2).

So God told Jonah to go there and "preach against it" (1:2). Jonah, who lived in northern Israel, instead went about as far from Nineveh as possible. It would be like someone living in Missouri being told to go to New York City—but instead he heads for Los Angeles. Jonah headed for Tarshish, which was at the western end of the Mediterranean Sea. But Nineveh was far to the north and east of where Jonah lived—across the Euphrates River and then to the Tigris River and to the north. Once Jonah got turned around (with the help of a mammoth fish), he reluctantly traveled to Nineveh, where he proclaimed God's message of repentance. The people of the city, even the king, repented and turned to the one true God. Even after such an amazing evangelistic success, Jonah became angry over Nineveh's transformation.

When

Jonah lived during the time of King Jeroboam II of Israel, who reigned from 793 BC until 753 BC. He would have lived in a time period soon after that of Elisha. The prophets Amos and Hosea were contemporaries of Jonah. During Jonah's time of preaching in Nineveh, the king of the Assyrians was probably Ashur-dan III.

Where

Jonah was from a Galilean town north of Nazareth called Gath-hepher. A mostly Muslim village called Mash Had is at the same site today. Gath Hepher was mentioned in Joshua 19:13 as being part of the territory the tribe of Zebulun was assigned when the Israelite tribes received their inheritance. Some ancient records suggest that Jonah's tomb is in this area, but others say he was buried near Nineveh, which is near present-day Mosul, Iraq. In 2014 the terrorist group ISIS blew up this traditional site of Jonah's tomb. Ironically, the destruction of the tomb allowed archaeologists (who entered the area after it had been liberated) to find evidence of an Assyrian palace that was located under the tomb site. In it, they found inscriptions that mentioned a king who was mentioned in the Bible.

Why

The message of the book of Jonah is at least twofold. It reminds its reader how important it is to obey God and follow His leading. Also, it shows how vital God's message is to any people—for God was relentless in getting Jonah to Nineveh to preach repentance.

Wow!

- A DC Comic called *Legions* includes a character named Jo-Nah from the planet Rimbor. He was swallowed by huge energy beast before escaping. Superman later explains to him that there is a similar story (the one of Jonah and a whale) on earth.
- Michelangelo depicted Jonah in one of his paintings on the Sistine Chapel ceiling at the Vatican in Rome.

Worth Remembering

- All the sailors were afraid and each cried out to his own god. And they threw the cargo into the sea to lighten the ship. But Jonah had gone below deck, where he lay down and fell into a deep sleep. The captain went to him and said, "How can you sleep? Get up and call on your god! Maybe he will take notice of us so that we will not perish." Then the sailors said to each other, "Come, let us cast lots to find out who is responsible for this calamity." They cast lots and the lot fell on Jonah. So they asked him, "Tell us, who is responsible for making all this trouble for us? What kind of work do you do? Where do you come from? What is your country? From what people are you?" He answered, "I am a Hebrew and I worship the LORD, the God of heaven, who made the sea and the dry land" (Jonah 1:5-9).

JONAH

- Now the LORD provided a huge fish to swallow Jonah, and Jonah was in the belly of the fish three days and three nights (Jonah 1:17).
- "In my distress I called to the LORD, and he answered me. From deep in the realm of the dead I called for help, and you listened to my cry" (Jonah 2:2).
- "But I, with shouts of grateful praise, will sacrifice to you. What I have vowed I will make good. I will say, 'Salvation comes from the LORD'" (Jonah 2:9).
- When God saw what they did and how they turned from their evil ways, he relented and did not bring on them the destruction he had threatened (Jonah 3:10).
- He prayed to the LORD, "Isn't this what I said, LORD, when I was still at home? That is what I tried to forestall by fleeing to Tarshish. I knew that you are a gracious and compassionate God, slow to anger and abounding in love, a God who relents from sending calamity" (Jonah 4:2).

Wonders from the Past

- Portions of the book of Jonah were found in the Dead Sea Scrolls.
- The ruins of Nineveh, which is located near Mosul, Iraq, are presently in danger from the encroaching city. Also, many of the ancient artifacts of Nineveh have fallen into the hands of looters. Archaeologists have discovered much, but organizations such as the Global Heritage Network fear much will be lost without a concerted drive to protect what is left of Nineveh's ruins.

MICAH

Judgment Now; Hope for the Future

Top Ten

1. Micah's name means "who is like the Lord." Notice that the book begins with his name and toward the

MICAH

end, Micah says, "Who is a God like you?" (7:18). So the book has that key idea as bookends.

2. If you are familiar with the phrase "beating swords into plowshares," you know a phrase from Micah (4:3; it also appears in Isaiah 2:4 and Joel 3:10).

3. Micah was a contemporary of the prophets Isaiah, Amos, and Hosea.

4. Because Micah came from a small, rural community, some scholars think he was a farmer or a sheepherder.

5. Some have referred to Micah as the "prophet of hope."

6. One of Micah's key prophetic statements is found in Micah 5:2, which says, "But you, Bethlehem Ephrathah, though you are small among the clans of Judah, out of you will come for me one who will be ruler over Israel, whose origins are from of old, from ancient times." This is a prophecy of Jesus' birth.

7. It would not be long before Micah's prophetic warnings came true—for both Samaria (2:3-7) and Jerusalem (5:1). This was in the 700s BC, meaning the Assyrian conquest of Israel was at hand, which would include the siege at Jerusalem.

8. One of the greatest passages pertaining to what God wants from His people is found in Micah 6:8: "to act justly and to love mercy and to walk humbly with your God."

9. Micah the prophet is mentioned in Jeremiah 26:17-19. Micah's ministry was used to help Jeremiah when some priests and false prophets attempted to do away with Jeremiah.

10. Those who study the literary aspects of the Bible note that Micah wrote beautiful poetry and used clever wordplay in his book.

MICAH

Who

Who Wrote It?
Micah hailed from Moresheth-Gath, a town of Judah not far from the border with Philistia. It was located on a road that went south toward Egypt. The archaeological tel called Tel ej-Judeideh is associated with that town. It was excavated in the nineteenth century. Micah lived and prophesied during the pre-exilic period of both Judah and Israel. He was the only prophet to speak to both kingdoms (see Micah 1:1, which addresses "Samaria and Jerusalem").

Who's in It?
The focus is on the kingdoms of Judah and Israel.

What

Micah turns his prophetic guns at Judah and Israel, letting both know that judgment is upon them for their idolatry and for their misuse of the land God had given them. He accurately assails the leaders of the two kingdoms for their lack of justice. Despite the people's efforts to use religious rituals to make things right with God, Micah implores them to be just, merciful, and humble—which, he tells them, is better than sacrificing. Despite the heavy warnings, Micah leaves the people with hope at the end of the last chapter.

When

Micah wrote during the same time Isaiah, Amos, and Hosea were speaking and writing their prophetic messages. This puts his time somewhere in the mid to late 700s BC—probably from 750 to 725—right before the Assyrian invasion.

Where

Although Micah lived in the Southern Kingdom of Judah, his message was directed at both the Northern Kingdom and the

Southern Kingdom. His words were aimed at the two capitals and worship centers: Samaria for Israel and Jerusalem for Judah.

Why

Here we go again. The heart of God is again grieved at the actions of His people—this time in both kingdoms. The people have broken covenant with the Father, and He must do something. The disobedience, judgment, and eventual hope and release continue to be the stories here—and Micah is the messenger. The grand surprise in Micah is the promise of the One to be born at Bethlehem, who will be the deliverer of the people. There is indeed hope ahead!

Wow!

In 2018, Micah was the 97th most popular name for baby boys born in the United States.

Worth Remembering

- Look! The LORD is coming from his dwelling place; he comes down and treads on the heights of the earth (Micah 1:3).
- I am filled with power, with the Spirit of the LORD, and with justice and might, to declare to Jacob his transgression, to Israel his sin (Micah 3:8).
- "But you, Bethlehem Ephrathah, though you are small among the clans of Judah, out of you will come for me one who will be ruler over Israel, whose origins are from of old, from ancient times" (Micah 5:2).
- He has shown you, O mortal, what is good. And what does the LORD require of you? To act justly and to love mercy and to walk humbly with your God (Micah 6:8).
- But as for me, I watch in hope for the LORD, I wait for God my Savior; my God will hear me (Micah 7:7).
- Who is a God like you, who pardons sin and forgives the transgression of the remnant of his inheritance? You do not stay angry forever but delight to show mercy (Micah 7:18).

MICAH

NAHUM
Bad News for Nineveh

Top Ten

1. The name Nahum appears just one time in Old Testament (Nahum 1:1). A different Nahum is mentioned in Luke 3:25 as a part of the lineage of Jesus.
2. Nahum's name means "consolation."
3. Nineveh is in the news again, and it doesn't look good for this large city. It is front and center in Nahum's presentation, and judgment time is ahead for the people who live there.
4. Think of the contrast between the book of Jonah and the book of Nahum. In the first one, the people repented and turned to God because of the message of His prophet. In Nahum, we read of Nineveh's demise, which happened perhaps 150 years after Jonah preached there.
5. Nahum was not alone in his pronouncement of gloom for post-revival Nineveh. Both Zephaniah and Isaiah wrote that Assyria was in for a bad conclusion.
6. Apparently, Nineveh had become quite prosperous. Nahum 3:16 says, "You have increased the number of your merchants till they are more numerous than the stars in the sky."
7. In 612 BC, the Babylonians, Medes, and Scythians defeated the city of Nineveh.
8. After a siege of several months, a river that ran through Nineveh overwhelmed its floodgates at flood stage and inundated the city—and allowed the attacking enemy to enter. Nahum had foretold the flood (1:8).

9. After Nineveh fell, it was apparently obliterated from the face of the earth, in a sense. It has been said that when Alexander the Great marched past the location of this former grand city, he didn't even know there had been a city there.

10. Nahum proclaimed his prophetic message during the reign of Manasseh, whose evil rule over Judah lasted fifty-five years.

Who

Who Wrote It?
All we are told about Nahum is that he is an Elkoshite (Nahum 1:1). No one has been able to identify his hometown. One theory is that it was in southern Judah; another is that the town was near the Tigris River and therefore relatively close to Nineveh.

Who's in It?
The city of Nineveh, the king of Assyria

What

The cruelty and savagery of the kingdom of Assyria was well-known in the region. So Nahum's prophecy of an end to the kingdom was welcome news to surrounding peoples. Look at how he ends the book: "All who hear the news about you clap their hands at your fall, for who has not felt your endless cruelty" (3:19).

When

Nahum lived during the mid to late years of the seventh century BC. The bookend events for the dating of this book are the destruction of the city of Thebes by the Assyrians (3:8) in 663 BC and the destruction of Assyria, which will occur in 612 BC.

Where

Most likely, Nahum was in Jerusalem when he prophesied against Nineveh.

Why

The sole purpose of this book is to pronounce the coming judgment on the land of Assyria through the destruction of Nineveh.

Worth Remembering

- The LORD is good, a refuge in times of trouble. He cares for those who trust in him (Nahum 1:7).
- "I am against you," declares the LORD Almighty. "I will burn up your chariots in smoke, and the sword will devour your young lions. I will leave you no prey on the earth. The voices of your messengers will no longer be heard" (Nahum 2:13).

Wonders from the Past

In recent years, archaeologists uncovered a cuneiform tablet, small enough to fit in a person's hand, that recounts an Assyrian official's anguish as he watches his empire being destroyed in the late sixth century BC. Among the statements: "How can I command? . . . Death will come out of it. No one will escape. I am done!"[10]

HABAKKUK

The Just Shall Live by Faith

Top Ten

1. Habakkuk seems like a really odd name to us, but it has a rather helpful meaning: "to cling," among others (see "Who"). This can remind us to cling to God in prayer, as Habakkuk did.
2. Rather than speaking out to the people of Judah, Habakkuk's message is directed at God.
3. Luke quotes Habakkuk in Acts 13:41.

4. Paul quotes Habakkuk 2:4 in Romans 1:17 and Galatians 3:11. All three passages address the pivotal concept that the just shall live by faith.
5. Habakkuk's use of the idea of the just living by faith, combined with the New Testament references to it, was a spark that helped ignite Martin Luther and the Protestant Reformation in the sixteenth century.
6. The prayer of Habakkuk in chapter 3 was likely a passage used in liturgy during public worship, perhaps in the temple. Indicators of that are that the word *selah* is used three times, that the subtitle "On *shigionoth*" appears in verse one, and that the notes "from the director of music" and "on my stringed instruments" are seen at the end. Some have suggested this meant Habakkuk was of the tribe of Levi—for it was the Levites who led temple worship and only Levites could use musical instruments in that capacity.
7. Habakkuk's chosen writing genre is poetry marked by the used of parallelism (for example, see 1:10–11: "they scoff. . ." "they laugh . . ." and "they sweep . . .").
8. Habakkuk also uses similes. See Habakkuk 1:14: "You have made people like the fish in the sea, like the sea creatures that have no ruler."
9. The historical background for the prophecy of Habakkuk can be found in 2 Kings 22:1–24 and 2 Chronicles 34:1–36.
10. Habakkuk 3:18 is a great reminder for us when things don't look good: "Yet I will rejoice in the LORD, I will be joyful in God my Savior."

Who

Who Wrote It?
Very little is known about Habakkuk. According to *Hitchcock's Bible Name Dictionary*, his name means "he that embraces; a

wrestler." He was a contemporary of the prophet Zephaniah and a prophet of the Southern Kingdom of Judah.

Who's in It?
Although Habakkuk doesn't address any nation specifically in his dialogue with God, he is referring to Judah.

What

Habakkuk does something different from other prophets with his prophetic words: instead of preaching to the people of Judah, he addresses God. Thus we get a glimpse into the prayer life of this prophet. And he doesn't hold back. Sounding a bit like David when he complained to God in the book of Psalms, Habakkuk begins right off with this: "How long, LORD, must I call for help, but you do not listen?" (1:2). And in verse 4 he says, "The wicked hem in the righteous, so that justice is perverted." He is writing after the reforms of Josiah had been instituted, but they were beginning to die out and the people were reverting to their sinful ways.

When

Habakkuk was a pre-exilic prophet for Judah. This means that he lived and prophesied in the years leading up to the Babylonian invasion of 586 BC. (Habakkuk 1:6 hints at this.) And since he served in the time after Josiah died in 609 BC, we know he lived at approximately the same time period as when the calendar changed centuries from the sixth to the fifth. He lived during the time of the prophet Jeremiah.

Where

Habakkuk lived in Jerusalem and wrote about Judah.

Why

Although Habakkuk used a different approach than other prophets, he was addressing the same questions that faced all eras of Judah's pre-exilic history. He seeks to understand why the injustices of Judah are ongoing, and he discovers the reasons for the upcoming invasion by Babylon.

Wow!

- In the Museo dell'Opera del Duomo, a museum in Florence, Italy, is sculptor Donatello's *Statue of the Prophet Habakkuk*. It is also known as *Lo Zuccone*, which means "pumpkin" in Italian—probably because Habakkuk is bald. Donatello created the sculpture in the 1420s.
- Paul Guldin (1577–1643) was a Swiss mathematician who came up with something called the Pappus-Guldinus theorem. Guldin's given name was Habakkuk Guldin.
- The story goes that reformer Martin Luther was taking part in a religious ritual in Rome when Habakkuk 2:4—"the just shall live by faith" (KJV)—came to mind. He stopped the ritual, and returned to Germany, where he took this passage as the basis of his doctrine of justification by faith.
- The opening of chapter 31 of Harriet Beecher Stowe's book *Uncle Tom's Cabin* quotes Habakkuk 1:13.

Worth Remembering

- How long, LORD, must I call for help, but you do not listen? Or cry out to you, "Violence!" but you do not save? (Habakkuk 1:2).
- LORD, are you not from everlasting? My God, my Holy One, you will never die. You, LORD, have appointed them to execute judgment; you, my Rock, have ordained them to punish. Your eyes are too pure to look on evil; you cannot tolerate wrongdoing. Why then do you tolerate the treacherous? Why are you silent while the wicked swallow up those more righteous than themselves? (Habakkuk 1:12–13).
- "The righteous person will live by his faithfulness" (Habakkuk 2:4).

HABAKKUK

- The Sovereign LORD is my strength; he makes my feet like the feet of a deer, he enables me to tread on the heights. For the director of music. On my stringed instruments (Habakkuk 3:19).

Wonders from the Past

"Habakkuk Commentary," part of the Dead Sea Scrolls, was found in Cave 1 in the Qumran area in 1947. This document was a scroll that contained notes and commentaries about the book of Habakkuk written by the people who hid the scrolls in the caves. It has been dated to the second half of the first century BC and has commentaries on the first two chapters of Habakkuk.

ZEPHANIAH
The Coming Day of the Lord

Top Ten

1. Some commentators find a play on words in Zephaniah 2:3, where the prophet says, "It may be that you will be hidden in the day of the LORD's anger" (NKJV). Because Zephaniah's name means "whom Jehovah hid," he could be using a play on words related to his name.
2. Zephaniah was related to Hezekiah, making him perhaps the only prophet descended from royalty.
3. Zephaniah 1:1 calls the prophet "son of Cushi." Some speculate that this meant Zephaniah was of Ethiopian descent and was therefore black.
4. In the book of Zephaniah, we get a prophecy directed not just at Judah and Israel but also to the rest of the world. In Zephaniah 2, the prophet speaks of judgment upon several nations (2:4–15).

5. The historical context for Zephaniah's life can be found in 2 Kings 21:16 and 2 Chronicles 33:1–10.
6. The book of Zephaniah uses the term "day of the LORD" more often than any other book of the Old Testament.
7. There are three other Zephaniahs in the Bible (see 1 Chronicles 6:36, Jeremiah 21:1, and Zechariah 6:10).
8. Statistics project that there are fewer than five hundred people in the United States whose parents gave the name Zephaniah.
9. Despite the ominous prophecy about the end of things in chapter 2, chapter 3 ends with rejoicing in coming salvation.
10. Zephaniah 3:17 gives us the unusual promise that God will sing.

Who

Who Wrote It?
In an unusual departure from the sketchy biographies of most minor prophets, Zephaniah is generous with his background, giving us an actual genealogy (Zephaniah 1:1). Included in his ancestral background is Hezekiah, indicating that the prophet was of the royal line of this king of Judah.

Who's in It?
Judah, people who live by the sea, the Philistines, Ammonites, Cushites, Assyria

What
This book is about judgment and restoration. In the first two chapters, a variety of nations, and then finally the whole world, face destruction brought on by God's judgment. And then in chapter three, we read about the restoration of Jerusalem and all nations of the world.

ZEPHANIAH

When

Using Zephaniah 1:1 again, we see that the prophet spoke and wrote during the reign of Josiah. Josiah's great, great grandfather Hezekiah, while the son of one of the worst kings in Judah's history (Ahaz), was noted as one of the godliest. Except for a prideful mistake late in life when he displayed Judah's treasures to the Babylonians, Hezekiah "did what was right in the eyes of the Lord" (2 Chronicles 29:2). Josiah was also one of the best kings of the kingdom period. He instituted major reforms to get the country back on track with God. The time period of Zephaniah's prophetic presence would have been from 640 to 605 BC. His contemporaries in prophecy were Jeremiah and Habakkuk.

Where

Zephaniah proclaimed his prophecy to the nation of Judah and nations beyond its borders. He lived in and prophesied from Jerusalem.

Why

We have seen this pattern repeated many times now: the people have violated God's covenant and have not repented—and they face judgment. However, hope still lives on the horizon as God offers to restore the people and offer salvation.

Wow!

A mosaic of Zephaniah, created in the twelfth century, graces the interior of St. Mark's Basilica in Venice, Italy.

Worth Remembering

- Be silent before the Sovereign LORD, for the day of the LORD is near. The LORD has prepared a sacrifice; he has consecrated those he has invited (Zephaniah 1:7).
- Seek the LORD, all you humble of the land, you who do what he commands. Seek righteousness, seek humility; perhaps

you will be sheltered on the day of the LORD's anger (Zephaniah 2:3).

- The LORD your God is with you, the Mighty Warrior who saves. He will take great delight in you; in his love he will no longer rebuke you, but will rejoice over you with singing (Zephaniah 3:17).

Wonders from the Past

In Zephaniah 2:4, the prophet foretold the overthrow of Ekron, a Philistine city. It was indeed overthrown in 605 BC. In 1997, archaeologists examining the ruins of a city where they thought Ekron should be discovered a stone with etching on it. Upon translating it, experts discovered that it not only identified the city of Ekron but also the king of the region at the time.

HAGGAI

It's Time to Rebuild the Temple

Top Ten

1. Ezra 3 and the book of Haggai tell the same story of the reconstruction of the Jerusalem temple.
2. Three waves of people returned from captivity. Zerubbabel led the first wave, Ezra led the second, and Nehemiah led the third. Haggai returned with Zerubbabel.
3. The people seemed to be content to refurbish their own homes, their "paneled houses" (1:4), instead of working on God's house.
4. Haggai addressed his comments specifically to Zerubbabel, who was governor of Judah (see 1:1).
5. It is possible (as suggested in 2:3) that Haggai may have been around when Solomon's temple was destroyed in 587. This means he would have gone into

exile and lived in Babylon throughout the captivity before being released to return to Judah.

6. Haggai is the tenth book in the collection known as The Twelve Prophets.

7. The only reference to the book of Haggai in the New Testament is in Hebrews 12:26, where the author refers to Haggai 2:6.

8. While the people began to reconstruct the temple during the time of Haggai, the book does not include the story of the work's completion.

9. Haggai is referenced by name two times in Ezra (5:1, 6:14) and nowhere else in Scripture (other than in the book of Haggai).

10. Haggai told us exactly when he delivered his messages from God. The first was on August 29, 520 BC (using our reckoning of dates and Haggai 1:1); the second on October 17, 520 BC; and the third and fourth on December 18, 520 BC.[11] (These were the findings of R.A. Parker and W.H. Dubberstein in their book *Babylonian Chronology, 626 BC–AD 75.*)

Who

Who Wrote It?
Haggai lived in the resettled Jerusalem after King Cyrus gave the people permission to return home (Ezra 1:1-4). His name means "my holiday." He, Zechariah, and Malachi were all post-exilic prophets.

Who's in It?
Zerubbabel, Joshua son of Jehozadak, the remnant

What
The people have misplaced priorities, and Haggai seeks to bring this to their attention. Despite the people's contention that "the time has not yet come to rebuild the LORD's house" (1:2), God's response indicates that they are wrong (vs. 4). They should

reconcentrate their efforts on rebuilding the temple, a task Ezra had begun about seventeen years earlier with the laying of the foundation. The project has been abandoned, and now Haggai is charged with getting the people involved in it again. As they work on the temple, they begin to notice that this new edifice is nothing like the magnificent temple of Solomon (2:3).

When

The prophecy and story of Haggai takes place after the people of Israel have returned from Babylonian captivity. Haggai 1:1 tells us his message began exactly on August 29, 520 BC ("in the second year of Darius, on the first day of the sixth month"). It has been almost twenty years since the people have returned from Babylon.

Where

This prophecy takes place in Jerusalem, for it is the people of Jerusalem who must rebuild the temple.

Why

Haggai's purpose in writing his short book was to remind the people returning from exile in Babylon that God had called them to rebuild the destroyed temple in Jerusalem. One of the techniques Haggai used to persuade the people to work on the temple was to criticize them for building "paneled houses" (1:4) as the temple remained in ruins.

Wow!

A marble sculpture called *The Prophet Haggai* resides in the Victoria and Albert Museum in London. The sculptor was Italian artist Giovanni Pisano, who crafted it between 1285 and 1297.

Worth Remembering

- This is what the LORD Almighty says: "These people say, 'The time has not yet come to rebuild the LORD's house.'" Then the word of the LORD came through the prophet Haggai: "Is it a time for you yourselves to be living in your paneled houses, while this house remains a ruin?" (Haggai 1:2-4).

- Now this is what the LORD Almighty says: "Give careful thought to your ways." (Haggai 1:5).

- "But now be strong, Zerubbabel," declares the LORD. "Be strong, Joshua son of Jozadak, the high priest. Be strong, all you people of the land," declares the LORD, "and work. For I am with you," declares the LORD Almighty. "This is what I covenanted with you when you came out of Egypt. And my Spirit remains among you. Do not fear" (Haggai 2:4-5).

- Then Haggai said, "'So it is with this people and this nation in my sight,' declares the LORD. 'Whatever they do and whatever they offer there is defiled. . . . From this day on, from this twenty-fourth day of the ninth month, give careful thought to the day when the foundation of the LORD's temple was laid'" (Haggai 2:14, 18).

- "'On that day,' declares the LORD Almighty, 'I will take you, my servant Zerubbabel son of Shealtiel,' declares the LORD, 'and I will make you like my signet ring, for I have chosen you,' declares the LORD Almighty" (Haggai 2:23).

- "The glory of this present house will be greater than the glory of the former house," says the LORD Almighty. "And in this place I will grant peace," declares the LORD Almighty" (Haggai 2:9).

ZECHARIAH
A Look Ahead

Top Ten

1. Zechariah's message from God came in the same year—year two of Darius' reign—that Haggai received his "word of the LORD" (Haggai 1:3).

2. In his own book, Ezra recognized both Haggai and Zechariah as prophets to the Jews in Judah and Jerusalem.
3. Zechariah's name means "Yahweh Remembers."
4. Zechariah's name was not unusual in Old Testament times. It was the name of nearly thirty characters in the Old Testament books.
5. Many of the messages Zechariah received and conveyed to the people were given during the same time period in which the much older Haggai prophesied (in 520 BC).
6. Zechariah was a bit unusual in that he was a Jewish person who was born in Babylon during the Captivity.
7. Zechariah has been dubbed "the little Isaiah" because, like Isaiah, he presented a messianic message.
8. The great news the prophet Zechariah presented is that salvation is available to all—regardless of background.
9. The book of Zechariah is noted for its prophecies about Jesus (See 2:10-12, 3:8-9, 13:1).
10. If you enjoy thinking about items that are "outside the box," you'll like Zechariah. Who else in Scripture tells of a flying scroll (chapter 5), four great horns (1:18-21), a man with a measuring line in his hand (2:1), and a man riding a red horse and standing under a myrtle tree (1:8)?

Who

Who Wrote It?

Zechariah was the son of Berekiah and the grandson of Iddo (1:1). Iddo was a Levite who was part of the return of Israelites to Judah under Zerubbabel's leadership (Nehemiah 12:1-4). According to Nehemiah 12:16, Iddo's grandfather was the head of a priestly family. This probably meant that Zechariah was a priest as well.

Who's in It?
Zechariah, Zerubbabel, Joshua, King Darius

What

God reveals eight visions to Zechariah, and Zechariah uses those vision to provide his message to the people. In those visions, God teaches about restoration, judgment, a coming Messiah, the completion of the temple, obedience, freedom from iniquity, and God's future kingdom of justice and peace.

When

As noted above, Zechariah received this word from the Lord early in the reign of Darius, king of Persia. The years for this book would have been between 520 and 518 BC.

Where

Zechariah had grown up in Babylon, but now he is back in the homeland of his family. From Jerusalem, Zechariah receives his visions from God and then conveys them to his people.

Why

Among the twelve Old Testament minor prophets, Zechariah stands out as the most messianic. He makes reference to Jesus' first coming when he writes, "See, your king comes to you, righteous and victorious, lowly and riding on a donkey" (9:9). He also refers to Jesus' second coming in the verses that follow (9:10–10:12).

Wow!

Michelangelo's painting of Zechariah graces the ceiling of the Sistine Chapel in the Vatican.

Worth Remembering

- "Therefore tell the people: This is what the LORD Almighty says: 'Return to me,' declares the LORD Almighty, 'and I will return to you,' says the LORD Almighty" (Zechariah 1:3).

- So he said to me, "This is the word of the LORD to Zerubbabel: 'Not by might nor by power, but by my Spirit,' says the LORD Almighty (Zechariah 4:6).
- Rejoice greatly, Daughter Zion! Shout, Daughter Jerusalem! See, your king comes to you, righteous and victorious, lowly and riding on a donkey, on a colt, the foal of a donkey (Zechariah 9:9).
- On that day his feet will stand on the Mount of Olives, east of Jerusalem, and the Mount of Olives will be split in two from east to west, forming a great valley, with half of the mountain moving north and half moving south (Zechariah 14:4).
- The LORD will be king over the whole earth. On that day there will be one LORD, and his name the only name (Zechariah 14:9).

Wonders from the Past

In 2011, archaeologists discovered a Byzantine-era church they think might contain Zechariah's tomb. The find was near Horbat Midras, a former Roman city. Sources suggest that the church at Horbat Midras was designed to mark the prophet's tomb.[12]

MALACHI
Ready for a Transition

Top Ten

1. While the book of Malachi comes at the end of the Old Testament, the content suggests that the author wrote in the time of Nehemiah, in the post-exilic days of Judah.

MALACHI

2. Not only is Malachi the last of the thirty-nine Old Testament books, it is also the last of the twelve minor prophets.

3. The next words you will read in the Bible after Malachi—in the book of Matthew—will cover a time more than 400 years after Malachi wrote.

4. According to babycenter.com, Malachi was the 175th most popular name for baby boys born in the United States in 2018. It was at its peak in 2006, when it was the 150th most popular given name.

5. The verse that identifies Malachi as the writer of his book (1:1) contains the only mention of that name in all of Scripture.

6. We know nothing about Malachi biographically. We can assume he lived in or around Jerusalem, for he mentions temple worship and things related to it in Malachi 1:6–10 and 2:11.

7. Malachi addresses a populace that has grown haphazard in its temple practices and a priesthood that is not leading the people toward God.

8. In Malachi 3:1 and 4:5, the prophet gives us a prophetic glimpse of the coming of John the Baptist.

9. Malachi 3:7–12, which discusses tithing, is a passage that creates discussion among Christians who want to obey God but are not sure which Old Testament practices carry over to the New.

10. The book of Malachi closes with a word of anticipation, for it refers to the day of the Lord and to a coming prophet. With those notes of anticipation, the Old Testament closes. Four hundred years later, inspired Scripture will open its New Covenant pages with a clear connection to the Old with the genealogy of the Messiah.

Who

Who Wrote It?

Was the name Malachi, which means "my messenger," a title or the name of an actual person? Most conservative scholars say he was a real person. Bible scholar Robert L. Alden writes, "If a man named Malachi did not write the book bearing his name, he would be the only exception."[13]

What

After the people returned from exile in Babylon, they did some good things. They rebuilt the temple and restored Jerusalem to safety by reconstructing the walls. But then they did what they had been doing for generations—they grew complacent. Therefore, God called Malachi to let the people know where they had been lacking. The prophet pointed out that their sacrifices were not acceptable, that they were again marrying pagan wives, and that the priests were not behaving as they should.

When

Since Malachi prophesied during the time of Nehemiah, this is clearly a post-exilic message to the Jews who had returned to Jerusalem. It is generally accepted that this book was written in the fifth century BC, probably in the 430s and 420s. There are no historical markers such as names of kings, but the events of the book match the time period of Nehemiah.

Where

If the events Malachi referred to in this book relate to the events Nehemiah described in chapter thirteen of his book (which appears to be the case), we know that Malachi was in Jerusalem. He saw how the people had declined in their interest in proper worship and in appropriate respect for the temple of God. So most probably, Malachi lived in or very near Jerusalem and wrote his book with Jerusalem and the temple in mind.

Why

There was a long list of ways in which the post-exilic people in Jerusalem failed to honor God. Among those was their lack of respect for the temple (see Nehemiah 13:4–7, for example), the poor behavior of the priests, and the failure to tithe properly.

MALACHI

While calling the people out for these things and asking them to return to righteousness, Malachi also points to a future when God's promises will be revealed and deliverance will come.

Worth Remembering

- "My name will be great among the nations, from where the sun rises to where it sets. In every place incense and pure offerings will be brought to me, because my name will be great among the nations," says the LORD Almighty (Malachi 1:11).
- "I will send my messenger, who will prepare the way before me. Then suddenly the Lord you are seeking will come to his temple; the messenger of the covenant, whom you desire, will come," says the LORD Almighty (Malachi 3:1).
- "I the LORD do not change. So you, the descendants of Jacob, are not destroyed. Ever since the time of your ancestors you have turned away from my decrees and have not kept them. Return to me, and I will return to you," says the LORD Almighty. "But you ask, 'How are we to return?'" (Malachi 3:6-7).
- "Will a mere mortal rob God? Yet you rob me. But you ask, 'How are we robbing you?' "In tithes and offerings" (Malachi 3:8).
- "Bring the whole tithe into the storehouse, that there may be food in my house. Test me in this," says the LORD Almighty, "and see if I will not throw open the floodgates of heaven and pour out so much blessing that there will not be room enough to store it" (Malachi 3:10).
- "But for you who revere my name, the sun of righteousness will rise with healing in its rays. And you will go out and frolic like well-fed calves" (Malachi 4:2).
- "See, I will send the prophet Elijah to you before that great and dreadful day of the LORD comes" (Malachi 4:5).

Wonders from the Past

- On an island in Upper Egypt, a collection of papyri documents, called the Elephantine Papers, seem to verify

MALACHI

that the situation Malachi faced in Jerusalem is historically accurate. The papers refer to legal documents of a Jewish community that settled in that region, and it appears that there is a connection between the practices of those people and the practices of the people back in Jerusalem—practices Malachi addressed.

- Non-biblical documents among the Dead Sea Scrolls, found in the Qumran region of Israel, referred, as Malachi did, to the anticipated coming of an Elijah-like person to Israel. This corresponds to what Malachi wrote in 3:1 and 4:5.

MALACHI

THE NEW TESTAMENT

MATTHEW
The Gospel of the Messiah

Top Ten

1. Although this gospel does not self-identify its author in the text, scholars agree that Matthew, one of the twelve apostles, is its author (see "Who").
2. Matthew makes great use of the Old Testament in his writings, referring to it more than one hundred times (according to some counts) in his gospel.
3. During the early days of Christianity, before the canon of Scripture was complete, Matthew was the most popular of the four Gospels.
4. One of the marks of the book of Matthew is that it records a series of long teaching sessions of Jesus Christ: the Sermon on the Mount, Christ's commissioning of His disciples, the Parables, His message on the Christian community, and His Mount of Olives Discourse.
5. Key to Matthew's presentation of Jesus in this gospel is the reality that He is the much-anticipated Messiah.
6. In chapter one, Matthew identifies Jesus as the Christ, the Messiah, the son of David, and Immanuel. After thirty-nine books about the promise, Matthew leaves no doubt about its fulfillment.
7. Matthew was primarily writing to an audience of Jewish believers who had begun to grow accustomed to this new development—the establishment of the church of Jesus Christ. They would have appreciated the Old Testament references and the names mentioned in the genealogy.
8. On the other hand, Jewish believers might have been a bit surprised to see such names as Rahab (a redeemed prostitute) and Ruth (from the hated nation of Moab) in Matthew's genealogy.

9. Matthew is one of what are called the "Synoptic Gospels" (the other two are Mark and Luke). This refers to the three gospels that are very much alike in the events they record and in the chronology in which they are recorded. John presents his gospel in a very different way from the other three.

10. Jesus and Matthew exchanged a meaningful encounter as recorded in Matthew 9:9–12. Jesus passed by Matthew's "tax collector's booth" (vs. 9) and simply said, "Follow me." He then joined Matthew for dinner at the taxman's house, which aroused the anger of the Pharisees.

Who

Both early church tradition and the early church fathers agree that Matthew the taxman was the author of this book. Matthew is also referred to as Levi in Scripture (in Mark and Luke). One element of the book that helps lead to the conclusion that Matthew/Levi is the writer is his numerous references to items dealing with money (something a tax collector would know something about). Matthew was a Jewish man from the Galilee region of Israel, and he became one of Jesus' twelve disciples. He is identified in Mark 2:14 as a "son of Alphaeus."

What

Matthew's first task was to introduce his readers to who Jesus was. He wanted them to know about His background (genealogy) and His birth. He introduced the concept of Jesus' virgin birth and the unusual circumstances that surrounded it— which established Him as a very different kind of king. Matthew then moved on to Jesus' life and work, starting with His baptism and the introduction at that moment of the all-important truth of the Trinity (God as Father, Son, and Holy Spirit). He told of Jesus' resistance to temptation and His selection of His disciples. Following that, Matthew recorded Jesus' five great teaching sessions and His miracles along the way. All this led up to the reason He came—to die on a cross and be resurrected for the sin of humankind. And at the end, Matthew records the challenge to all believers: to spread the word about Jesus.

When

It is generally accepted that Matthew wrote his gospel twenty or more years after Jesus' death, burial, resurrection, and ascension—somewhere between AD 55 and AD 85. It is believed that the Gospel of Mark was written before Matthew.

Where

You almost need a GPS to keep track of the locations of the events in Matthew. You can start at the Sea of Galilee area, where Mary and Joseph lived before they traveled south to Bethlehem for Jesus' birth. Then it was off to Egypt to escape Herod's wrath. The family later returned to Nazareth, where Jesus grew up. He was baptized in the Jordan River, faced temptation in the wilderness, and then moved to Capernaum, where much of His ministry took place. He and His disciples journeyed north to Caesarea-Philippi, and then it was south to Jerusalem, where He faced His crucifixion.

Why

Imagine what it must have been like to be a Jewish person in Jesus' day and have it dawn on you that *this* was the plan—that the Jewish Messiah had come, and because of Him your whole system of worship was changing. In one sense, Matthew wrote his gospel to help that transition. The Jewish believers had to be reminded that Jesus was Jewish, that He was the fulfillment of the Old Testament promise, and that it was right for them to embrace Him and what would become Christianity.

Wow!

- The following phrases based on the book of Matthew are still used in popular conversation: "eye for an eye" (5:38), "go the extra mile" (5:41), "wolves in sheep clothing" (7:15), "the blind leading the blind" (15:13-14), "signs of the times" (16:3), and "live by the sword, die by the sword" (26:52).

- In Shakespeare's *Hamlet*, the prince himself speaks of God's will by saying, "Not a whit, we defy augury. There is a special providence in the fall of the sparrow" (see Matthew 10:29).
- In Charles Dickens' novel *Oliver Twist*, one character describes Oliver as a "millstone around the parochial throat." This is an allusion to Matthew 18:6.

Worth Remembering

- This is how the birth of Jesus the Messiah came about: His mother Mary was pledged to be married to Joseph, but before they came together, she was found to be pregnant through the Holy Spirit (Matthew 1:18).
- Jesus answered, "It is written: 'Man shall not live on bread alone, but on every word that comes from the mouth of God'" (Matthew 4:4).
- "Come, follow me," Jesus said, "and I will send you out to fish for people" (Matthew 4:19).
- "You are the light of the world. A town built on a hill cannot be hidden" (Matthew 5:14).
- "In the same way, let your light shine before others, that they may see your good deeds and glorify your Father in heaven" (Matthew 5:16).
- "You have heard that it was said, 'Love your neighbor and hate your enemy.' But I tell you, love your enemies and pray for those who persecute you" (Matthew 5:43-44).
- "This, then, is how you should pray: 'Our Father in heaven, hallowed be your name'" (Matthew 6:9).
- "Do not store up for yourselves treasures on earth, where moths and vermin destroy, and where thieves break in and steal" (Matthew 6:19).
- "But seek first his kingdom and his righteousness, and all these things will be given to you as well" (Matthew 6:33).

- "Not everyone who says to me, 'Lord, Lord,' will enter the kingdom of heaven, but only the one who does the will of my Father who is in heaven" (Matthew 7:21).
- "But go and learn what this means: 'I desire mercy, not sacrifice.' For I have not come to call the righteous, but sinners" (Matthew 9:13).
- "Come to me, all you who are weary and burdened, and I will give you rest" (Matthew 11:28).
- Jesus looked at them and said, "With man this is impossible, but with God all things are possible" (Matthew 19:26).
- Jesus replied: "'Love the Lord your God with all your heart and with all your soul and with all your mind'" (Matthew 22:37).
- "Therefore go and make disciples of all nations, baptizing them in the name of the Father and of the Son and of the Holy Spirit" (Matthew 28:19).

Wonders from the Past

- In Matthew 11:21, Jesus pronounced a curse on the town of Chorazin. "Woe to you, Chorazin!" He said. This town, which was near the Sea of Galilee, dropped out of existence, but archaeologists have rediscovered it.
- Similarly, Jesus condemned Bethsaida in Matthew 11:21. The actual location of the town of Bethsaida is in question. Archaeologists differ on whether it was located at a dig called el-Araj or at another dig called el-Tell. An article by Samuel Pfister at the website "Bible History Daily" (biblicalarchaeology.org) concludes, "As it stands, archaeologists from two separate sites now claim to be excavating biblical Bethsaida." Either way, we know that the town Jesus cursed ceased to exist as an inhabited place, just as He said it would. In Matthew 8:14, Jesus visited Peter's house in Capernaum. Archaeologists have discovered what they think is that house in that city. It is now a major attraction for people visiting Israel.

- In 2008, officials took possession of a stone box tomb-robbers had removed from its intended location. It was an ossuary, or bone box, from the first century AD. These boxes were used to store bones after the body had decomposed in a cave tomb for about a year. This ossuary had an inscription on the outside that read, "Miriam daughter of Yeshua son of Caiapha, priest of Ma'azya from Beit Imri." Experts believe this is a reference to Caiaphas, the high priest who was responsible for Jesus' death (see Matthew 26:3 and Matthew 26:57).

What's Unique in This Gospel?

- Joseph's angelic visit (1:18–25)
- The visit of the wise men (2:1–12)
- Joseph's family's flight to Egypt (2:13–15)
- The death of the children in Bethlehem (2:16–18)
- Judas' death (27:3–5)
- Pilate's wife's dream (27:19)
- The Great Commission (28:18–20)

MARK
The Gospel of Hope

Top Ten

1. Mark is the shortest of the four gospels.
2. This gospel has a fast-moving feel to it. Mark immediately gets into Jesus' ministry at age 30, and off he goes.
3. If you like numbers, you might like this little tidbit: Mark speaks of things in threes—Peter's three denials, the crowds were with Jesus three days without food before the feeding of the four thousand, three

predictions of Jesus' death, Peter wanted to erect three shelters at the transfiguration, three different boat scenarios, three situations when the disciples were asleep, the area where Jesus was crucified went dark at three in the afternoon on that day.

4. Mark uses two words more than the other three gospel writers: the word *gospel* itself (five times in the NIV) and the word *immediately* (thirty-six times in the NKJV).

5. In two instances, Mark uses Aramaic terms Matthew and Luke don't use when telling the same story. In Mark 5:41, where he tells the story of Jesus healing a little girl, he uses the Aramaic *Talitha koum*, which means a tender-sounding, "Little girl, get up." The other time is in Mark 7:34, when he describes the healing of the man who couldn't hear or speak. Mark uses the word *Ephphatha*, meaning, "be opened."

6. One of the characteristics of Jesus' ministry as pictured in the book of Mark is secretiveness. In Mark 1:34, we are told that Jesus "would not let the demons speak because they knew who he was." After healing a man with leprosy, Jesus told him, "See that you don't tell this to anyone" (1:44). In the incident in which He healed Jairus' daughter, Mark records, "He gave strict orders not to let anyone know about this" (5:43).

7. Many scholars believe the book of Mark was written when the author was living in Rome.

8. Mark reports twenty of Jesus' miracles in his short (sixteen chapters) book.

9. In his book *De Viris Illustribus*, which means *On Illustrious Men*, Latin Church Father and historian Jerome wrote this about the book of Mark: "Mark the disciple and interpreter of Peter wrote a short gospel at the request of the brethren at Rome embodying what he had heard Peter tell."

10. The final twelve verses of Mark are not found in the oldest manuscripts. Some conservative scholars

MARK

suggest that while much in those verses is based on other verses (except some of the statements about signs), it is best to be careful in considering those verses as part of the inspired text.

Who

There is no lack of information about Mark, also called "John Mark," in the Bible. We probably know more about him than anyone except Paul, Jesus, and John from the New Testament. It was at his mother's house that the friends of Peter met to pray when Peter was in prison (see Acts 12). Paul and Barnabas had a tiff over Mark during one of their missionary journeys (see Acts 15:36-41). Paul and Barnabas later resolved that disagreement, and Mark became a great help to Paul. We can assume that Mark had met Jesus, but it probably would have happened when he was younger, perhaps as a teenager. So in addition to observing Jesus then, he was also able to use the testimonies of Peter and others—through the guidance of the Holy Spirit—to write his gospel.

What

Without mention of the Nativity, Mark dives right into the action—beginning with Jesus' forerunner, John the Baptist. We read of Jesus' baptism and His overcoming temptation in the wilderness—and the narration continues. Jesus starts accumulating His disciples and then heads off with them to Capernaum. This gospel hardly lets us catch our breath as we see the Messiah drive out a demon and heal the sick and possessed. Jesus takes a brief prayer break, and then more healing. It is with breakneck speed that Mark reveals the Savior's words and actions. Jesus takes time to preach by the Sea of Galilee before He sets off to heal and feed the people. In Mark, we get a condensed version of the much longer Matthew—while at the same time getting a few new details not included in the first book of the New Testament canon.

When

A respectable number of scholars suggest that Mark was written before Matthew—and that it was the first of the gospels to be put into writing. The time period suggested for its creation is about AD 70. There is not universal agreement here; some think it could have been penned fifteen years or so earlier.

Where

The area Mark covers is not as expansive as that of Matthew's gospel. This is because Mark chose not to include many of the stories Matthew recounts. It starts at the Jordan River, moves to the Galilee area and Capernaum. Crossing the Sea of Galilee a little later, Jesus and His disciples arrive at the region of the Gerasenes, where they are urged to leave after the people's pigs drowned. Back in Capernaum, Jesus visits the synagogue before visiting surrounding villages. It's about thirty miles to Tyre, but Jesus goes there because a little girl needs Him. After healing her, it's back to Galilee. Jesus' last long trip was to take His disciples to Caesarea-Philippi, then back to Jerusalem for Passion Week.

Why

When Jesus came up out of the Jordan River after John baptized Him, the Father spoke from heaven, saying, "You are my Son" (1:11). This was an important title for Mark. He used it in Mark 1:1, and he recorded the centurion saying the same thing in Mark 15:39. This is a vital designation, one John used in 1 John 5:5–9 as a proof of who Jesus is. One of the keys to understanding Mark is to know that Jesus is the Son of God.

Wow!

In Abraham Lincoln's June 16, 1858 "House divided" speech, he alluded to Mark 3:25 when he proclaimed, "A house divided against itself cannot stand."

MARK

Worth Remembering

- And so John the Baptist appeared in the wilderness, preaching a baptism of repentance for the forgiveness of sins (Mark 1:4).
- "I baptize you with water, but he will baptize you with the Holy Spirit" (Mark 1:8).
- Then he said to them, "The Sabbath was made for man, not man for the Sabbath" (Mark 2:27).
- Then he called the crowd to him along with his disciples and said: "Whoever wants to be my disciple must deny themselves and take up their cross and follow me" (Mark 8:34).
- "If anyone is ashamed of me and my words in this adulterous and sinful generation, the Son of Man will be ashamed of them when he comes in his Father's glory with the holy angels" (Mark 8:38).
- "For even the Son of Man did not come to be served, but to serve, and to give his life as a ransom for many" (Mark 10:45).
- "Love the Lord your God with all your heart and with all your soul and with all your mind and with all your strength" (Mark 12:30).
- "The second is this: 'Love your neighbor as yourself.' There is no commandment greater than these" (Mark 12:31).
- "Heaven and earth will pass away, but my words will never pass away" (Mark 13:31).
- He said to them, "Go into all the world and preach the gospel to all creation" (Mark 16:15).
- "Whoever believes and is baptized will be saved, but whoever does not believe will be condemned" (Mark 16:16).
- After the Lord Jesus had spoken to them, he was taken up into heaven and he sat at the right hand of God (Mark 16:19).
- Then the disciples went out and preached everywhere, and the Lord worked with them and confirmed his word by the signs that accompanied it (Mark 16:20).

Wonders from the Past

According to Mark 1:21, Jesus taught in the synagogue of Capernaum, His second hometown after Nazareth. While the current archaeological site in Capernaum where a synagogue stands is from three centuries after Jesus appeared there, it is significant. Studies have revealed that the foundation of the synagogue where Jesus taught 2,000 years ago is still there, beneath the third-century worship center.

What's Unique in This Gospel?

- Unlike Matthew, Luke, and John, Mark does not cite any Old Testament prophecies.
- In Mark alone, Jesus foretells the destruction of the temple (chapter 13).
- Mark doesn't include anything about Jesus' birth or childhood. In Matthew and Luke, we have the birth story. In John, we see His arrival noted in different terms: He "became flesh and made his dwelling among us" (John 1:14)

LUKE
The Gospel of Certainty

Top Ten

1. How cool would it be to be Theophilus? Not just because he may have been some kind of high-ranking official (scholars are not certain who he was), but also because Dr. Luke specifically wrote a gospel for his use (see Luke 1:3).
2. The book of Luke begins like no other in the Bible— spelling out its apologetic approach: "an orderly account" to the story of Jesus "so that you may know the certainty of the things you have been taught."

LUKE

This sounds a lot like a thesis sentence for a college research paper.

3. Actually, Luke didn't stop with the gospel that bears his name. He also wrote the book of Acts, which does for the apostles what he does for Jesus here: show that their activities were real and that they were done for God's glory.

4. Luke records more parables in his gospel than any of the other gospel writers.

5. Luke's gospel is the longest book in the New Testament. It is a distant twelfth, though, when compared with the books of the Old Testament (right after 1 Kings). The next longest book in the New Testament is also Luke's: Acts, which rests in fifteenth place overall.

6. It is possible but not certain that Luke's brother was Titus (2 Corinthians 8:16).

7. Think of all the things we learn when we read Luke's exclusive account of Jesus being taken to the temple when He was eight days old (see 2:22-41). We realize the importance of His Jewish heritage, and we see His parents obeying God's command to name Him Jesus, indicating that He would save people from their sin. We see the importance of the Levitical law (Leviticus 12:2-4). We see the relative poverty of the family, whose offering was just two birds. We see Simeon verifying the baby Jesus' Messiahship. It was an auspicious day.

8. Women were important to Jesus' mission. In Luke 8, the writer explains that a small group of women He had healed had been added to the entourage traveling with Him. The disciples plus this group of dedicated followers must have made up quite the traveling contingent.

9. The term "Son of Man" appears fifteen times in the book of Luke. This phrase reminds us that Jesus was not only fully deity, but also fully human.
10. Some Bible scholars, including Dr. David L. Allen of Southwestern Baptist Theological Seminary, are convinced that in addition to writing his gospel and the book of Acts, Luke also wrote Hebrews.

Who

It is widely accepted that Luke is the author of the third gospel and the book of Acts. Luke was not a Jew, which sets him apart from the others who wrote gospels. Also, Luke was a physician, a fact that comes through a few times in his prose. He is noted for doing meticulous research on the topics he wrote about. Luke was able to put into writing such accurate accounts partly because of his close association with the apostle Paul, who mentions Luke in Colossians 4:14, in 2 Timothy 4:11, and in Philemon 24.

What

Luke's purposeful recounting of the life of Jesus allows us to follow chronologically the vital information we need to know about the life of our Savior. Starting with the story of His forerunner, John the Baptist, and continuing on into the vital details about His incarnation, Luke creates a beautiful narrative of the Messiah's coming to earth.

When

It is assumed that Luke, who was a good historian and researcher, used information gleaned from Matthew and Mark to write his gospel. Estimates suggest that he wrote this book in the late 50s to mid-60s AD.

Where

The book starts in the hill country of Judea, probably west of Jerusalem. Zechariah, the father of John the Baptist, was a priest,

LUKE

so Luke includes his visit to the temple in chapter one. The scene shifts to Nazareth, hometown of Joseph and Mary, but Mary soon treks out to the hills to see Elizabeth (her relative and John the Baptist's mother). Jesus is born in Bethlehem, and when He is eight days old, His parents take Him to the temple in Jerusalem. Luke records the story of the family traveling from Nazareth to Jerusalem. From there, as in Matthew, Luke recounts Jesus moving from place to place as He heals and teaches before eventually heading for Jerusalem.

Why

Luke made it obvious from the beginning of his gospel that one of his objectives was to make sure Theophilus knew for sure that the story of Jesus was trustworthy and true. He chose the events he recorded specifically to help the new believer or the seeking believer see that the story really took place and is worth believing. How could someone from a different background or who was naturally skeptical be convinced of the gospel of Jesus? The reader could have checked the facts with people living in that day, and even now we have enough evidence to support the truth of what Luke has told us.

Wow!

Russian writer Fyodor Dostoevsky's book *Devils* is an allegory about the political state of Russia in the 1860s. Before the second part of this three-part novel, Dostoevsky quotes Luke 8:32–36.

Worth Remembering

- With this in mind, since I myself have carefully investigated everything from the beginning, I too decided to write an orderly account for you, most excellent Theophilus, so that you may know the certainty of the things you have been taught (Luke 1:3–4).

LUKE

- But the angel said to her, "Do not be afraid, Mary; you have found favor with God. You will conceive and give birth to a son, and you are to call him Jesus" (Luke 1:30–31).
- When Elizabeth heard Mary's greeting, the baby leaped in her womb, and Elizabeth was filled with the Holy Spirit (Luke 1:41).
- But the angel said to them, "Do not be afraid. I bring you good news that will cause great joy for all the people. Today in the town of David a Savior has been born to you; he is the Messiah, the Lord. This will be a sign to you: You will find a baby wrapped in cloths and lying in a manger." Suddenly a great company of the heavenly host appeared with the angel, praising God (Luke 2:10–13).
- And Jesus grew in wisdom and stature, and in favor with God and man (Luke 2:52).
- John answered them all, "I baptize you with water. But one who is more powerful than I will come, the straps of whose sandals I am not worthy to untie. He will baptize you with the Holy Spirit and fire" (Luke 3:16).
- And the Holy Spirit descended on him in bodily form like a dove. And a voice came from heaven: "You are my Son, whom I love; with you I am well pleased" (Luke 3:22).
- "Why do you call me, 'Lord, Lord,' and do not do what I say?" (Luke 6:46).
- "For whoever wants to save their life will lose it, but whoever loses their life for me will save it" (Luke 9:24).
- He told them, "The harvest is plentiful, but the workers are few. Ask the Lord of the harvest, therefore, to send out workers into his harvest field" (Luke 10:2).
- "So I say to you: Ask and it will be given to you; seek and you will find; knock and the door will be opened to you" (Luke 11:9).
- But Jesus called the children to him and said, "Let the little children come to me, and do not hinder them, for the kingdom of God belongs to such as these" (Luke 18:16).

LUKE

- "Father, if you are willing, take this cup from me; yet not my will, but yours be done" (Luke 22:42).
- Jesus called out with a loud voice, "Father, into your hands I commit my spirit." When he had said this, he breathed his last (Luke 23:46).

Wonders from the Past

- Luke 3:1 says, "In the fifteenth year of the reign of Tiberius Caesar—when Pontius Pilate was governor of Judea . . ." In 1961, a stone slab bearing the name of Pontius Pilate was unearthed at Caesarea Maritima, a town northwest of Jerusalem. In Luke 23, we read that Pontius Pilate sentenced Jesus to be crucified. In one of his accounts of first-century Rome, historian Cornelius Tacitus (c. 56–c. 120 AD) also mentioned Pontius Pilate.
- Early in church history, a specific cave or animal shelter was recognized as the place where Jesus was born (see Luke 2:1-20). What is now called The Church of the Nativity was built over this site somewhere between the fourth and sixth centuries. It can still be visited today in Bethlehem.

What's Unique in This Gospel?

- While Matthew and Luke both include genealogies, they are different from one another. One reason for this could be that Matthew provides Jesus' genealogy through Joseph, who was not Jesus' birth father but His legal father. On the other hand, Luke's genealogy is through Mary, Jesus' birth mother.
- Only in Luke do we see the story of Mary visiting Elizabeth when both women were pregnant.
- Only Luke includes Jesus' presentation in the temple when He was eight days old.
- We learn more about the Holy Spirit in Luke's gospel than we do in the other three.

LUKE

- Only Luke gives us Mary's Song, which we can read in chapter 1.

JOHN

The Gospel of Jesus' Deity

Top Ten

1. The Gospel of John is not considered one of the Synoptic Gospels because it presents the story of Jesus differently from Matthew, Mark, and Luke.

2. Do you recall how your English teacher described metaphors? John will give you a refresher. He recorded that Jesus called himself "the bread of life" (6:35). He also referred to himself as "the light of the world" (8:12). And in John 15:5, the Lord said, "I am the vine."

3. Two keywords in the book of John are *believe* and *life*. "Belief" occurs eighty-four times and "life" appears forty-one times in the gospel (niv).

4. In the book of John, Jesus clearly let His listeners know that He was not just a special man but was, in fact, God. In John 10:30, He said, "I and the Father are one."

5. John contains the story of Jesus' first miracle: turning water into wine at a wedding in Cana.

6. At the beginning of the book of John, we see several important facts about Jesus: He is known as "the Word," He is eternal with God, "through him all things were made," and "in him was life."

7. John gives his thesis for this book—his goal in writing it—in John 20:31: "that you may believe that Jesus is the Messiah, the Son of God, and that by believing you may have life in his name."

8. Scholars have concluded that upwards of 90 percent of what John recorded in his gospel is unique to this book when compared with the other three gospels.
9. The Gospel of John records an incident in which Jesus knew the people He had been ministering to wanted to forcibly make Him the king (John 6:15).
10. The seven miracles John recorded in his gospel help us see that Jesus was the Son of God.

Who

The man dubbed "the beloved disciple" is the penman for the fourth gospel, which bears his name. He was given that moniker because he identified himself as "the disciple whom Jesus loved" (John 13:23). There seemed to be a special bond in the friendship between John and Jesus. John and his brother James were known as the "sons of thunder" (Mark 3:17), an appellation Jesus himself gave them—and it may reflect their temperament. Later in his life, John apparently left Jerusalem for Ephesus, which is where he wrote his gospel in about AD 90. John also wrote 1, 2, and 3 John, and the book of Revelation.

What

John's gospel is the record of someone who knew Jesus on a personal level. Some have suggested that they were cousins and may have grown up knowing each other. But the most important thing John recognized about Jesus—and made clear in his book—was His deity. Imagine what it was like to realize that your best friend was not just a man but God incarnate! So toward the end of his life, while serving the church Paul had started at Ephesus, John sat down to write Jesus' story. He saw in the young Christian church a growing gap between this new faith and traditional Judaism. Through the Holy Spirit's guidance, John set out to make sure people recognized that Jesus was God, that He was the Redeemer, and that abundant life was available to all who would believe in Him. He did this by selecting the miracles and stories about Jesus that would best help people believe. After all, he had plenty of material from which to choose (see John 21:25).

When

John doesn't start with the beginning of Jesus' earthly life in Bethlehem. He starts "in the beginning" (1:1), which connotes that Jesus existed with God from eternity past. This "Word" that "became flesh and dwelt among us" (1:14) then began His public ministry at age thirty with the help of John the Baptist. From there, He called His disciples—and then the stories began: the water turned into wine, the conversion of Nicodemus, the amazing conversation with the Samaritan woman, and several healing miracles. Through John's selection of stories, we move with Jesus to Jerusalem for the Triumphal Entry and the events of Holy Week. After the resurrection, we see some interesting stories other gospel writers didn't record—namely Thomas' recognition of who Jesus was and Jesus' reinstatement of Peter into leadership after His denials.

Where

The first action in the book of John takes place near the Jordan River "where John was baptizing." After spending a couple of days there with John and some disciples, Jesus moves on to Galilee, where he calls several more of His disciples. At Cana, the location of which is not known today, Jesus performs His first miracle. Jesus' travels take Him to Capernaum, His new hometown, then to Jerusalem for Passover and to clear the temple of moneychangers. After a trip into the Judean countryside, Jesus stops by the well in Samaria while his followers went to get lunch. He moves on to the Galilee region before returning to Jerusalem, where He heals a blind man by rubbing mud in his eyes and then telling him to go to the Pool of Siloam to wash his face. After another stay in Galilee, Jesus returns to Jerusalem for the Feast of the Tabernacles and later the Festival of Dedication. After a short stay in Bethany, where

JOHN

He raises Lazarus from the dead, Jesus returns to Jerusalem at His Triumphal Entry.

Why

One way to look at the purpose of John's gospel is to review the seven things Jesus said about himself in that book. These "I am" statements present us with an overview of God Incarnate. He said the following: "I am the bread" (6:35), "I am the light" (8:12), "I am the gate" (10:9), "I am the good shepherd" (10:11), "I am the resurrection and the life" (11:25), "I am the way, the truth, and the life" (14:6), and "I am the true vine" (15:1). No one but someone who is completely man and completely God could be all of these things—and that is what John set out to prove.

Wow!

Charles Dickens' great novel *A Tale of Two Cities* presents a character who is willing to die in someone else's place. Sydney Carton takes Charles Darnay's place at Darnay's execution. Before he dies, Carton quotes John 11:25: "I am the resurrection and the life."

Worth Remembering

- In the beginning was the Word, and the Word was with God, and the Word was God. He was with God in the beginning. Through him all things were made; without him nothing was made that has been made. In him was life, and that life was the light of all mankind. The light shines in the darkness, and the darkness has not overcome it (John 1:1-5).
- "For God so loved the world that he gave his one and only Son, that whoever believes in him shall not perish but have eternal life" (John 3:16).
- Jesus answered, "Everyone who drinks this water will be thirsty again, but whoever drinks the water I give them will never thirst. Indeed, the water I give them will

become in them a spring of water welling up to eternal life" (John 4:13-14).

- "All those the Father gives me will come to me, and whoever comes to me I will never drive away" (John 6:37).
- To the Jews who had believed him, Jesus said, "If you hold to my teaching, you are really my disciples. Then you will know the truth, and the truth will set you free" (John 8:31-32).
- "I am the good shepherd; I know my sheep and my sheep know me" (John 10:14).
- "A new command I give you: Love one another. As I have loved you, so you must love one another. By this everyone will know that you are my disciples, if you love one another" (John 13:34-35).
- Jesus answered, "I am the way and the truth and the life. No one comes to the Father except through me" (John 14:6).
- "Greater love has no one than this: to lay down one's life for one's friends" (John 15:13).

Wonders from the Past

- A well near the village of Sychar has been identified as likely being the one where Jesus met with a Samaritan woman in John 4.
- The Pool of Siloam to which Jesus sent the blind man in John 9 has been discovered at the end of Hezekiah's tunnel in Jerusalem.

What Is Unique in This Gospel?

- John's gospel does not include these things that are in the other three: Jesus' baptism, the transfiguration, the parables.
- John presents some information found only on his pages: the water turned to wine, Jesus washing the disciples' feet, the story of Lazarus being raised from the dead, and Jesus' encounter with the woman at the well.

ACTS
The New Church in Action

Top Ten

1. The book of Acts puts us in familiar territory—the church age. We see things such as the establishment of the local church, evangelism, missionary work, and the changes resulting from people putting their faith in Jesus Christ.

2. We could call this book "the Acts of Peter and Paul." The first dozen chapters mostly give us details about Peter's ministry, and the final chapters introduce us to Paul's work as the church gets started.

3. Or perhaps we could call it "Luke: The Sequel," since Luke clearly wrote this book as a follow-up to his gospel.

4. How exciting it must have been for the disciples when, after Jesus answered their question about the kingdom and promised them the coming Holy Spirit, He suddenly arose out of their sight on His way to heaven (see Acts 1:1–11).

5. But the excitement was not about to end. Imagine the scene a little later, on the Day of Pentecost, when God sent the promised Holy Spirit: flames top the heads of the apostles and a violent wind rushed through the crowd. Then people began witnessing to others in languages they had never learned.

6. Jesus left the disciples with clear marching orders—and even a plan for accomplishing it: witness about Him in Jerusalem, then move out into Judea and Samaria, and then expand the message to the ends of the earth.

7. Acts reveals that there is a new paradigm—the Holy Spirit now equips each believer to carry out the important work of spreading the gospel of Jesus Christ.

8. In the book of Acts, a major transition takes place as followers of Jesus move from worship in the temple to getting together in homes for church meetings.
   If you thought Billy Graham was a great evangelist (and he was), think about this: when Peter preached his sermon to the people of Jerusalem, three thousand people put their faith in Christ and were baptized.

9. Another important transition happened in Acts 10: God told Peter that because of the new system of belief, which based everything on faith in Christ, there would be no more prohibitions regarding the kind of food believers could eat.

Who

Dr. Luke is credited with writing Acts. Again, as he did in his gospel, Luke addresses the book to Theophilus. Luke had accompanied Paul on some of his missionary excursions. Beginning in Acts 16:10, Luke began including himself in the narrative as he wrote about Paul's journeys.

What

Jesus' work on earth is complete, and He is about to return to heaven to continue His work from there. He has promised the disciples everything they will need—including the soon-coming Holy Spirit. Upon arrival, the Spirit empowers the people, and they are off and running as the New Testament church gets off to a rousing beginning. Soon enough, officials get wind of the amazing conversions taking place, and they call on Peter and John to meet with them. They order the two to stop speaking out about Jesus, but this doesn't stop the church from growing. The opposition to this growing faith continues, leading to the death of the first martyr, Stephen. Attending Stephen's murder and applauding it is a man named Saul—who would soon become a great missionary for the gospel. Once the man now called Paul trusts Jesus, he is relentless in his mission as he crisscrosses the area around the Mediterranean to preach

ACTS

the gospel. He leads several missionary journeys, taking with him some of the church's top people, men such as Luke, Barnabas, and John Mark. Those missionary journeys lead to the formation of churches in Ephesus, Philippi, Corinth, and other places. Paul's preaching gets him into trouble, and as the book ends, he is in Rome, where he continues to teach and write while awaiting trial.

When

Scholars can date the events of the book of Acts with confidence because so much is known about first-century events. Jesus' ascension took place in AD 30, so the events relating to the coming of the Holy Spirit took place that same year. The persecutions of this new faith came in the next few years, and Paul's conversion was in about AD 37. His missionary journeys took place in the 40s and 50s. He arrived in Rome early in the next decade.

Where

Jesus told His disciples to wait in Jerusalem, and it's a good thing they did, because they experienced first-hand some of the seminal events of the beginning of church history: Jesus' ascension, the coming of the Holy Spirit, and Peter's huge evangelistic meeting, when 3,000 people trusted the Savior. The ascension took place on the Mount of Olives, just outside the city. The coming of the Holy Spirit took place in a house in Jerusalem, and Peter's sermon most likely took place on the southern steps of the temple. The next few events of Acts took place in Jerusalem, including the persecutions of the Christians, which led to them being scattered throughout the land. For instance, Philip went to Samaria (chapter 8), and spread the gospel there. Soon Peter and John joined him. Paul was on his way to Damascus to spread his hate for the Way (what the new faith was called back then) when Jesus intercepted him and changed his life forever. Christians continued to scatter and evangelize. In Acts 11, we see the extent of the missionary work: Phoenicia, Cyprus, Antioch. Then came the work of Paul, Barnabas, John Mark, and others as they took the gospel message into what is now Turkey and Greece.

Why

Dr. Luke granted us a grand blessing when he penned the book of Acts. Just as it is interesting to read the history of the local church and how its founding men and women labored to bring it into existence, it is also fascinating and inspiring to see how Christianity, which started with one man and twelve followers, quickly grew into an international movement. Acts shows us how it all happened, and that reminds us that God's Holy Spirit is behind any work of spreading the gospel of Jesus Christ.

Wow!

- The first signed painting of the Dutch master Rembrandt was his *The Stoning of Saint Stephen*, which he painted at age 19. It is on display in a museum in Lyon, France.
- Michelangelo's painting *The Conversion of Saul* hangs in the museum of the Vatican in Italy.

Worth Remembering

- Then they gathered around him and asked him, "Lord, are you at this time going to restore the kingdom to Israel?" (Acts 1:6).
- "But you will receive power when the Holy Spirit comes on you; and you will be my witnesses in Jerusalem, and in all Judea and Samaria, and to the ends of the earth" (Acts 1:8).
- When the day of Pentecost came, they were all together in one place. Suddenly a sound like the blowing of a violent wind came from heaven and filled the whole house where they were sitting. They saw what seemed to be tongues of fire that separated and came to rest on each of them. All of

ACTS

them were filled with the Holy Spirit and began to speak in other tongues as the Spirit enabled them (Acts 2:1-4).

- Peter replied, "Repent and be baptized, every one of you, in the name of Jesus Christ for the forgiveness of your sins. And you will receive the gift of the Holy Spirit" (Acts 2:38).
- They devoted themselves to the apostles' teaching and to fellowship, to the breaking of bread and to prayer. Everyone was filled with awe at the many wonders and signs performed by the apostles. All the believers were together and had everything in common. They sold property and possessions to give to anyone who had need. Every day they continued to meet together in the temple courts. They broke bread in their homes and ate together with glad and sincere hearts, praising God and enjoying the favor of all the people. And the Lord added to their number daily those who were being saved (Acts 2:42-47).
- All the believers were one in heart and mind. No one claimed that any of their possessions was their own, but they shared everything they had (Acts 4:32).
- Peter and the other apostles replied: "We must obey God rather than human beings!" (Acts 5:29).
- Then Peter began to speak: "I now realize how true it is that God does not show favoritism but accepts from every nation the one who fears him and does what is right" (Acts 10:34-35).
- When the Gentiles heard this, they were glad and honored the word of the Lord; and all who were appointed for eternal life believed. The word of the Lord spread through the whole region (Acts 13:48-49).
- In this way the word of the Lord spread widely and grew in power (Acts 19:20).

Wonders from the Past

- Scholars have verified that the names and locations of people and places mentioned in the Acts are historically true. Here are some examples:

- In Acts 17:6–8, Luke refers to city officials in Thessalonica "politarchs" (translated as "city officials" or "rulers of the city" in different Bible versions). Ancient inscriptions discovered in that city verify the use of that word.
- The names of Felix and Festus, both procurators of Judea named in Acts, have been historically verified.
- Luke mentions a man named Sergius Paulus in Acts 13:7. Archaeological proof has been found that a man by this name lived at the time.
- Luke's comments regarding the city of Ephesus in Acts 19:18–41 have been verified: sorcery was practiced there, trade in silver idols was prevalent, a temple dedicated to the false deity Artemis was located there, and there was a theater in the city. For more on this, go to inplainsite.org /html/acts_and_archaeology.html.

ROMANS
Doctrine and Practice of the Christian Faith

Top Ten

1. Through the years, many have waxed eloquently about the book of Romans. Martin Luther said of the book: "the more it is dealt with, the more precious it becomes, and the better it tastes."
2. We can surmise by reading Acts 2:10 that some of the people Paul wrote to in the church at Rome could have been present at the coming of the Holy Spirit on the Day of Pentecost (before Saul/Paul was a Christian).
3. Paul quotes from the Old Testament (which he would have known well because of his strong Jewish education) nearly sixty times in this book.

4. Unlike the churches in Ephesus and Philippi, Paul did not found the church in Rome.

5. Paul apparently greatly valued the work of the women in the church he addressed in this book (see Romans 16:1–15). Many of the people mentioned in this passage are women.

6. The book of Romans, specifically Romans 3:21–26, helped provide the spark that ignited the Protestant Reformation under the leadership of Martin Luther.

7. Paul's travel plans outlined in this book included a stop in Rome to visit the people at the church there before making his way to Spain (see Romans 15:24–28).

8. Romans sets forth the vital truth that the knowledge of God is innate in all humankind and has been made plain to all, making all humans without excuse regarding the knowledge of His existence (see Romans 1:18–20).

9. Romans also clearly points out that every human has sinned and must be reconciled to God. This establishes the absolute necessity of the gospel and of faith for each person.

10. Paul also sets a standard for believers in regard to how they should respond to their governmental leaders. Imagine how this was received by the Christians in Rome, who lived under often oppressive leadership.

Who

Paul self-identifies as the author of this letter in the first verse. He also gives credit to his scribe, Tertius, who actually recorded the words on the scroll. It is thought that Paul was in Corinth when he wrote this letter to fellow believers in Rome. He planned to deliver the letter himself.

What

Paul's declaration in Romans 1:16 that he is not ashamed of the gospel is as much a testimony as it is a teaching. Paul clearly

ROMANS

demonstrates through his efforts that he will take the gospel anywhere and explain it to anybody. In Romans, he takes the opportunity to record for all time the theology behind the gospel, and as a result he has provided for us an abundantly clear explanation of the importance of God's solution for humankind's deadly problem of sin. In the doctrinal part of Romans, we read about the universality of sin, righteousness before God (with Abraham as an illustration), the advantages of justification by faith, and the results of our relationship with Jesus Christ, our Savior. Paul then moves on to spell out how we should live in light of our salvation.

When

Unlike Acts, this book is not based on events as much as it is on teaching and principals. As we read Romans, we don't follow a series of activities being described in a certain time frame. We know that Paul wrote the book while visiting Corinth— probably in AD 57 or 58.

Where

Paul mentions some of the people with whom he interacted in Corinth. According to 16:23, a person named Gaius was apparently Paul's host in that city. He also sends greetings from a city official named Erastus, from a person in the church named Quartus, from his coworker Timothy, and from a few others in the city.

Why

Paul was a missionary, not a pastor, but he had a pastor's heart. He knew that there was plenty of room for division in the new churches—all of which were just three decades old or younger. He knew there was tension between Jewish believers and gentile believers regarding which practices Christians needed to participate in. That's why Paul tried to unify the believers by repeating the basics, such as justification through the righteousness of God—plus nothing. Paul wanted the churches

ROMANS

to rally around that principle and set aside the differences that resulted from their coming from diverse cultures.

Worth Remembering

- For I am not ashamed of the gospel, because it is the power of God that brings salvation to everyone who believes: first to the Jew, then to the Gentile (Romans 1:16).
- For since the creation of the world God's invisible qualities—his eternal power and divine nature—have been clearly seen, being understood from what has been made, so that people are without excuse (Romans 1:20).
- As it is written: "There is no one righteous, not even one" (Romans 3:10).
- For all have sinned and fall short of the glory of God (Romans 3:23).
- Therefore, since we have been justified through faith, we have peace with God through our Lord Jesus Christ (Romans 5:1).
- But God demonstrates his own love for us in this: While we were still sinners, Christ died for us (Romans 5:8).
- For the wages of sin is death, but the gift of God is eternal life in Christ Jesus our Lord (Romans 6:23).
- Because through Christ Jesus the law of the Spirit who gives life has set you free from the law of sin and death (Romans 8:2).
- And we know that in all things God works for the good of those who love him, who have been called according to his purpose (Romans 8:28).
- If you declare with your mouth, "Jesus is Lord," and believe in your heart that God raised him from the dead, you will be saved (Romans 10:9).
- For, "Everyone who calls on the name of the Lord will be saved" (Romans 10:13).
- Therefore, I urge you, brothers and sisters, in view of God's mercy, to offer your bodies as a living sacrifice, holy and

ROMANS

pleasing to God—this is your true and proper worship. Do not conform to the pattern of this world, but be transformed by the renewing of your mind. Then you will be able to test and approve what God's will is—his good, pleasing and perfect will (Romans 12:1-2).

Wonders from the Past

- As archaeologists poked around in Corinth, they found a stone block that had this inscription on it: "Erastus, commissioner of public works, bore the expense of this pavement" (see Romans 16:23).
- Of the twenty-six Roman Christians Paul mentions by name at the end of this book, thirteen of the names have been discovered inscribed on items that relate to the palace of the Roman emperor. This shows that these were common names at the time in the Roman capital.
- In 1972, Dr. John McRay was doing archaeological research at Caesarea Maritima when he found a mosaic inscription of Romans 13:3. The inscription dates back to the fifth century AD.

1 CORINTHIANS

Trouble in the Church

Top Ten

1. Paul seems to have his hands full with this group of believers in a city called Corinth. These people lived in a prosperous city that offered all kinds of activities that were not exactly Sunday school-approved.
2. When you add up all the things Paul wrote in Scripture, he used up more ink writing to the folks at Corinth than to believers in any other city.

3. Among the issues Paul addressed in 1 Corinthians were divisions based on personalities, divisions based on intellectual background, sexual immorality, civil actions of Christian vs. Christian, marriage in general, food offered to idols, and the proper use of spiritual gifts (all pretty modern issues, except the food thing).

4. Paul was not in Corinth to observe the issues he addressed in this letter. He was probably in Ephesus at the time. He mentioned that he had heard about the division issues through a report from "Chloe's household" (1:11).

5. Paul was familiar with the people in the church at Corinth because he had lived there for eighteen months in AD 51–52. He had stayed with a married couple named Aquila and Priscilla (they had been kicked out of Rome because they were Jewish). It was here that Paul worked making tents alongside that couple. Paul had preached in the synagogue for a while until he was opposed. Then he simply moved next door to the synagogue and had church at Titius Justus' house.

6. While staying in Corinth, Paul wrote the letters we now call 1 and 2 Thessalonians.

7. Sexual immorality was ingrained even in the pagan worship of the people of Corinth. That worship was based in the Temple of Aphrodite, a place noted for its immoral sexual practices under the auspices of "worship."

8. In the midst of all of the problems Paul had to address in this letter, he taught some amazing truths and practices: the Lord's Supper, love, and a grand explanation of the resurrection.

9. For a close-up view of the kinds of people who lived in Corinth—and the change salvation could bring—look at 1 Corinthians 6:9–11. Redemption brought huge lifestyle changes to many in the city.

10. The people in the church at Corinth were mostly gentiles, and they represented a wide socioeconomic range.

Who

Paul had been away from the Christians in Corinth for a few years, and he had received a negative report about them. To address what he had heard, he sat down in Ephesus to write a letter to instruct, rebuke, and educate his friends in the church. Paul started this church, so he had an intense interest in seeing the people live as godly Christians should.

What

When whoever read this letter to the people in the church at Corinth got started, you can picture the people calmly listening and soaking up Paul's gentle beginning. A word about himself, a word about the people, a friendly, "grace and peace to you" benediction, a thoughtful note about how thankful he was for them. And then, bam! Paul gets to his point: there's trouble in Corinth, and he was going to do something about it. As gentle as Paul was, he had to get to the point. Paul explained in clear terms the problems he had heard about, and then he explained what the people would have to do to reverse course and follow Jesus as they should. Paul spoke prophetically (explaining what they needed to know, not foretelling the future), just as a pastor does today when a problem creeps into a local church. His purpose was to correct a myriad of problems that were killing the effectiveness of Christ's local body of believers in Corinth.

When

Paul wrote this letter to the folks at Corinth in about AD 55, three or so years after he had left Corinth after spending eighteen months there. He was living in Ephesus at the time.

Where

Geography is not an issue in this letter. We know that the people lived in Corinth, a city steeped in idolatry and immorality. It was probably not possible for the people of Corinth to escape the presence and overall influence of the Temple of Aphrodite, a temple to the goddess of love. However, Paul wanted the Christians in Corinth to avoid having it negatively affect their lives.

Why

What Paul wanted from the church in Corinth is no different from what a godly pastor wants from the people in his own church: a recognition that Christ is supreme and an acknowledgement that the things the community outside the church offers, while inviting, can be harmful. Paul set out to help these people understand what true Christianity looks like so that they could enjoy its benefits and strengthen their relationship with God. Paul was loving but direct in his message to them.

Wow!

- In J.K. Rowling's *Harry Potter and the Deathly Hallows* is a reference to 1 Corinthians 15:26: "The last enemy to be destroyed is death."
- In the 1984 award-winning movie *Places in the Heart*, the key scene is based on a reading of 1 Corinthians 13 and the result of understanding authentic love in Christ.

Worth Remembering

- So neither the one who plants nor the one who waters is anything, but only God, who makes things grow (1 Corinthians 3:7).
- Or do you not know that wrongdoers will not inherit the kingdom of God? Do not be deceived: Neither the sexually immoral nor idolaters nor adulterers nor men who have sex with men (1 Corinthians 6:9).
- No temptation has overtaken you except what is common to mankind. And God is faithful; he will not let you be tempted beyond what you can bear. But when you are

tempted, he will also provide a way out so that you can endure it (1 Corinthians 10:13).

- So whether you eat or drink or whatever you do, do it all for the glory of God (1 Corinthians 10:31).
- But in fact God has placed the parts in the body, every one of them, just as he wanted them to be (1 Corinthians 12:18)
- If I speak in the tongues of men or of angels, but do not have love, I am only a resounding gong or a clanging cymbal (1 Corinthians 13:1).
- Love is patient, love is kind. It does not envy, it does not boast, it is not proud (1 Corinthians 13:4).
- For what I received I passed on to you as of first importance: that Christ died for our sins according to the Scriptures (1 Corinthians 15:3).
- After that, he appeared to more than five hundred of the brothers and sisters at the same time, most of whom are still living, though some have fallen asleep. Then he appeared to James, then to all the apostles, and last of all he appeared to me also, as to one abnormally born (1 Corinthians 15:6–8).

Wonders from the Past

In AD 51, the Isthmian Games were held near Corinth. In 1 Corinthians 9:24–27, Paul uses athletic terminology, perhaps as a way to connect with people who had interest in the Games.

2 CORINTHIANS

Things Get Personal for Paul

Top Ten

1. Although Paul's first letter to the Corinthians was generally well received, there were some in the church

who opposed him. In part, 2 Corinthians is a response to those people.

2. Paul had received Titus' report stating that much good had come as a result of his first letter, but that there were still some issues. One was that some people did not consider Paul a legitimate apostle.

3. In order to explain his legitimacy, Paul included considerable biographical information in 2 Corinthians. After he completed this letter, Titus delivered it to the church.

4. Paul also had to deal with false teachers who had come to the church to preach "a Jesus other than the Jesus we preached" (2 Corinthians 11:4).

5. It appears that Paul wrote four letters to the Corinthians. One that no longer exists is mentioned in 1 Corinthians 5:9, and the other not in the canon of Scripture is mentioned in 2 Corinthians 2:4.

6. Paul ended up making three trips to Corinth. The first time was when he started the church; he was there a year and a half. The second is referred to in 2 Corinthians 2:1 as a "painful visit." And he wintered there after he had written 2 Corinthians. Paul wrote the book of Romans on this visit.

7. Although Corinth was in Greece, it had a heavy Roman influence. You can see that in names of people Paul mentioned (Aquila, Crispus, Gaius). The Romans had rebuilt the city in 44 BC—about one hundred years before Paul first visited it. Despite the Roman influence, Paul wrote his two letters to the Corinthians in Greek.

8. In 2 Corinthians 8–9, Paul writes the most extensive teaching in the New Testament about giving.

9. In 2 Corinthians 11:12 and following, it appears that Paul could be telling readers that he was going back to his vocation of tent making ("I will keep on doing what I am doing in order to cut the ground

from under those who want an opportunity to be considered equal with us in the things they boast about"). He was making sure they knew that he was not sharing the gospel for financial gain—and that his way of earning a living was by making tents. If he was in the city near the time of the Isthmian Games (an Olympic-like event), there would be plenty of work to do because people coming to town for the Games would be staying in tents.

10. Second Corinthians 1:3–7 is one of the most helpful passages in Scripture for those who are grieving, for it reminds us that our heavenly Father is the God of all comfort.

Who

The evidence is strong that Paul wrote 2 Corinthians. The book has too many autobiographical details to be considered to have come from anyone else's pen. It appears that he wrote this letter from Macedonia, somewhere between AD 54 and 56.

What

Through no fault of his own, Paul is forced to defend himself. Certain factions in the Corinthian church had begun to question his authority, and at the same time, false teachers had crept into the church to throw into the mix confusion about doctrine and sound teaching. As he presents his case, Paul also provides teaching on subjects such as the New Covenant, giving to the Lord's work, reconciliation, and warnings to those who are in rebellion.

When

The letter seems to be a preparation for Paul's next visit to Corinth (Acts 20:2–3). It arrived to the people of the church via Titus. Later, after they had time to digest its contents and work through some of the issues it addressed, Paul arrived to spend the winter there.

2 CORINTHIANS

Where

Geography is not an issue in this letter. We know it is addressed to the church in in Corinth, a city steeped in idolatry and immorality. It was probably not possible for the people of Corinth to escape the presence and overall influence of the Temple of Aphrodite, a temple to the goddess of love. However, Paul wanted the Christians in Corinth to avoid having it negatively affect their lives.

Why

Paul, the founding father of the Corinthian church, is deeply concerned about the direction the congregation is going. Because of what we know about Paul, it seems hard to believe that the people were able to make the accusations they did about him. But dealing with people can be difficult, and their concerns and their sometimes-erroneous understanding of doctrine must be addressed. Paul's handling of these situations is a great lesson for ministers of the gospel today as they deal with similar issues.

Wow!

- In Thornton Wilder's Pulitzer Prize-winning novel *The Bridge of San Luis Rey*, one of the characters, Marquesa de Montemayor, refers to a letter exchanged between him and his daughter as her 2 Corinthians letter—probably referencing the fact that Paul's letter was meant to iron out difficulties in the church.
- In Shakespeare's play *Macbeth*, the main character says, "No boasting like a fool; This deed I'll do before this purpose cool" (Act 4, Scene 1, Lines 71-72). This is an allusion to 2 Corinthians 11:16: "Let no one take me for a fool. But if you do, then tolerate me just as you would a fool, so that I may do a little boasting."

Worth Remembering

- Praise be to the God and Father of our Lord Jesus Christ, the Father of compassion and the God of all comfort, who comforts us in all our troubles, so that we can comfort those in any trouble with the comfort we ourselves receive from God (2 Corinthians 1:3-4).

- For our light and momentary troubles are achieving for us an eternal glory that far outweighs them all. So we fix our eyes not on what is seen, but on what is unseen, since what is seen is temporary, but what is unseen is eternal (2 Corinthians 4:17-18).
- We are confident, I say, and would prefer to be away from the body and at home with the Lord. So we make it our goal to please him, whether we are at home in the body or away from it (2 Corinthians 5:8-9).
- For we must all appear before the judgment seat of Christ, so that each of us may receive what is due us for the things done while in the body, whether good or bad (2 Corinthians 5:10).
- Therefore, if anyone is in Christ, the new creation has come: The old has gone, the new is here! (2 Corinthians 5:17).
- For he says, "In the time of my favor I heard you, and in the day of salvation I helped you." I tell you, now is the time of God's favor, now is the day of salvation (2 Corinthians 6:2).
- The weapons we fight with are not the weapons of the world. On the contrary, they have divine power to demolish strongholds. We demolish arguments and every pretension that sets itself up against the knowledge of God, and we take captive every thought to make it obedient to Christ (2 Corinthians 10:4-5).
- We do not dare to classify or compare ourselves with some who commend themselves. When they measure themselves by themselves and compare themselves with themselves, they are not wise (2 Corinthians 10:12).
- And I know that this man—whether in the body or apart from the body I do not know, but God knows—was caught up to paradise and heard inexpressible things, things that no one is permitted to tell (2 Corinthians 12:3-4).
- May the grace of the Lord Jesus Christ, and the love of God, and the fellowship of the Holy Spirit be with you all (2 Corinthians 13:14).

2 CORINTHIANS

Wonders from the Past

About twenty years after Paul's last visit to Corinth, a devastating earthquake hit the city.

GALATIANS
Paul's Handwritten Note

Top Ten

1. In Galatians 6:11, Paul told the people of the churches in the region of Galatia that he had penned his own letter to them in large letters. Scholars have surmised that it was in his own hand because of its urgency, and that he wrote it in large letters because he had poor eyesight.
2. In this letter, Paul addressed an issue similar to one facing the church at Corinth: false teachers trying to sway believers away from the true gospel.
3. The false teachers Paul referred to in this letter were called "Judaizers." They told the people that, in keeping with Jewish law, all males (Jew or gentile) had to be circumcised as a prerequisite for salvation. This question had been settled at the Council of Jerusalem (see Acts 15), but some continued to teach this false doctrine.
4. Martin Luther was fond of the book of Galatians because of Paul's emphasis on salvation by faith alone.
5. When Paul writes of the churches of Galatia (1:2), he is referring to assemblies of believers in Lystra, Antioch, Iconium, and Derbe.
6. In this letter, Paul lets his readers in on a little squabble he'd had with Peter in the town of Antioch (2:11–13). Peter had been afraid to associate with gentile believers because of his association with those who thought Jewish believers should keep practicing Jewish customs.

7. In Acts 15, we read about a council in Jerusalem to discuss the same issue raised in Galatians 2:11–21. Bible scholars sometimes debate this premise: these two accounts describing this discussion about faith in Christ alone were actually separate accounts of the same incident.

8. One of the most instructive passages for Christians seeking to live a godly life is found in Galatians 5. It contrasts two ways of living: one controlled by the sinful nature (19-21) and one controlled by the indwelling Holy Spirit (22-23).

9. Not many people quote Habakkuk. But Paul did, and it was pivotal to his argument: "The righteous will live by his faith" (Habakkuk 2:4; Galatians 3:11).

10. In order to teach the contrast between the law and grace, Paul uses the word *law* twenty-eight times in this short book.

Who

As in 2 Corinthians, the autobiographical information contained in this book confirms that Paul wrote it.

What

The gospel of Jesus Christ is the centerpiece of this book. Paul sets out to show that Jesus had come to rescue lost sinners, and that they need nothing but faith in Him for salvation. He seems a bit perturbed that the people have so quickly gone astray from truth and headed toward a "different gospel" (1:6). He launches into a biographical sketch to establish his own faith through grace before using numerous examples to support this doctrine (chapter 3). He concludes by reminding his readers about the great power of the Holy Spirit.

When

If this is Paul's first letter to a church, as some say, and if he wrote it in about 48 AD, then he penned this letter just fifteen or so years after the ascension of Jesus. This fast-spreading faith

GALATIANS

was already being tested, so it was vital that Paul nip any heresy in the bud.

Where

This message went to several churches in Galatia, which was an area west of Israel and north of the Mediterranean Sea. Paul had visited the area on his first missionary journey (see Acts 13:4-14:28).

Why

Paul did not set out to argue with the Judaizers who had come into these towns to sow seeds of heresy. Instead, he addressed the Galatian Christians themselves, hoping to dissuade them from leaving their faith behind and depending on works for salvation. It was a direct approach that was powerful then—and it still packs a punch today.

Wow!

In his "I Have a Dream" speech in 1963, Dr. Martin Luther King Jr. wished for the day "when all God's children, black men and white men, Jews and Gentiles and Catholics, will be able to join hands and sing the words of the old Negro spiritual, 'Free at last!'" Many have assumed that he was alluding to Galatians 3:28: "There is neither Jew nor Gentile, neither slave nor free, nor is there male and female, for you are all one in Christ Jesus."

Worth Remembering

- For through the law I died to the law so that I might live for God. I have been crucified with Christ and I no longer live, but Christ lives in me. The life I now live in the body, I live by faith in the Son of God, who loved me and gave himself for me (Galatians 2:19-20).

GALATIANS

- There is neither Jew nor Gentile, neither slave nor free, nor is there male and female, for you are all one in Christ Jesus (Galatians 3:28).
- It is for freedom that Christ has set us free. Stand firm, then, and do not let yourselves be burdened again by a yoke of slavery (Galatians 5:1).
- For in Christ Jesus neither circumcision nor uncircumcision has any value. The only thing that counts is faith expressing itself through love (Galatians 5:6).
- You, my brothers and sisters, were called to be free. But do not use your freedom to indulge the flesh; rather, serve one another humbly in love (Galatians 5:13).
- So I say, walk by the Spirit, and you will not gratify the desires of the flesh (Galatians 5:16).
- But the fruit of the Spirit is love, joy, peace, forbearance, kindness, goodness, faithfulness, gentleness and self-control. Against such things there is no law (Galatians 5:22-23).
- Carry each other's burdens, and in this way you will fulfill the law of Christ (Galatians 6:2).
- Let us not become weary in doing good, for at the proper time we will reap a harvest if we do not give up (Galatians 6:9).
- Therefore, as we have opportunity, let us do good to all people, especially to those who belong to the family of believers (Galatians 6:10).

Wonders from the Past

In the 1930s, archaeologists excavated the ancient city of Antioch (one of the Galatian cities Paul visited and wrote to) and found the first-century main street. Paul most probably walked that street. According to the *Archaeological Study Bible*, the street had broad walkways, temples, shops, and baths.[14]

GALATIANS

EPHESIANS
An Encouraging Note from a Friend in Jail

Top Ten

1. Unity is an important theme in this letter to Ephesians, especially in 4:4-6.
2. One key to the unity Paul refers to in this letter is existing together in the community of believers called the church.
3. Another important element of unity, according to Ephesians 1:10, is that believers are all under the authority of one person: Jesus.
4. This is the first of the four letters Paul wrote from prison. The other three are Philippians, Colossians, and Philemon.
5. It is possible that Ephesians, like Galatians, was meant to go to a number of churches, not just one (like a circular letter for many to read). One factor pointing to this is that the phrase "in Ephesus" does not appear in some of the early manuscripts of this letter.
6. The term "in Christ" appears thirty-two times in the book of Ephesians, reinforcing the position of the Christian in relation to Jesus.
7. In this letter, Paul presents a pattern for the godly family—spelling out roles for wives, husbands, and children (see 5:21-6:9).
8. One of Paul's subthemes in Ephesians is the Trinity. In several passages, he makes mention of the Father, the Son, and the Spirit (4:4-6 and 5:18-20, for example).
9. A man named Tychicus delivered this letter from Paul to the church. Paul respected Tychicus, calling him a "dear brother and faithful servant in the Lord" (6:21). Tychicus sometimes traveled with Paul (see Acts 20:4)

and also helped him communicate with the church at Colossae (see Colossians 4:7–9).

10. During the missionary journey phase of Paul's ministry, he stayed in Ephesus longer than in any other of the cities where he had planted churches. He spent more than two years there (see Acts 19:8–10).

Who

Paul is generally accepted as this letter's writer. The introductory statement supports this, as do factors such as his mention of his friend Tychicus, the fact that the early church supported Pauline authorship, and the pattern of the book, which matches that of Paul's other epistles. He probably wrote Ephesians in the early 60s AD, while a prisoner in the city of Rome.

What

It was important to Paul, and to other leaders of the first-century church, to dispel the thinking that Jews and gentiles were to be divided at all in this new faith. A new community was being formed, and it was simply the Christian church. The idea of unity of believers was vital to melding these two groups into "one new man," as Paul put it in Ephesians 2:15 (NKJV). The believers were then to walk in unity and holiness as they lived and worshiped together. This was the direction in which Paul guided the people of Ephesus and the surrounding region.

When

Paul visited and wrote to Ephesus during a time of a huge emphasis on the Temple of Artemis in the city. The goddess Artemis was just one of nearly twenty false deities the people of this vibrant city worshiped. Paul and his friends faced strong cultural backlash in Ephesus. Remember, Paul was arrested in Ephesus after a silversmith named Demetrius accused the apostle of taking business away from the people who crafted Artemis shrines (see Acts 19:23–41). The power of the gospel,

however, proved strong enough to establish a church in this
idol-loving community.

Where

Ephesus was a port city on the Aegean Sea. It was a trading
center, a governmental judicial center, and the home of the
grand Temple of Artemis. This building was one of the Seven
Wonders of the Ancient World, and it dominated the landscape
in Ephesus.

Why

Unlike the ones Paul wrote to the people of Corinth, he did
not send this letter to the people to address major problems.
Instead, he wanted to make sure the people at the church he had
founded in Ephesus did not drift from the faith. So he wrote to
them to exhort them to stay strong in the unity they could find
in Jesus and to live according to the doctrines and teachings they
had already received.

Wow!

- William Shakespeare's play *The Comedy of Errors* has the city
  of Ephesus as its setting.
- In President Ronald Reagan's address to the nation on
  April 2, 1983, observing Easter and Passover, he quoted
  from Ephesians 2:17–19.

Worth Remembering

- Praise be to the God and Father of our Lord Jesus Christ,
  who has blessed us in the heavenly realms with every
  spiritual blessing in Christ (Ephesians 1:3).
- In him we have redemption through his blood, the
  forgiveness of sins, in accordance with the riches of God's
  grace (Ephesians 1:7).

- I have not stopped giving thanks for you, remembering you in my prayers. I keep asking that the God of our Lord Jesus Christ, the glorious Father, may give you the Spirit of wisdom and revelation, so that you may know him better. I pray that the eyes of your heart may be enlightened in order that you may know the hope to which he has called you, the riches of his glorious inheritance in his holy people (Ephesians 1:16–18).

- For it is by grace you have been saved, through faith—and this is not from yourselves, it is the gift of God—not by works, so that no one can boast (Ephesians 2:8–9).

- This mystery is that through the gospel the Gentiles are heirs together with Israel, members together of one body, and sharers together in the promise in Christ Jesus (Ephesians 3:6).

- There is one body and one Spirit, just as you were called to one hope when you were called; one Lord, one faith, one baptism; one God and Father of all, who is over all and through all and in all (Ephesians 4:4–6).

- Be kind and compassionate to one another, forgiving each other, just as in Christ God forgave you (Ephesians 4:32).

- Follow God's example, therefore, as dearly loved children and walk in the way of love, just as Christ loved us and gave himself up for us as a fragrant offering and sacrifice to God (Ephesians 5:1–2).

- Submit to one another out of reverence for Christ (Ephesians 5:21).

- Wives, submit yourselves to your own husbands as you do to the Lord (Ephesians 5:22).

- Husbands, love your wives, just as Christ loved the church and gave himself up for her (Ephesians 5:25).

- This is a profound mystery—but I am talking about Christ and the church (Ephesians 5:32).

- Children, obey your parents in the Lord, for this is right (Ephesians 6:1).

- Fathers, do not exasperate your children; instead, bring them up in the training and instruction of the Lord (Ephesians 6:4).
- Finally, be strong in the Lord and in his mighty power. Put on the full armor of God, so that you can take your stand against the devil's schemes (Ephesians 6:10–11).

Wonders from the Past

Ephesians 2:14 says, "He himself is our peace, who has made the two groups one and has destroyed the barrier, the dividing wall of hostility." In the 1800s, a stone slab was found in Jerusalem. On it was written in Greek, "No gentile may enter within this Temple barrier." The historian Josephus wrote that these kinds of dividers were hung in the temple to remind people that only Jews were to enter. That sounds like a physical example of a "dividing wall of hostility."

PHILIPPIANS
The Joy of Shared Service

Top Ten

1. The church at Philippi was first both in Paul's mission and in his heart. This was his first church plant, and the feelings of mutual love and admiration are on display in this letter.
2. The church had sent a financial gift to Paul when he was in Rome (in prison), so one of his reasons for writing was to say, "Thank you."
3. The words *joy* and *rejoice* appear a combined eleven times in this upbeat letter.
4. Paul's first visit to Philippi took place because God had redirected his itinerary. In Acts 16, we read that Paul planned to go north to Bithynia, but God

prevented that move. Then he had a vision of a man telling him and his companions to go to Macedonia. The next thing you know, he's in Philippi, leading a woman named Lydia to salvation in Jesus Christ.

5. Philippians contains the interesting story of Epaphroditus, who was so sick that he almost died. But "God had mercy on him" (2:27) and he got better. Later in that passage, Paul revealed even more: "He almost died for the work of Christ. He risked his life to make up for the help you yourselves could not give me" (vs. 30). It was probably Epaphroditus who delivered the scroll from Paul to the Philippian church.

6. Ironically, while Paul was in Rome, the people in Philippi (which was in Macedonia) were in a Roman city. The people of Philippi were considered Roman, and many of the city's citizens were retired soldiers of the Roman army. They were afforded retirement land in the city, so Roman influence was great in Philippi. The people realized that their governmental leadership came from Rome itself.

7. As Paul wrote his encouraging letter to the Philippian church, he reminded them that believers in Jesus had been promised that the Lord would someday return. And he spelled out the hope of heaven in Philippians 3:20–21.

8. Although most of this epistle is about joy and thankfulness and the future hope of heaven, Paul still has a few words for people who want to require Christians to take part in Jewish ceremonies. And those words aren't soft, either. In chapter three, he calls those people "dogs," "evildoers," and "mutilators of the flesh." Not exactly PC language!

9. One of the most misapplied Bible verses appears in Philippians. In 4:13, Paul writes, "I can do all this through him who gives me strength." In context, he explains that he has suffered greatly for the cause of

PHILIPPIANS

Christ. He has known great need, and he has known times of plenty. He has learned to be content even if he is hungry and in want. In God's service, he can endure anything with His strength. This is not about athletes hitting home runs or being able to accomplish something you could not normally do. This is not doing anything we set our minds to—and waiting for God to make it happen.

10. Imagine what it must have meant to the people at Philippi when Paul says, "All God's people here send you greetings, especially those who belong to Caesar's household" (4:22). It's likely that a buzz went through the crowd when people realized that Paul had led people in the retinue of the supreme ruler of the land to faith in Christ.

Who

There is little doubt that the apostle Paul, apparently with the assistance of Timothy (1:1), wrote this letter to his beloved congregation. He was in a Roman jail, or at least under house arrest, when he wrote this letter in about AD 61 or 62.

What

Paul's first order of business in this letter is to convey hearty thanks to his friends and fellow believers in Philippi. There seems to be a great deal of mutual admiration going on. He recognizes that he has suffered, but he rejoices nonetheless. He requests that his friends live in unity and conduct themselves in a manner worthy of their professions of faith in Christ. One of the key passages for them—and for us—is the beginning of chapter two, where he pleads for humility in the light of Jesus' great example of setting aside heaven's glories to come to earth. Paul tells his friends to press on, and he gives them the hope of finding God's peace.

When

It seemed to be a time of peace and contentment in the church at Philippi. Churches often enjoy good times, but even then, they need encouragement and instruction. This letter was, we can imagine, received with great joy. Paul let these Christians enjoy the confidence and contentment found in Christ. Yet he still addressed such things as the problem of Judaizers, the need for humility, and the comfort of looking forward to Christ's return.

Where

Philippi was located in northeastern Greece, near the Aegean Sea. One of the primary roads to the city was the Via Egnatia (or Egnatian Way), which was Rome's primary east-west corridor. Paul probably took the Via Egnatia as he traveled to new cities.

Why

This book was deeply personal. Paul wanted to thank his dear friends in Philippi for their generous support of his ministry. At the same time, he had a few words of advice for them regarding false teachers. He also reminded them of the importance of being unified in their faith.

Wow!

In Johnny Cash's song "Man in White," he told of the conversion of the apostle Paul. He referred to Paul with terms related to Philippians 3:5 when he sang, "I was born of the Tribe of Benjamin, I was a Pharisee."

Worth Remembering

- Being confident of this, that he who began a good work in you will carry it on to completion until the day of Christ Jesus (Philippians 1:6).
- Who, being in very nature God, did not consider equality with God something to be used to his own advantage; rather, he made himself nothing by taking the very nature of a servant, being made in human likeness (Philippians 2:6–7).
- Brothers and sisters, I do not consider myself yet to have taken hold of it. But one thing I do: Forgetting what is

behind and straining toward what is ahead, I press on toward the goal to win the prize for which God has called me heavenward in Christ Jesus (Philippians 3:13–14).

- But our citizenship is in heaven. And we eagerly await a Savior from there, the Lord Jesus Christ, who, by the power that enables him to bring everything under his control, will transform our lowly bodies so that they will be like his glorious body (Philippians 3:20–21).
- And the peace of God, which transcends all understanding, will guard your hearts and your minds in Christ Jesus (Philippians 4:7).
- I know what it is to be in need, and I know what it is to have plenty. I have learned the secret of being content in any and every situation, whether well fed or hungry, whether living in plenty or in want. I can do all this through him who gives me strength (Philippians 4:12–13).
- My God will meet all your needs according to the riches of his glory in Christ Jesus (Philippians 4:19).

Wonders from the Past

Excavations of ancient Philippi have revealed such things as a theater, a forum called the Agora, the possible site of the jail where Paul was incarcerated (Acts 16), and a number of churches from his era. The churches demonstrate the importance of Paul's influence for Christianity in the city.

COLOSSIANS

Addressing Major Error

Top Ten

1. While Paul's letter to the Philippians was sent to dear friends with whom he had lived and worked, his letter

to the people at Colossae was written for Christians
he did not know personally.

2. Paul wanted the Christians in Colossae to circulate this
letter to other churches in the region after they had
read it.

3. In Colossians 4:11, Paul mentions a man named Jesus,
who also went by the name Justus. Apparently, the
people at Colossae knew this man, who was with Paul
as he wrote the letter.

4. According to Colossians 1:7–8, it appears that
Epaphras was the founder of the church at Colossae.

5. Epaphras had delivered some bad news to Paul: new
heresy was creeping into the church. Part of the reason
for Paul's letter was to correct these errors and get the
people back on track doctrinally.

6. Because Paul does not name the errors he is addressing
in Colossians, we have to make some inferences. The
errors could be related to the continuing controversy
over how Judaism should interact with the church
or to a heresy called Gnosticism. The points Paul
makes relate specifically to not being attached to
ceremonialism (2:11, 16–17; 3:11) and to the sufficiency of
Christ (1:15–20; 2:2–3:9).

7. In Colossians 3:18–21, Paul repeats his instructions for
family life from Ephesians.

8. In this letter, Paul gives us a great definition of false
teaching: "hollow and deceptive philosophy, which
depends on human tradition and the elemental spiritual
forces of this world rather than on Christ" (2:8).

9. The city of Colossae no longer exists as a habitation.
It was damaged by an earthquake in the first century
AD and rebuilt. Invaders defeated the city in the eighth
century. The site under the rubble of Colossae has
never been excavated.

10. The much wealthier nearby city of Laodicea also was damaged by the same earthquake. There was a church in Laodicea at the time as well.

Who

This was another of the letters Paul wrote during his Roman incarceration in AD 60–61. Timothy is mentioned in Colossians 1:1, but this does not mean he wrote the book. This may have been Paul's way of getting people who had not heard of him but who knew Timothy to trust the letter. It may also mean that Timothy was Paul's scribe until he got to Colossians 4:18, where Paul added his own greeting.

What

Paul takes the right track in countering an erroneous argument. He doesn't call names and accuse; he simply explains correct doctrine and expects his hearers to understand what he is refuting. The key element to getting people on the right track is to explain fundamental truths such as the supremacy of Jesus Christ and the fullness of Christ. He told the Colossians to remain strong by staying connected to the Head: Jesus. He followed the teaching on doctrine with some instruction on Christian living.

When

Paul wrote this letter in the early 60s AD.

Where

The town of Colossae was east of Ephesus in Asia Minor. The more affluent cities of Laodicea and Hierapolis were nearby. Colossae had a vibrant economy until the Romans changed the road leading into the city, thus benefiting the two cities mentioned above.

Why

Many religions make room for Jesus while adding other elements of worship, making Jesus just *one* of the ideas or *one* of the key

COLOSSIANS

people. Christianity cannot stand with this kind of teaching. Jesus does not share space in matters of faith. He is supreme and exclusive, so when Paul heard that false teachers were suggesting otherwise, he had to correct the error. Therefore, he wrote this letter to reemphasize the supremacy of Jesus Christ. Christ is above all and He is complete. Any other teaching is erroneous and dangerous.

Wow!

The rock band Thrice uses the words of Colossians 1:15 as the title its song "Image of the Invisible."

Worth Remembering

- The Son is the image of the invisible God, the firstborn over all creation. For in him all things were created: things in heaven and on earth, visible and invisible, whether thrones or powers or rulers or authorities; all things have been created through him and for him (Colossians 1:15–16).
- Once you were alienated from God and were enemies in your minds because of your evil behavior. But now he has reconciled you by Christ's physical body through death to present you holy in his sight, without blemish and free from accusation (Colossians 1:21–22).
- See to it that no one takes you captive through hollow and deceptive philosophy, which depends on human tradition and the elemental spiritual forces of this world rather than on Christ (Colossians 2:8).
- When you were dead in your sins and in the uncircumcision of your flesh, God made you alive with Christ. He forgave us all our sins, having canceled the charge of our legal indebtedness, which stood against us and condemned us; he has taken it away, nailing it to the cross (Colossians 2:13–14).
- Set your minds on things above, not on earthly things. For you died, and your life is now hidden with Christ in

COLOSSIANS

God. When Christ, who is your life, appears, then you also will appear with him in glory. Put to death, therefore, whatever belongs to your earthly nature: sexual immorality, impurity, lust, evil desires and greed, which is idolatry (Colossians 3:2–5).

- Here there is no Gentile or Jew, circumcised or uncircumcised, barbarian, Scythian, slave or free, but Christ is all, and is in all (Colossians 3:11).
- Therefore, as God's chosen people, holy and dearly loved, clothe yourselves with compassion, kindness, humility, gentleness and patience (Colossians 3:12).
- Bear with each other and forgive one another if any of you has a grievance against someone. Forgive as the Lord forgave you (Colossians 3:13).
- Let the peace of Christ rule in your hearts, since as members of one body you were called to peace. And be thankful (Colossians 3:15).

Wonders from the Past

As of now, no one has come forward to explore the remains of Colossae.

---

1 THESSALONIANS

Encouragement and Instruction

Top Ten

1. You can read how the church at Thessalonica got its start in Acts 17. Paul preached to the Jews in the synagogue and ended up being run out of town. However, some Jews and many Gentiles believed, and the church was started.

2. Luke specifically stated that many "prominent women" had been among the first converts in Thessalonica (see Acts 17:4).

3. Paul had to leave Thessalonica suddenly because rabble-rousers had forced him out, so he didn't know how things were going with the church there until he got a report from Timothy (see 1 Thessalonians 3).

4. The charges against Paul and those who aided him (including the unfortunate Jason, who had to post bond) were based on Roman decrees, which Paul violated when he proclaimed the kingdom of God.

5. The Roman presence in Thessalonica would have been strong because it was the capital city of the Roman province of Macedonia.

6. Thessalonica was on the road called the Via Egnatia (or the Egnatian Way), the same road that ran through the city of Philippi.

7. Paul stayed at least three weeks during his first visit to Thessalonica; in Acts 17, Luke says he spoke in the synagogue on three consecutive Sabbaths.

8. Paul attempted to return to Thessalonica, but according to 1 Thessalonians 2:18, Satan prevented his return. He prayed over and over to be able to go back there (3:10).

9. First and 2 Thessalonians may have been the first two letters Paul wrote to New Testament churches.

10. One of the key elements of Paul's first letter to the church at Thessalonica was his teaching about the second coming of Jesus.

Who

Clearly, Paul is the author of 1 Thessalonians. He wrote it from Corinth in response to what he had heard about this new assembly of believers. He probably wrote this letter around AD 50.

What

During Paul's short visit to Thessalonica, his message of the gospel turned the lives of these new Christians upside down. Because they embraced this new faith, their lives were deeply affected; they even faced persecution. Paul had left town when things got tough, so some people wondered whether or not he was the real deal. Therefore, the first thing he did in his initial letter was defend his ministry, which he did in 1 Thessalonians 2:1–16. Second, he gave these believers guidelines on how to live holy lives. Also, the people were concerned about death and the return of Christ, so he addressed that topic in 4:13–5:11.

When

It was not easy to carve out a new church in a community so heavily involved in Roman culture and so strongly Jewish in background. But it took place just a couple of decades after Jesus' death, burial, resurrection, and ascension. This was all new to these people, so they needed the help of someone as wise and learned as Paul to instruct them in living out the Christian faith.

Where

Thessalonica was an important city for both political and commercial reasons. It was situated on the vital Egnatian Way, midway between its eastern terminus in Byzantium and its western end at the Adriatic Sea. This twenty-foot-wide road spanned 1,100 miles and linked Italy to Asia. This put Thessalonica in a strategic location for spreading the gospel message.

Why

Paul was the great encourager of the churches he served. The new church at Thessalonica needed Paul's positive message, so he penned them a note of encouragement and instruction. As he wrote, he instructed them on the confusing subject of the Lord's return and on holy living. He had heard a good report from Timothy, so he used that as part of his positive approach.

Wow!

Paul's phrase, "the Lord will come like a thief in the night" (1 Thessalonians 5:2) has been used in numerous ways in movies, music, and print. Here is a sampling of people who used that phrase as a title: the Rolling Stones, Nutshell (a musical group), Ernest William Hornung (a collection of short stories), William Sears (a book), Russell Doughten (an early 1970s Christian movie about the second coming). Edgar Allen Poe also used the line in his grotesque short story, "The Masque of the Red Death."

Worth Remembering

- We always thank God for all of you and continually mention you in our prayers (1 Thessalonians 1:2).
- Because our gospel came to you not simply with words but also with power, with the Holy Spirit and deep conviction. You know how we lived among you for your sake (1 Thessalonians 1:5).
- Encouraging, comforting and urging you to live lives worthy of God, who calls you into his kingdom and glory (1 Thessalonians 2:12).
- May he strengthen your hearts so that you will be blameless and holy in the presence of our God and Father when our Lord Jesus comes with all his holy ones (1 Thessalonians 3:13).
- It is God's will that you should be sanctified: that you should avoid sexual immorality (1 Thessalonians 4:3).
- For God did not call us to be impure, but to live a holy life (1 Thessalonians 4:7).
- Make it your ambition to lead a quiet life: You should mind your own business and work with your hands, just as we told you (1 Thessalonians 4:11).
- Brothers and sisters, we do not want you to be uninformed about those who sleep in death, so that you do not grieve like the rest of mankind, who have no hope. For we believe that Jesus died and rose again, and so we believe that God

will bring with Jesus those who have fallen asleep in him. According to the Lord's word, we tell you that we who are still alive, who are left until the coming of the Lord, will certainly not precede those who have fallen asleep. For the Lord himself will come down from heaven, with a loud command, with the voice of the archangel and with the trumpet call of God, and the dead in Christ will rise first. After that, we who are still alive and are left will be caught up together with them in the clouds to meet the Lord in the air. And so we will be with the Lord forever. Therefore encourage one another with these words (1 Thessalonians 4:13–18).

- For you know very well that the day of the Lord will come like a thief in the night. While people are saying, "Peace and safety," destruction will come on them suddenly, as labor pains on a pregnant woman, and they will not escape. But you, brothers and sisters, are not in darkness so that this day should surprise you like a thief. You are all children of the light and children of the day. We do not belong to the night or to the darkness. So then, let us not be like others, who are asleep, but let us be awake and sober (1 Thessalonians 5:2–6).

- Therefore encourage one another and build each other up, just as in fact you are doing (1 Thessalonians 5:11).

- Pray continually, give thanks in all circumstances; for this is God's will for you in Christ Jesus. Do not quench the Spirit (1 Thessalonians 5:17–19).

- The grace of our Lord Jesus Christ be with you (1 Thessalonians 5:28).

Wonders from the Past

In Acts 17:6, Luke used the word *politarches* to describe the city officials Jason was taken to because he had welcomed Paul into his house. In archaeological excavations, an inscription from the same time period was found that bore the word *politarches*. According to BiblePlaces.com, the word doesn't appear in any other Greek literature.

2 THESSALONIANS
Correction and Assurance

Top Ten

1. First Thessalonians is Paul's shortest letter to the churches.
2. In this letter, Paul introduces the idea of the coming antichrist.
3. Paul refers to our Savior as the Lord Jesus Christ ten times in this letter—the most in any New Testament book.
4. Apparently, confusion about eschatology (a branch of theology having to do with the end times) is not new. The people of the church at Thessalonica were as fuzzy about the details as we sometimes are today.
5. Apparently, someone had sent the Thessalonian Christians a note Paul had supposedly written, giving them bad information about the Lord's return. Paul wrote this second letter, in part, to straighten out that problem.
6. Paul wrote this letter in his own handwriting, just so the people would know it was his and not a forgery.
7. This letter is valuable to us as well because it reminds us how to live as we await the Lord's return.
8. In order to further encourage the church, as he did in 1 Thessalonians, Paul told the people that he had been boasting about them to other church congregations.
9. While Paul wrote this second letter to the Thessalonians to explain things about the future, one of his terms was less than clear. In 2 Thessalonians 2:6–7, he speaks of someone "holding back" the power of the "lawless one." There is not total consensus about who is the one doing the holding back,

although people have made several suggestions. Many believe Paul was referring to the Holy Spirit.

10. While explaining his teaching about the coming of the Lord, Paul drew on his knowledge of the Old Testament. Some of his teaching was based on Daniel 7, 8, and 11.

Who

Again, Paul writes to the church at Thessalonica. This letter probably arrived just a few months after the initial one was delivered to the new church in this Macedonian provincial capital.

What

It didn't take long for people to try to mislead the new Christians about what was true. Once Paul heard about this, he sat down (he was in Corinth at the time) and wrote another encouraging, edifying, teaching letter to guide the people into sound doctrine and practice as they followed their Savior, the Lord Jesus Christ.

When

Still a new congregation, the Thessalonians were afraid they had already missed the day of the Lord. Paul wrote this letter to a church that was less than a year old, in AD 51 or 52, so Jesus' earthly ministry was still recent history.

Where

Today, the city Thessaloniki sits on the remains of the ancient Thessalonica. When Paul visited this city, it had a population of about 200,000 people. In Acts 17, Paul visited the synagogue there, so it can be surmised that there was a strong Jewish population. One of the key geographic features of Thessaloniki is that its residents can see Mount Olympus, the highest mountain in Greece.

Why

Similar to 1 Thessalonians, Paul sent this letter to encourage the believers in Thessalonica and to teach them sound doctrine. The letter also included some correction of error that had been introduced. Paul took great pains to show how much he as a leader cared for this new flock of believers.

Wow!

In 1609, Captain John Smith, who was a leader of the people living in Jamestown, the first English settlement in the New World, proclaimed that one tenet of their philosophy was "He that will not work shall not eat" (see 2 Thessalonians 3:10).

Worth Remembering

- We ought always to thank God for you, brothers and sisters, and rightly so, because your faith is growing more and more, and the love all of you have for one another is increasing (2 Thessalonians 1:3).
- God is just: He will pay back trouble to those who trouble you (2 Thessalonians 1:6).
- With this in mind, we constantly pray for you, that our God may make you worthy of his calling, and that by his power he may bring to fruition your every desire for goodness and your every deed prompted by faith (2 Thessalonians 1:11).
- Concerning the coming of our Lord Jesus Christ and our being gathered to him, we ask you, brothers and sisters, not to become easily unsettled or alarmed by the teaching allegedly from us—whether by a prophecy or by word of mouth or by letter—asserting that the day of the Lord has already come. Don't let anyone deceive you in any way, for that day will not come until the rebellion occurs and the man of lawlessness is revealed, the man doomed to destruction (2 Thessalonians 2:1–3).

2 THESSALONIANS

- For the secret power of lawlessness is already at work; but the one who now holds it back will continue to do so till he is taken out of the way. And then the lawless one will be revealed, whom the Lord Jesus will overthrow with the breath of his mouth and destroy by the splendor of his coming (2 Thessalonians 2:7–8).
- But we ought always to thank God for you, brothers and sisters loved by the Lord, because God chose you as firstfruits to be saved through the sanctifying work of the Spirit and through belief in the truth (2 Thessalonians 2:13).
- For even when we were with you, we gave you this rule: "The one who is unwilling to work shall not eat." We hear that some among you are idle and disruptive. They are not busy; they are busybodies (2 Thessalonians 3:10–11).

Wonders from the Past

The road Paul (and perhaps Peter and others) traveled as he made his way around Greece, the Egnatian Way (or Via Egnatia), can still be seen in parts of Greece. It is possible to hike certain portions of the Via Egnatia today.

1 TIMOTHY

Guidance for a Young Pastor

Top Ten

1. The New Testament letters immediately following 2 Thessalonians in the canon of Scripture has been dubbed the "Pastoral Epistles." Instead of being written to the church at large, as were the letters to Thessalonica and others, these three letters were written to pastors.

2. These three pastoral letters are 1 and 2 Timothy and Titus—and they are called by the names of the two pastors to whom Paul wrote.

3. Have you ever noticed that the five letters between Colossians and Philemon are arranged in alphabetical order? That might help you when you look up the three Pastoral Epistles: 1 and 2 Thessalonians, 1 and 2 Timothy, Titus.

4. A young pastor named Timothy was the recipient of 1 and 2 Timothy. He was well acquainted with Paul; they had traveled extensively—to Troas, Philippi, Thessalonica, Berea, Athens, and Corinth. He was with Paul in Rome when the apostle wrote Philippians. He was pastor of the church at Ephesus when Paul wrote him.

5. As one would assume, the content of the pastoral letters is quite different from the previous epistles. These three letters had to do with church governance, worship, and leadership.

6. As in Thessalonica, false teachers had risen up in the churches, and Paul wrote the pastoral letters to head them off before they could corrupt the church.

7. Timothy's church at Ephesus is the same church John attended in his old age as he wrote his books of the Bible.

8. Timothy had a distinct advantage in the ongoing effort to meld Jews and gentiles into one church. His mother was a Jewish believer, and his father was Greek (see Acts 16:1).

9. To give you an idea of the depth of Timothy's commitment to serving others, in order to have a better relationship with the Jews, he allowed himself to be circumcised before he went with Paul on his second missionary journey (see Acts 16:1).

10. Timothy's relative youth may have been a bit of a stumbling block to some older people in the church, but Paul urged him not let that bother him (see 1 Timothy 4:12).

1 TIMOTHY

Who

Paul is the penman of this letter, which he wrote between AD 64 and AD 66, when he was out of prison in Rome.

What

Paul's first directive to Timothy was to encourage him to stop false teachers from causing controversies and divisions in the church. Paul even named names—pinpointing Hymenaeus and Alexander as men Timothy needed to extract from the church. Paul's next admonition was about prayer and its importance in the church. He then mentions women and their role in worship services. He continues by giving guidelines for selecting church leadership, the dangers of error in the church, and the absolute value of simply preaching the Word of God.

When

It is getting late in Paul's life. He had been imprisoned in Rome, but he has been released and is visiting various cities. It is time to turn leadership over to young Timothy, whom Paul left in Ephesus during his travels. The church is maturing, and it needs direction and proper leadership to move into the future as a body of believers.

Where

The scene shifts back to Ephesus, a city mentioned in Acts 19. Paul had written to this church about other issues, and now, a few years later, he writes to Timothy, the new leader of the church. Ephesus, located on the western coast of what is now Turkey, had about 250,000 residents.

Why

Many problems in churches today stem from issues similar to the ones the believers in Ephesus faced: doctrinal error and lack of godly leadership. Paul, hoping to guide Timothy as he leads his congregation, addresses those exact issues.

1 TIMOTHY

Wow!

Each of these famous writers used their own variations of
1 Timothy 6:10, which warns that the love of money is a root of
all kinds of evil, in their own writing:

- Carl Sandburg: "Money is power, freedom, a cushion, a root
  of all evil . . . "
- Louisa May Alcott: "Money is the root of all evil, and yet it
  is such a useful root that we cannot go on without it."
- George Bernard Shaw: "Lack of money is the root of all evil."

Worth Remembering

- As I urged you when I went into Macedonia, stay there in
  Ephesus so that you may command certain people not to
  teach false doctrines any longer or to devote themselves
  to myths and endless genealogies. Such things promote
  controversial speculations rather than advancing God's
  work—which is by faith. The goal of this command is love,
  which comes from a pure heart and a good conscience and
  a sincere faith (1 Timothy 1:3-5).
- Here is a trustworthy saying that deserves full acceptance:
  Christ Jesus came into the world to save sinners—of whom
  I am the worst (1 Timothy 1:15).
- I urge, then, first of all, that petitions, prayers, intercession
  and thanksgiving be made for all people—for kings and all
  those in authority, that we may live peaceful and quiet lives
  in all godliness and holiness (1 Timothy 2:1-2).
- For there is one God and one mediator between God and
  mankind, the man Christ Jesus, who gave himself as a
  ransom for all people. This has now been witnessed to at
  the proper time (1 Timothy 2:5-6).
- Now the overseer is to be above reproach, faithful to his
  wife, temperate, self-controlled, respectable, hospitable, able
  to teach, not given to drunkenness, not violent but gentle,
  not quarrelsome, not a lover of money (1 Timothy 3:2-3).

1 TIMOTHY

- Have nothing to do with godless myths and old wives' tales; rather, train yourself to be godly. For physical training is of some value, but godliness has value for all things, holding promise for both the present life and the life to come (1 Timothy 4:7–8).
- Don't let anyone look down on you because you are young, but set an example for the believers in speech, in conduct, in love, in faith and in purity. Until I come, devote yourself to the public reading of Scripture, to preaching and to teaching (1 Timothy 4:12–13).

Wonders from the Past

In his book *Wealth in Ancient Ephesus and the First Letter to Timothy*, Gary G. Hoag suggests that the braided hair mentioned 1 Timothy 2:9 is a reference to something Ephesian women did in deference to the goddess Artemis. Not wearing their hair that way would have been a sign they had rejected that idol.

2 TIMOTHY

A Farewell Letter from Prison

Top Ten

1. Paul's living conditions have worsened. This letter, written during his second imprisonment, indicates that he is no longer under house arrest (as with his first imprisonment) in Rome. He was perhaps being held in the Mamertine Prison in Rome, and he had asked for a cloak to be brought to him (2 Timothy 4:13), suggesting the coldness of this dungeon prison.
2. Before being arrested again, Paul had visited Ephesus and left Timothy there to pastor that group of Christians.

3. This would be Paul's final letter. His concluding statements in 2 Timothy indicate that he knew his time was short.

4. Tradition suggests that Paul was taken outside the city limits of Rome and beheaded.

5. One of the key statements in 2 Timothy is Paul's assertion that the Scriptures were divinely inspired, or "Godbreathed" (3:16–17).

6. Historically, Paul wrote this letter during the time of Emperor Nero, who famously burned down Rome (probably so he could rebuild it on a grander scale) and then blamed Christians for the conflagration.

7. Whereas Paul had earlier been in prison because he requested a Roman trial (see Acts 25), this time he may have been caught up in Nero's persecution of Christians. As a church leader, he would have been a likely target.

8. Paul's famous words "come before winter" (2 Timothy 4:21 NKJV) indicate the urgency of his situation as he pleads with his good friend Timothy to visit him soon—before it's too late.

9. The Mamertine Prison is also thought to be where Peter was incarcerated in Rome. The building still stands and can be visited today.

10. Paul's final words had to bring comfort to Timothy and the people of Ephesus: "The Lord be with your spirit. Grace be with you" (4:22). And with those words, Paul was ready to go "safely to his heavenly kingdom" (4:18).

Who

After Paul spent some time as a free man, it appears that he was arrested again and returned to prison in Rome. He wrote 2 Timothy while serving that second stint in Roman incarceration. Some had abandoned him (see 2 Timothy 1:15; 4:9-10), but 2 Timothy 4:11 suggests that Luke was the lone friend who stayed with him. Luke may have helped Paul write this letter to Timothy.

What

Despite the discouraging situation Paul found himself in—imagine being arrested again after thinking you were now a free man—Paul took the time to encourage Timothy. In this note to his "dear son" (1:2), Paul reminded Timothy of his heritage, encouraged him not to be ashamed of the testimony of Jesus, and exhorted him to keep preaching what Paul had modeled. He told him to be bold in the grace of Jesus. In 2 Timothy 2, Paul gave some pastor-to-pastor advice about dealing with false teaching and foolish arguments. He told Timothy to persevere during the hard times that were to come.

When

One era was coming to a close and a new one was beginning. Paul was passing the torch of leadership as he faced his imminent execution. It was about AD 67 when Paul wrote this letter to Timothy. It was a difficult time for the new church of Jesus Christ. The people faced persecution from the Roman government and testing from false teachers, and Paul was trying to prepare Timothy for what lay ahead.

Where

Two cities are in focus here: Ephesus and Rome. Because of Paul's influence and Timothy's leadership, Ephesus had become a key city for Christianity. It would be one of the churches the apostle John mentioned in Revelation 2. Despite the rampant idolatry in Ephesus (the Temple of Artemis being the main feature of pagan worship) and its opulent wealth, the gospel of Jesus Christ made a big impact on the city.

Why

Timothy was apparently no Paul. It appears that he may have been a bit timid, and Paul felt the need to encourage him to be bold in his work. Timothy was leading one of the most important churches in the thirty-year history of the Christian faith, and Paul knew he needed a boost. He also needed help in battling those who wanted to dismantle the solid doctrine of this growing faith. Paul, sensing his own mortality, wrote this uplifting and edifying note to Timothy.

Wow!

- The Awana program for children uses 2 Timothy 2:15 as the basis for the acronym that is its name: "Approved Workmen Are Not Ashamed."
- President Barack Obama quoted 2 Timothy 4:7 during a memorial service for Senator Robert Byrd in 2010: "The time of my departure has come. I have fought the good fight, I have finished the race, I have kept the faith."
- The phrase "Come before winter" in 2 Timothy 4:21 (NKJV) is also the title of a 2017 documentary about the final days of World War II-era German pastor and martyr Dietrich Bonhoeffer.

Worth Remembering

- For the Spirit God gave us does not make us timid, but gives us power, love and self-discipline (2 Timothy 1:7).
- And the things you have heard me say in the presence of many witnesses entrust to reliable people who will also be qualified to teach others (2 Timothy 2:2).
- Do your best to present yourself to God as one approved, a worker who does not need to be ashamed and who correctly handles the word of truth (2 Timothy 2:15).
- Flee the evil desires of youth and pursue righteousness, faith, love and peace, along with those who call on the Lord out of a pure heart (2 Timothy 2:22).
- In fact, everyone who wants to live a godly life in Christ Jesus will be persecuted (2 Timothy 3:12).

- All Scripture is God-breathed and is useful for teaching, rebuking, correcting and training in righteousness (2 Timothy 3:16).
- Preach the word; be prepared in season and out of season; correct, rebuke and encourage—with great patience and careful instruction. For the time will come when people will not put up with sound doctrine. Instead, to suit their own desires, they will gather around them a great number of teachers to say what their itching ears want to hear (2 Timothy 4:2-3).
- For I am already being poured out like a drink offering, and the time for my departure is near (2 Timothy 4:6).

Wonders from the Past

Ephesus has been one of the most highly researched archaeological biblical sites. Archaeologists have uncovered numerous historical sources that verify what is recorded about Ephesus in Acts and in the Epistles. For instance, Luke's story about people of Ephesus rushing to the theater, shouting, "Great is Artemis of the Ephesians!" (Acts 19:34) mirrors exactly the phrase Ephesians used when they spoke of that pagan goddess. Also, a carved Menorah discovered in the steps to the great Library of Celsus verifies Luke's account that Paul went to the synagogue in Ephesus to preach (Acts 19:8)—there was a Jewish population in Ephesus at the time.

TITUS

Ministry to a Greek Island

Top Ten

1. Paul called Titus "my true son," which indicates that the apostle likely led Titus to faith in Jesus Christ.
2. Titus was of Greek descent (see Galatians 2:3).

3. Titus delivered Paul's second letter to the Corinthians to the church in Corinth and was expected to help them as Paul's representative.

4. During the time between Paul's two imprisonments in Rome, he visited Titus in Crete. And when Paul was in Rome for his second imprisonment, Titus visited him (2 Timothy 4:10).

5. Paul left Titus in Crete to "put in order what was left unfinished and appoint elders in every town" (Titus 1:5).

6. According to Titus 3:12, Paul was planning to replace Titus in Crete with either Artemas or Tychicus so that Titus could join him on another mission.

7. Paul mentions Titus nine times in 2 Corinthians.

8. The genesis of the church at Crete may have been at Pentecost, when people from the island heard the disciples preaching the gospel in various languages—presumably including theirs (see Acts 2:11).

9. Titus 1:5 indicates that Paul and Titus had earlier been to Crete, perhaps on one of Paul's missionary journeys. It was now time to establish an organization for the Christians there—a church.

10. Crete is known as the birthplace of the mythological deity Zeus.

Who

Paul wrote his letter to Titus in about AD 66, while he was between his two imprisonments in Rome—at about the same time he wrote 1 Timothy. Paul wrote his letter from a city called Nicopolis, which was located in western Greece.

What

While a group of Christians had been established on the island of Crete, they had not yet been organized into a true New Testament church. Paul left Titus there to appoint elders and give the church a framework. Paul recognized that it was a tough crowd in Crete (see his reference to "many rebellious people" in Titus

TITUS

1:10), so he made clear the kind of person who should serve as an elder (1:7-9). Beyond that, Paul gave Titus help with how to handle various groups within the church (older people, younger people, slaves). Paul also wrote about encouraging the people toward good works and good behavior.

When

Titus received this letter in about AD 67. Among the new and growing churches, false teachers were springing up—especially Judaizers (called "those of the circumcision group" in 1:10). Being a Greek who had chosen not to be circumcised (see Galatians 2:3), Titus would have been the right person to address this situation. This church had much to learn about church organization and about how to live the Christian life.

Where

Crete is a small island (150 miles long and 35 miles wide) located southeast of Greece. It appears that more than one church had been established there. Crete was a Roman-occupied island, and it had a Roman governor. The Old Testament indicates that the Philistines originated in Crete before moving to Canaan. We read in Amos 9:7: "'Are not you Israelites the same to me as the Cushites?' declares the LORD. 'Did I not bring Israel up from Egypt, the Philistines from Capthor and the Arameans from Kir?'" Scholars suggest that Capthor and the island of Crete are one and the same.

Why

We can look at the church or churches in Crete as missions churches—established because people had come to faith in Christ but were unable to govern themselves without someone to explain what church was supposed to look like. So Paul sent Titus there and later followed up with this letter of instruction. While we can learn by looking over Titus' shoulder and see what truths are meant for us, Paul's primary reason for writing the letter was to give structure to the church at Crete.

Worth Remembering

- The reason I left you in Crete was that you might put in order what was left unfinished and appoint elders in every town, as I directed you (Titus 1:5).
- He must hold firmly to the trustworthy message as it has been taught, so that he can encourage others by sound doctrine and refute those who oppose it (Titus 1:9).
- For the grace of God has appeared that offers salvation to all people (Titus 2:11).
- These, then, are the things you should teach. Encourage and rebuke with all authority. Do not let anyone despise you (Titus 2:15).
- He saved us, not because of righteous things we had done, but because of his mercy. He saved us through the washing of rebirth and renewal by the Holy Spirit (Titus 3:5).

Wonders from the Past

In Gortyn, Crete, are the ruins of a church called the Basilica of St. Titus. It is not of Titus' era (it was built in the 500s), but it does reflect the fact that Titus had a big impact on Crete.

PHILEMON
Uncommon Love and Concern

Top Ten

1. At 445 words, Philemon is the third shortest book in the Bible.
2. The name Philemon means "kind" or "affectionate."
3. Philemon lived in Colossae, so when Paul sent his letter to the church there (which met in Philemon's home), he also sent this private note to Philemon.

PHILEMON

4. Philemon was apparently a well-to-do citizen of Colossae.

5. An unknown writer has remarked that this letter is "a little idyll of the progress of Christianity." It shows what Christlike love can do in the life of a person who had no status in society in Roman culture—a slave.

6. The subject of the letter is the slave Onesimus, whose name, interestingly, means "profitable."

7. According to Colossians 4:7–9, Paul sent Onesimus (in the company of Tychicus) from Rome (where Paul was) to Philemon.

8. Onesimus had run away from Philemon, had ended up in Rome, and had come into contact with Paul (small world, huh?). He had trusted Christ as Savior.

9. Paul was sending Onesimus back to his master, even though he could have used his help in Rome (Paul was under house arrest and not in a prison at the time).

10. Paul asked Philemon to receive Onesimus back not as a slave any longer, but as a brother in Christ. Paul also said he would pay anything Onesimus' departure might have cost Philemon. It's all an amazing testimony to the changing power of the gospel.

Who

There is no doubt that Paul wrote this letter. He penned it, along with the letter to Colossae, in around AD 60. Paul was a prisoner in Rome when he first encountered Onesimus.

What

Notice the irony of the first sentence of Philemon: "Paul, a prisoner of Jesus Christ." He is a prisoner of Christ and a prisoner of the Roman state—yet he seeks to set free a slave from the prison of slavery. Paul heartily commends Philemon for his faith and then tells him he is praying that Philemon understand his coming difficult request regarding Onesimus. He pleads with Philemon to let his faith guide his reaction to Onesimus' return

PHILEMON

and to respond to it in a godly way. Then Paul invites himself for a visit at Philemon's house after his release. True Christlike hospitality is key to everything that happens in the book of Philemon.

When

During this era, the use of slaves was widespread in the Roman Empire. One estimate holds that slaves numbered in the tens of millions in that time and place. Slavery did not last a lifetime; most slaves were allowed to leave that life in their thirties or forties. Slaveholders were expected to treat their workers with respect and fairness. That Onesimus ran away, though, suggests that it was not an ideal situation in which to live.

Where

Philemon lived in Colossae, a city in Asia Minor Paul had visited. It was about one hundred miles from Ephesus and just a few miles from Laodicea.

Why

The essence of this letter is forgiveness. Onesimus has wronged Philemon, but now that Onesimus has trusted Jesus and become a part of the family of believers, Paul asks Philemon to be gracious and forgiving toward him. While Paul does not call for an overthrow of the slavery system, he implies that the gospel itself can do this by changing people's hearts.

Wow!

- Afro-pop gospel singer Armstrong Kalua took the stage name Onesimus Muzik as a tribute to the meaning of the name of Paul's friend in the book of Philemon.
- At the 2013 168 Film Project Awards, a movie short called *Useless*, which is based on Philemon 1:10–11, won awards for best actor and best film.

PHILEMON

Worth Remembering

- I always thank my God as I remember you in my prayers (Philemon 1:4).
- I pray that your partnership with us in the faith may be effective in deepening your understanding of every good thing we share for the sake of Christ (Philemon 1:6).
- I appeal to you for my son Onesimus, who became my son while I was in chains (Philemon 1:10).
- Formerly he was useless to you, but now he has become useful both to you and to me (Philemon 1:11).
- No longer as a slave, but better than a slave, as a dear brother. He is very dear to me but even dearer to you, both as a fellow man and as a brother in the Lord (Philemon 1:16).
- So if you consider me a partner, welcome him as you would welcome me (Philemon 1:17).
- If he has done you any wrong or owes you anything, charge it to me (Philemon 1:18).
- Confident of your obedience, I write to you, knowing that you will do even more than I ask (Philemon 1:21).

Wonders from the Past

At the British Museum in London is a Roman slave tag that states, "Hold me, if I run off, and return me to my master Viventius on the estate of Callistus."

HEBREWS
The Promise of a Better Hope

Top Ten

1. One of the distinguishing marks of the book of Hebrews is that scholars have not determined who wrote it. Paul, Luke, Apollos, Clement, Barnabas, and

Timothy are among the names that have been considered. One third-century church father declared, "Who wrote the epistle of Hebrews? In truth, only God knows."

2. When the King James Version of the Bible was first published, Hebrews had a heading suggesting that Paul wrote it. However, scholars later concluded there was no definitive proof of his authorship.

3. The book is called "Hebrews" because its message is directed at Jewish Christians. Paul's epistles were written primarily to gentile believers.

4. The person who wrote the book was familiar with Jewish worship routines.

5. Hebrews makes more than eighty direct or indirect references to the Old Testament.

6. Hebrews speaks of "a better hope," "a better covenant," "better promise," "a better country," and "an even better resurrection" as it explains that the gospel of Jesus Christ and the New Covenant is far "better" than the Old Covenant.

7. In Hebrews 9, the author shows the contrast between the tabernacle in the Old Testament and the true tabernacle, Jesus Christ.

8. One of the most popular sections of Hebrews is chapter 11, which some call "God's Hall of Faith." This chapter tells short stories of people who lived out their faith in God in exemplary ways.

9. Hebrews 11 mentions twenty-two examples of Bible characters who lived by faith.

10. The writer's closing benediction in Hebrews 13:20–21 provides a great wrap-up for all believers: a reminder of Jesus' work and an exhortation to do God's will.

Who

Because the author of Hebrews did not identify a specific audience, it is not absolutely clear to whom it was written. However, it is clear that the original recipients were mostly, if not exclusively, Jewish believers (and perhaps some nonbelievers). These Christians faced persecution, and they apparently felt discouraged, with many wondering if they had chosen wisely in rejecting their ancient Jewish traditions for this new faith.

What

This book was apparently written to Jewish believers who were reconsidering their commitment to Jesus Christ, and the author is trying to encourage them to stay in the faith.

When

This book may have been written in the 60s AD. It refers to the temple in Jerusalem, which was destroyed in AD 70 during the Siege of Jerusalem. The persecution referred to in this book was perhaps a result of Nero and his hatred of Christians.

Where

One popular theory is that the audience of Hebrews lived in or near Rome. Christians had established a strong presence in the capital city. Hebrews 13:24 mentions "those from Italy," but it's not clear if that refers to where the letter was written or where it was going.

Why

To believers who have questions about their faith, the solution always comes down to understanding who Jesus is and why He is superior to every other answer. The writer of Hebrews, recognizing the tenuous nature of the people being addressed, encourages them to continue to trust Jesus as God's final Word. His plan of salvation is far better than the old system of continual sacrifices, so they should have the courage to keep going forward in the faith. This letter exhorts Hebrew believers to stick with Jesus and continue to trust and serve Him.

Wow!

Canada's coat of arms quotes Hebrews 11:16. It reads, "*desiderantes meliorem patriam*," which is Latin for "desiring a better country."

Worth Remembering

- The Son is the radiance of God's glory and the exact representation of his being, sustaining all things by his powerful word. After he had provided purification for sins, he sat down at the right hand of the Majesty in heaven (Hebrews 1:3).
- Let us then approach God's throne of grace with confidence, so that we may receive mercy and find grace to help us in our time of need (Hebrews 4:16).
- We have this hope as an anchor for the soul, firm and secure. It enters the inner sanctuary behind the curtain (Hebrews 6:19).
- Because of this oath, Jesus has become the guarantor of a better covenant (Hebrews 7:22).
- But in fact the ministry Jesus has received is as superior to theirs as the covenant of which he is mediator is superior to the old one, since the new covenant is established on better promises (Hebrews 8:6).
- Now faith is confidence in what we hope for and assurance about what we do not see (Hebrews 11:1).
- Therefore, since we are surrounded by such a great cloud of witnesses, let us throw off everything that hinders and the sin that so easily entangles. And let us run with perseverance the race marked out for us, fixing our eyes on Jesus, the pioneer and perfecter of faith. For the joy set before him he endured the cross, scorning its shame, and sat down at the right hand of the throne of God (Hebrews 12:1-2).

JAMES

JAMES
How Faith and Works Work

Top Ten

1. The writer of this book knew Jesus in a special way; he was His younger brother.

2. James, a Jewish person himself, wrote this book as a way of helping Jews stay strong in this new faith.

3. According to Galatians 1:18–19, James had become a leader in the church at Jerusalem.

4. While the Jewish community had at one time settled in Israel with each tribe (except the Levites) having its own land, when James writes to the Hebrew people, they are "scattered among the nations" (1:1).

5. James alludes to the Sermon on the Mount twenty-three times in this letter.

6. One of the key points of tension in the book of James is between faith (eleven mentions NIV) and works (ten mentions NKJV).

7. Reformer Martin Luther, worried that the book of James emphasized works to the detriment of faith, called it, "an epistle of straw."

8. James enunciates fifty commands in his letter.

9. Some believe the book of James was one of the earliest books of the New Testament written.

10. According to the Jewish historian Josephus, James died a martyr for the cause of his brother.

Who

James grew up in the same household as Jesus, but he did not become a believer until he saw his brother in person after the crucifixion and resurrection. James was among the people who received a personal visitation from the risen Lord (1 Corinthians 15:7). For years after Jesus departed into heaven, James served as a pastor. He became known as James the Just.

What

James used a great deal of ink in this book to explain to his readers how to handle trials and temptations.

When

It is possible that James wrote this book as recently as ten years after Jesus' ascension to heaven—in the mid-40s AD. According to James 2:2, believers were still meeting in synagogues (the word *meeting* in this verse is translated "synagogue" in some Bible versions), which would indicate an early date. His many references to what Jesus taught would make sense; the lessons were still relatively fresh in his mind.

Where

Jewish believers were scattered throughout Asia Minor, Greece, and even Egypt, so it is hard to say exactly where James' target audience was located. Since he used the term "scattered abroad among the nations," one can assume that this letter would have been delivered to known churches throughout a large region.

Why

As is so often true with the churches who received letters from Paul and others, the people James addressed were just learning to negotiate the waters of this new journey into Christianity. Therefore, there were a number of areas of mystery. For instance, what were they to do with trials that infiltrated their lives? Why were bad things happening to them, even though they were following the right way? How were they to understand the relative importance of riches and poverty? James addressed these questions in his letter. And, as a helpful pastor will do, he supplied his readers with wisdom in a number of areas as they sought to live the Christlike life.

Wow!

Among the favorite Bible passages of former New York Yankees manager Joe Girardi and former Los Angeles Angels outfielder Tim Salmon is James 1:2–3.

JAMES

Worth Remembering

- Consider it pure joy, my brothers and sisters, whenever you face trials of many kinds (James 1:2).
- If any of you lacks wisdom, you should ask God, who gives generously to all without finding fault, and it will be given to you (James 1:5).
- Blessed is the one who perseveres under trial because, having stood the test, that person will receive the crown of life that the Lord has promised to those who love him (James 1:12).
- When tempted, no one should say, "God is tempting me." For God cannot be tempted by evil, nor does he tempt anyone (James 1:13).
- Do not merely listen to the word, and so deceive yourselves. Do what it says (James 1:22).
- Those who consider themselves religious and yet do not keep a tight rein on their tongues deceive themselves, and their religion is worthless. Religion that God our Father accepts as pure and faultless is this: to look after orphans and widows in their distress and to keep oneself from being polluted by the world (James 1:26–27).
- In the same way, faith by itself, if it is not accompanied by action, is dead (James 2:17).
- Likewise, the tongue is a small part of the body, but it makes great boasts. Consider what a great forest is set on fire by a small spark (James 3:5).
- Out of the same mouth come praise and cursing. My brothers and sisters, this should not be (James 3:10).
- What causes fights and quarrels among you? Don't they come from your desires that battle within you? (James 4:1).
- Submit yourselves, then, to God. Resist the devil, and he will flee from you. Come near to God and he will come near to you. Wash your hands, you sinners, and purify your hearts, you double-minded (James 4:7–8).

Wonders from the Past

"There is evidence that early Jewish Christians sometimes met in synagogues," says archaeologist John McRay. "The New Testament letter of James refers to Christians (undoubtedly Jewish) meeting in a synagogue (2:2), but bear in mind that at this time Jews probably met most often in homes and rented halls."[15]

1 PETER
An Encouraging Word

Top Ten

1. Jesus referred to Peter's death in John 21:18. Peter may have written this letter near the time of his death in Rome.
2. When Peter used the word *Babylon* in 5:13, it was probably a metaphorical reference to Rome—a city with similar godless characteristics. Some believe he may have used this word to disguise his actual location.
3. Peter mentioned in this letter that he had witnessed Jesus' sufferings, which could be seen as an encouragement to people going through hard times.
4. Peter wrote this letter to a group of churches scattered throughout what is today Turkey. Included were the Galatian churches, which Paul also wrote to.
5. This letter references several Old Testament passages: Psalm 118:22, Isaiah 53:9, and Psalm 34:12–16, for example.
6. Times were very tough for Christians during this era in church history. For example, their neighbors harassed them for not participating in their pagan activities (see 4:3-4).

7. When Peter uses the term "strangers in the world" (2:11 CEB), he is telling his readers that he understands how they stand out from others—from the nonbelieving Jewish community and from pagan neighbors—because of their faith.

8. Peter uses the word *suffering* seven times in this book.

9. First Peter has been called "The Job of the New Testament" because of its emphasis on suffering.

10. It is believed that Silas, who is mentioned in 1 Peter 5:12, delivered this letter to the churches.

Who

It would have been a great encouragement for the churches to get a letter from someone who had walked with Jesus through His earthly life. And for that person to be Peter, who was so closely aligned with Jesus, would have been even better. Peter wrote this book in the mid-60s AD. This was during the persecution of the Christians in Rome at the hands of Nero, and it would have been in close proximity to the martyrdom of Paul. Some surmise that Paul and Peter were both held prisoner in the Mamertine Prison in Rome.

What

In order to properly encourage his readers as they faced hard times, Peter first reinforces the great rewards of salvation in Jesus Christ. Then he calls on his fellow believers to strive for a holy life both in the Christian community and before those outside the church. As an encouragement, he reminds them of Jesus' suffering and also proposes to them the idea that it is a privilege to suffer for His sake.

When

The church of Jesus Christ was around thirty years old at the time, and it was facing tough times due to both governmental and societal pressures. Peter's reference to the devil being a roaring lion (5:8) would remind the people that the persecution they faced from many sources was actually spiritual in nature—and that their response to it should also be spiritual.

Where

The church locations mentioned in 1 Peter 1:2 are references to churches Paul had founded, but Peter had probably visited them as well. Pontus was a province in northeastern Asia Minor that bordered Galatia and Cappadocia. Aquila was from Pontus (Acts 18:2). People from Pontus were in Jerusalem at Pentecost (see Acts 2) and heard the gospel in their own language. Galatia, which had already received a letter from Paul, was a neighbor to Pontus. Cappadocia was in eastern Asia Minor. It too had citizens visiting Jerusalem at Pentecost. Bithynia was a planned destination of Paul and his traveling companions, but he didn't go because the Holy Spirit told them not to (see Acts 16:7).

Why

Peter understood suffering and knew Jesus face-to-face, so he was the right person to give comfort and instruction to churches facing difficult times. His reminders that these believers could have hope in the midst of suffering, his promise of their bright future (1:4–5), and the prospect of the "Chief Shepherd" appearing (5:4) were just what the people needed to hear, when they needed to hear it.

Wow!

- Any number of writers have used Peter's phrase "All flesh is as grass" (1 Peter 1:24 KJV). Here is a short list of artists who have alluded to this line in their works: poet Christina Rossetti, poet T.S. Eliot, science fiction writer Clifford Simak, and composer Brahms.
- Charles Dickens uses the "roaring lion" image of 1 Peter 5:8 in his book *Hard Times* to describe one of his characters, James Harthouse.

1 PETER

- In Shakespeare's *Othello*, this description mirrors 1 Peter 3:4–5: "A maiden never bold; Of spirit so still and quiet that her motion Blushed at herself" (Act 1, Scene 3, lines 94-96).

Worth Remembering

- Praise be to the God and Father of our Lord Jesus Christ! In his great mercy he has given us new birth into a living hope through the resurrection of Jesus Christ from the dead (1 Peter 1:3).
- But you are a chosen people, a royal priesthood, a holy nation, God's special possession, that you may declare the praises of him who called you out of darkness into his wonderful light (1 Peter 2:9).
- "He himself bore our sins" in his body on the cross, so that we might die to sins and live for righteousness; "by his wounds you have been healed" (1 Peter 2:24).
- Be alert and of sober mind. Your enemy the devil prowls around like a roaring lion looking for someone to devour. Resist him, standing firm in the faith, because you know that the family of believers throughout the world is undergoing the same kind of sufferings (1 Peter 5:8-9).

2 PETER

A Warning and a Promise

Top Ten

1. Peter specifically refers to another letter to this same group of believers in 2 Peter 3:1. This may or may not have been 1 Peter.
2. Peter gives autobiographical information that would have reminded his readers who he was (he referenced the transfiguration in 1:18 and Jesus' allusion to Peter's subsequent death in 1:14).

3. Jude and 2 Peter have many similarities in content, particularly their focus on false teachers.
4. Scholars see parts of 2 Peter as coming from Jude's writing; thus, they see Jude as having written his epistle first.
5. Before Peter began addressing some key negative influences in the churches of Asia, he pointed to eight key characteristics for believers: faith, goodness, knowledge, self-control, perseverance, godliness, mutual affection, and love. Apparently, the people who were disrupting the church were missing these characteristics.
6. Even though this was still the first century, people were already doubting the Lord's return, so Peter wrote to reassure them.
7. "To know" is a key concept in 2 Peter. The word *know* is used eleven times and *knowledge* is used six times in this book.
8. There is a harshness to Peter's condemnation of false teachers who are wreaking havoc on churches, and it's because of the destructive nature of their actions.
9. Peter introduces the idea that the earth will one day be burned up and that there will a new heaven and a new earth (3:11-13).
10. Peter commends Paul's letters to the people, saying that they contained the "wisdom that God gave him" (3:15).

Who

Peter introduces the letter by telling his readers that it came from his pen. He called himself a "servant and apostle of Jesus Christ." Since he referred to his first letter in 3:1, we can assume that this letter went to the same people to whom he sent the first.

What

Peter wanted to remind believers that they already had what they needed through God's "divine power" and that they could escape the world's corruption. He then gave them eight traits (see number 5 of Top Ten) that could help them stay strong in Jesus. They were then equipped to hear the bad news—that there were others out to deceive them for their own gain. The strength and godly power with which he introduced the book were vital, as the people became aware of charlatans and false teachers in the church.

When

Peter wrote this letter about thirty years after Jesus' death, burial, resurrection, and ascension. It had been a time of region-wide growth for the church, and now, as a new generation was being raised in the church, new challenges arose.

Where

As in 1 Peter, the people he addressed in this letter lived and worshiped in Asia Minor. They had probably been connected to Paul and his missionary work and letters.

Why

Peter was concerned. What if these false teachers and purveyors of negativity became dominant in these churches? Could the gospel message be in jeopardy? Peter wanted to use his final years to make sure the church returned to its roots in the gospel of Jesus, so he took on the task of warning these individual churches.

Wow!

Second Peter 1:3–11 is CBS sports commentator and NCAA men's basketball expert Clark Kellogg's favorite Bible passage.

Worth Remembering

- For this very reason, make every effort to add to your faith goodness; and to goodness, knowledge; and to knowledge, self-control; and to self-control, perseverance; and to perseverance, godliness; and to godliness, mutual affection; and to mutual affection, love (2 Peter 1:5-7).
- Above all, you must understand that no prophecy of Scripture came about by the prophet's own interpretation of things. For prophecy never had its origin in the human will,

but prophets, though human, spoke from God as they were carried along by the Holy Spirit (2 Peter 1:20-21).

- But there were also false prophets among the people, just as there will be false teachers among you. They will secretly introduce destructive heresies, even denying the sovereign Lord who bought them—bringing swift destruction on themselves (2 Peter 2:1).
- Above all, you must understand that in the last days scoffers will come, scoffing and following their own evil desires. They will say, "Where is this 'coming' he promised? Ever since our ancestors died, everything goes on as it has since the beginning of creation" (2 Peter 3:3-4).
- The Lord is not slow in keeping his promise, as some understand slowness. Instead he is patient with you, not wanting anyone to perish, but everyone to come to repentance (2 Peter 3:9).
- But the day of the Lord will come like a thief. The heavens will disappear with a roar; the elements will be destroyed by fire, and the earth and everything done in it will be laid bare (2 Peter 3:10).
- But grow in the grace and knowledge of our Lord and Savior Jesus Christ. To him be glory both now and forever! Amen (2 Peter 3:18).

Wonders from the Past

Some church traditions say Peter was buried in Rome—specifically at the present-day location of the Vatican—but this has not been corroborated archaeologically.

1 JOHN

Reality Check

Top Ten

1. This is one of the last books of the Bible written—toward the final decade of the first century.

2. The apostle John, who wrote this book, lived into his nineties—perhaps to one hundred years old.
3. John had a direct influence on some of the men we call the early church fathers—leaders in the church into the second century. That includes Ignatius, bishop of Antioch, and Polycarp, bishop of Smyrna.
4. John, who was originally from Bethsaida in Galilee, lived in the city of Ephesus during his later years.
5. Christianity had been around for about sixty years when John wrote this letter. One of the problems the church faced was Gnosticism—a heretical belief that there were two entities: body and spirit. Gnostics held that the physical body was the residence of sin, so Jesus could not have existed in bodily form, for He would have had sin.
6. Three of the four biblical uses of the word *antichrist* appear in 1 John (2:18, 2:22, 4:3). The other is in 2 John 1:7.
7. This letter was meant to be circulated among the churches near Asia Minor—the region of Ephesus.
8. While John was addressing specific problems threatening the first-century church, he did so in a way that allows us to learn twenty centuries later about things such as living *in* the world while not being *of* the world (see 1 John 2:15; also, John 17:14–15).
9. The deity of Christ is important in this book. John refers to Jesus as the "Son of God" nine times in 1 John, emphasizing His deity.
10. John often uses contrasts in this book as he tries to counter the false teaching of the Gnostics: light and darkness, love and hate, and truth and lies, for example.

Who

The elder statesman of the church and the last remaining disciple, John was a link between the first and second centuries. He had known Jesus personally as a close friend and he knew

Him as his Savior, so it was important to him late in his life to write down what he knew and what the Holy Spirit had directed him to write. Probably a nonagenarian at the time, John would have been highly respected in Ephesus, where he lived, and throughout Asia Minor. It was vital for John to stem the tide of false teaching that threatened Ephesus and other nearby churches and to bring the church as a whole back to the concept of love.

What

John was not one to waste a good introduction. Both this letter and his gospel (which he probably wrote after this letter) begin similarly by emphasizing Jesus' existence with God from eternity past. He then tackled the subject of sin—which some in the church claimed to be free from. John emphasized love and its essential nature for Christians. And he reiterated how important it is to recognize Jesus for who He really is.

When

The best estimate is that John wrote this letter between AD 85 and AD 90. He probably wrote this before he wrote his gospel record.

Where

By now the temple at Jerusalem had been destroyed (AD 70), and Asia Minor had become the center of Christianity. We see evidence of that in Revelation 2–3, where John addresses seven churches, all of which were in that region.

Why

It is time for a reality check for the young church. A number of competing philosophies and belief systems were already twisting and distorting the gospel message, and John wanted to draw people back to the reality of true faith in the God-man Jesus. He also emphasized the importance of obedience and the essential

1 JOHN

nature of Christian love—for one another and for those outside the church.

Worth Remembering

- If we walk in the light, as he is in the light, we have fellowship with one another, and the blood of Jesus, his Son, purifies us from all sin (1 John 1:7).
- The one who does what is sinful is of the devil, because the devil has been sinning from the beginning. The reason the Son of God appeared was to destroy the devil's work (1 John 3:8).
- You, dear children, are from God and have overcome them, because the one who is in you is greater than the one who is in the world (1 John 4:4).
- Dear friends, let us love one another, for love comes from God. Everyone who loves has been born of God and knows God. Whoever does not love does not know God, because God is love (1 John 4:7-8).
- No one has ever seen God; but if we love one another, God lives in us and his love is made complete in us (1 John 4:12).
- We love because he first loved us (1 John 4:19).
- For everyone born of God overcomes the world. This is the victory that has overcome the world, even our faith (1 John 5:4).
- And if we know that he hears us—whatever we ask—we know that we have what we asked of him (1 John 5:15).

Wonders from the Past

- Some scholars have found similarities between books such as 1 John and writings from the Qumran region, where the Dead Sea Scrolls were found.
- Archaeological discoveries have verified that the Gnosticism John opposed was an issue in his day. A Gnostic library discovered in Egypt has given scholars evidence of this heresy in the first-century church.

2 JOHN
To the Chosen Lady

Top Ten

1. Second John is the second shortest book in the Bible.
2. Unlike 1 John, which was apparently meant to be read in a number of churches in the region, 2 John appears to be a personal note meant for one person.
3. Paul's letter to Philemon had a similar concept in that it was a message written to one person: Onesimus' master, Philemon.
4. This letter is addressed to "the lady chosen by God and her children." Whether this is an actual woman or a symbolic reference to a church and its members is not known.
5. This book is the only one in the New Testament addressed to a woman.
6. John, the longest-living disciple, refers to himself in this letter as "the elder" (vs. 1).
7. John speaks as a pastor to the church in this letter.
8. The message of 2 John is similar to that of 1 John— it's about love and truth, and about standing against falsehoods.
9. A heresy called Docetism (the Gnostic doctrine holding that Christ's body was not human in the physical sense) was prevalent at the time John wrote this letter, and he addressed how to avoid it.
10. John writes on the subject of hospitality in 2 John; however, he instructs Christians not to extend hospitality to false teachers (see vs. 10).

Who

Scholars are sure 2 John is from the pen of the aged apostle John. Its style and contents align with John's other writings, especially 1 and 3 John.

2 JOHN

What

The essence of John's teaching in this short letter can be summed up with two words: love and truth. He writes of the truth, "which lives in" believers, and he finds great joy in discovering that his spiritual children are "walking in the truth." Next, he implores his reader to "walk in love."

When

John probably wrote 2 John around the same time he wrote 1 John.

Where

The "chosen lady," whether this means a person or a church, lived in the same region John addressed in 1 John—in Asia Minor, around Ephesus.

Why

The heart of the "elder" was simple: he wanted his readers to honor God's truth and live in His love. To encourage this, he took "paper and ink" to convey a written message—hoping to later visit his recipients in person (vs. 12).

Wow!

In 2016, the Christian rock band Sanctus Real released the song "This Is Love," which mirrors 2 John 1:6: "And this is love: that we walk in obedience to his commands."

Worth Remembering

- Because of the truth, which lives in us and will be with us forever (2 John 2).
- Grace, mercy and peace from God the Father and from Jesus Christ, the Father's Son, will be with us in truth and love (2 John 3).

2 JOHN

- It has given me great joy to find some of your children walking in the truth, just as the Father commanded us (2 John 4).
- And now, dear lady, I am not writing you a new command but one we have had from the beginning. I ask that we love one another (2 John 5).
- I say this because many deceivers, who do not acknowledge Jesus Christ as coming in the flesh, have gone out into the world. Any such person is the deceiver and the antichrist (2 John 7).

3 JOHN
Personal Note to a Faithful Man

Top Ten

1. At 219 words, 3 John is the shortest book in the Bible.
2. John sent this letter to a faithful man named Gaius (vs. 1).
3. Verse 4 implies that John had led Gaius to faith in Christ.
4. John had received a good report about Gaius' faithfulness to the truth.
5. John calls out a person named Diotrephes, perhaps a pastor, for spreading what he calls "malicious nonsense." (1 John 9–10)
6. Diotrephes even refused to allow other believers to come and talk with him (vs. 10).
7. In verse 12, John also mentions a man named Demetrius, who may have delivered his letter to Gaius.
8. As in 2 John, the elder statesman tells his reader he would like to drop by for a visit.

9. Third John is the only book in the New Testament that does not contain the names Jesus or Christ. The name of God appears twice (vss. 6 and 11).
10. Verse 7 mentions "the Name," which is usually meant in reference to "the name of Jesus."

Who

Third John begins with the identifier "The elder," which scholars agree refers to John, who was both an elder statesman and an elder in his church at Ephesus.

What

Simply put, this was a thank-you note to Gaius, accompanied by a word of warning about a man in the church who was causing trouble. John thanked Gaius for being hospitable to people he didn't even know when they paid him a visit. Then there is Diotrephes, who did everything wrong: he wouldn't listen to John, he didn't want visiting teachers participating at his church, and he rejected good hospitality. He was everything a Christian leader should not be.

When

Scholars believe John wrote this epistle between AD 85 and AD 95.

Where

We are not told the name of the city Gaius or Diotrephes lived in. There are a few men named Gaius in the New Testament, but it is not clear which one this is—or whether it's another Gaius. We can only surmise that the letter's recipient lived somewhere in the region around Ephesus.

Why

John's letter to Gaius is a wise mixture of love and truth. He pours out appreciation to Gaius for the good work he is doing then condemns the negative influence of Diotrephes. The truth that results from this criticism of a failed church member is this: "Do not imitate what is evil but what is good" (vs. 11). We see both in this book. Follow people like Gaius, not people like Diotrephes, John teaches.

Wow!

Singer Johnny Cash wrote and performed a song called "My Children Walk in Truth," which is based on 3 John 1:4. He wrote, "My greatest joy is knowing that my children walk in truth and that they are giving you, Lord, of their fire and strength of youth. Yes, I've found the greatest joy of my salvation is knowing that my children walk in truth."

Worth Remembering

- It gave me great joy when some believers came and testified about your faithfulness to the truth, telling how you continue to walk in it. I have no greater joy than to hear that my children are walking in the truth (3 John 3–4).
- It was for the sake of the Name that they went out, receiving no help from the pagans. We ought therefore to show hospitality to such people so that we may work together for the truth (3 John 7–8).
- Dear friend, do not imitate what is evil but what is good. Anyone who does what is good is from God. Anyone who does what is evil has not seen God (3 John 11).

JUDE

JUDE
Addressing Church Trouble

Top Ten

1. Matthew 13 and Mark 6 tell us that Jesus had a brother named Judas, or Jude. This is the man who wrote this short epistle.

2. Jude identifies himself as James' (and therefore Jesus') brother in Jude 1:1.

3. Jude's letter was not included in the official canon of Scripture until the fourth century.

4. Jude does not hold back in his harsh words for the false teachers he warns about in this letter. He calls them "godless men," "dreamers," "blemishes at your love feasts," and "clouds without rain," among other things.

5. In Jude 1:14–15, the writer quotes from an apocryphal First Book of Enoch. Part of the quotation from Enoch can also be attributed to Deuteronomy 33:2. Enoch is not considered an inspired book so it was not accepted in the canon of Scripture.

6. Second Peter and Jude are similar in content, as they both alert Christians to false teaching.

7. Jude changes his theme as he begins to write. He starts by telling his readers he intended to write about salvation, but he ends up addressing the problem of false teachers.

8. One of the interesting features of Jude's letter is his recounting of a battle between Michael and the devil over Moses' body (vs. 9). This is the only mention of this skirmish in the Bible.

9. Jude may have been included in Paul's statement about "the Lord's brothers" taking their wives with them on missions trips (see 1 Corinthians 9:5).

10. The book of Jude ends in a beautiful doxology preachers often use as they speak God's blessing over their people (24–25).

Who

The evidence is clear that Jesus' brother Jude (referred to as Judas in Matthew and Mark) wrote this book. This means two of Jesus' brothers, James and Jude, were authors of Bible books. Interestingly, both were reluctant followers of their brother—trusting in Him only after His death, burial, and resurrection.

Jude addresses himself as a "servant of Jesus Christ," similar to the way other New Testament writers self-identify.

What

Error is creeping into the church of Jesus Christ, so Jude moves from writing about salvation to addressing this growing problem of false teaching. Using Old Testament stories as his jumping-off point, Jude speaks of people who are rejecting authority, speaking abusively, and looking out for themselves only. He says they "boast among themselves and flatter others for their own advantage" (vs. 16). He then offers an antidote: be built up in the faith, pray in the Spirit, remain in God's love, show mercy to doubters, and witness to them.

When

Scholars are not sure when Jude wrote this letter, but it appears he penned it in the late 60s AD.

Where

While it is not known who Jude's "dear friends" he was writing to were, we can assume that he wrote this book for a certain body of believers and not as a general epistle, like ones that were meant to circulate among several different congregations. Jude may have written it to the same people Peter addressed in his second letter.

Why

You can sense the passion Jude has for this topic. First, the proliferation of the error he addresses was serious, and second, that error makes him shift the direction of his subject matter. Clearly, these are serious problems, and they have to be addressed in order for the gospel to continue in its pure state.

Worth Remembering

- Mercy, peace and love be yours in abundance (Jude 2).
- Dear friends, although I was very eager to write to you about the salvation we share, I felt compelled to write and

JUDE

urge you to contend for the faith that was once for all entrusted to God's holy people (Jude 3).

- To him who is able to keep you from stumbling and to present you before his glorious presence without fault and with great joy—to the only God our Savior be glory, majesty, power and authority, through Jesus Christ our Lord, before all ages, now and forevermore! Amen (Jude 24-25).

REVELATION
The Revelation of Jesus Christ

Top Ten

1. The book of Revelation is considered "apocalyptic literature," which indicates an "unveiling" of hopefulness for a society facing difficult times.
2. Revelation can be interpreted in several ways. One is to see everything as symbolic and not historic. Another is to view the book as related only to the time period in which it is written. A third method sees the book as a record of church history—beginning to end. And the fourth method is to see it as futuristic—that John was conveying what will happen in prophetic history all the way to the coming of the new heaven and new earth.
3. John wrote this book while he was in exile on the Island of Patmos; Roman officials had sent him there for preaching God's Word (1:9).
4. John was told, "Write, therefore, what you have seen, what is now and what will take place later" (1:19).
5. What John has written in Revelation is the result of a vision God has given him. He writes in the best words he could find about things that are nearly incomprehensible.

REVELATION

6. One of the key numbers in the book of Revelation is 7: seven churches, seven bowls, seven seals, seven lampstands, seven angels, and on it goes.

7. John delivered God's message to seven key churches in Asia Minor before he began revealing the prophetic nature of the book.

8. Revelation reminds us that our God is the Alpha and the Omega—meaning He represents the beginning of the world and the end of the world as we know it—and then on into eternity. One of the key statements of God's eternal nature is Revelation 1:8: "'I am the Alpha and the Omega,' says the Lord God, 'who is and who was, and who is to come.'"

9. The book of Revelation provides the perfect capstone for human story as it is recorded in the Bible. The story began with creation, continued through the fall of humanity, was explained in the long story of re-creation and salvation, and leads to the final culmination of Revelation 21–22.

10. The best news of all is contained in this book: in the end, God wins.

Who

The gospel writer John, one of Jesus' twelve apostles, is the author of this book. While enduring his exile on the small Greek island of Patmos, John was "in the Spirit" when God told him to write down Jesus' messages to the seven churches. Then, beginning in Revelation 4, he communicates a vision of heaven and multitudes of other mysterious scenes that encompass the rest of the book. John received God's message and wrote this book in the late 80s or early 90s AD.

What

The seven churches of Asia Minor had received various messages from the writers of the Epistles, but the ones in Revelation 2–3 were different. This was a series of word-for-word messages from

REVELATION

Jesus himself—with each specifically crafted to meet the key need of each church. Next, things got fantastic for John. He was transported to a place where he was before the throne of God himself. Before him were opened amazing visions of seals and scrolls, and he heard trumpets and singing. He witnessed God's ultimate victory over evil, and at the end, he was introduced to the new heaven and the new earth. In events that can hardly be described with words, John opened up a new world of hope and grandeur—all reflecting the glory and majesty of God.

When

The first three chapters of Revelation (after a brief doxology and greeting in chapter 1) are addressed to seven churches in Asia Minor. The rest of the book presents pictures of what will someday take place in God's economy. We can't fathom the reality of what these pictures represent, but we know that even in our days of crisis, we have the sure hope that God will someday make all things right and that we will bask in His presence for eternity.

Where

The message of Revelation is for all believers everywhere. We can learn from what the churches learned from Jesus' evaluation of their state of affairs, and we can look forward with anticipation to God's future plan for all who have put their faith in Jesus Christ.

Why

Whether you lived in John's day, a time of persecution by the Roman government, or whether you lived at any time in the intervening history of the world, when life was tough and troubles of all kinds visited you each day, you could find solace in Revelation. The heart of this book is the sure hope and comforting knowledge that God is in control and that there will come a day when evil will be eradicated forever. The joy of God's perfection will be our eternal reality. God gave John this vision to show us that His story has an incredibly joyous ending, and all who put their faith in Jesus will one day sing, "Holy, holy, holy is the Lord God Almighty" (Revelation 4:8) as we marvel in the place God has prepared for us. That is the wonderful "Why" of the book of Revelation.

Wow!

- Michelangelo's *The Last Judgment*, which covers the entire altar wall of the Sistine Chapel, represents vividly one of the themes of Revelation: Christ's return and God's final judgment on all humanity.
- Think of the many classic hymns written using the words and ideas we will experience someday in heaven. Here are just three of them: "Worthy Is the Lamb," "Holy, Holy, Holy," and "Crown Him with Many Crowns."
- The Irish rock band U2 has recorded several songs referencing Revelation, including "Fire" (Revelation 6) and "Where the Streets Have No Name" (Revelation 22:1).
- Perhaps the most prevalent of John's visions is found in Revelation 6:1–8—what is popularly called the Four Horsemen of the Apocalypse. Here is a short list of cultural references to this biblical picture: the Four Horsemen of Notre Dame (the four football players who made up the Irish's offensive backfield and played under Knute Rockne in 1924); Four Horsemen of the Supreme Court (four justices who opposed Franklin Roosevelt's New Deal agenda); movies by that name (1921 and 1962); the song "The Man Comes Around" by Johnny Cash, which refers to the four horsemen; multiple TV programs and video games have used the term.

Worth Remembering

- "Look, he is coming with the clouds," and "every eye will see him, even those who pierced him"; and all peoples on earth "will mourn because of him." So shall it be! Amen.

REVELATION

"I am the Alpha and the Omega," says the Lord God, "who is, and who was, and who is to come, the Almighty" (Revelation 1:7–8).

- When I saw him, I fell at his feet as though dead. Then he placed his right hand on me and said: "Do not be afraid. I am the First and the Last. I am the Living One; I was dead, and now look, I am alive for ever and ever! And I hold the keys of death and Hades" (Revelation 1:17–18).

- "I know your deeds. See, I have placed before you an open door that no one can shut. I know that you have little strength, yet you have kept my word and have not denied my name" (Revelation 3:8).

- "Here I am! I stand at the door and knock. If anyone hears my voice and opens the door, I will come in and eat with that person, and they with me. To the one who is victorious, I will give the right to sit with me on my throne, just as I was victorious and sat down with my Father on his throne" (Revelation 3:20–21).

- Whenever the living creatures give glory, honor and thanks to him who sits on the throne and who lives for ever and ever (Revelation 4:9).

- The twenty-four elders fall down before him who sits on the throne and worship him who lives for ever and ever. They lay their crowns before the throne and say: "You are worthy, our Lord and God, to receive glory and honor and power, for you created all things, and by your will they were created and have their being" (Revelation 4:10–11).

- I saw thrones on which were seated those who had been given authority to judge. And I saw the souls of those who had been beheaded because of their testimony about Jesus and because of the word of God. They had not worshiped the beast or its image and had not received its mark on their foreheads or their hands. They came to life and reigned with Christ a thousand years (Revelation 20:4).

- And the devil, who deceived them, was thrown into the lake of burning sulfur, where the beast and the false prophet had been thrown. They will be tormented day and night for ever and ever (Revelation 20:10).

- And I saw the dead, great and small, standing before the throne, and books were opened. Another book was opened, which is the book of life. The dead were judged according to what they had done as recorded in the books (Revelation 20:12).
- Then I saw "a new heaven and a new earth," for the first heaven and the first earth had passed away, and there was no longer any sea. I saw the Holy City, the new Jerusalem, coming down out of heaven from God, prepared as a bride beautifully dressed for her husband (Revelation 21:1-2).
- And I heard a loud voice from the throne saying, "Look! God's dwelling place is now among the people, and he will dwell with them. They will be his people, and God himself will be with them and be their God" (Revelation 21:3).
- "'He will wipe every tear from their eyes. There will be no more death' or mourning or crying or pain, for the old order of things has passed away" (Revelation 21:4).
- He said to me: "It is done. I am the Alpha and the Omega, the Beginning and the End. To the thirsty I will give water without cost from the spring of the water of life. Those who are victorious will inherit all this, and I will be their God and they will be my children" (Revelation 21:6-7).
- No longer will there be any curse. The throne of God and of the Lamb will be in the city, and his servants will serve him. They will see his face, and his name will be on their foreheads. There will be no more night. They will not need the light of a lamp or the light of the sun, for the Lord God will give them light. And they will reign for ever and ever (Revelation 22:3-5).
- "Look, I am coming soon! My reward is with me, and I will give to each person according to what they have done" (Revelation 22:12).
- The Spirit and the bride say, "Come!" And let the one who hears say, "Come!" Let the one who is thirsty come; and let the one who wishes take the free gift of the water of life (Revelation 22:17).

REVELATION

Wonders from the Past

Archaeologists have found ruins from each of the seven cities
John wrote to in Revelation 2–3, verifying that he indeed wrote to
real churches in real cities.

REVELATION

SOURCES

- *Adventuring through the Bible*, Ray C. Stedman, Discovery House, Grand Rapids, 2012.
- *All the Men of the Bible*, Herbert Lockyer, Zondervan, Grand Rapids, 1958.
- *Amos, Hosea, Micah—An Archaeological Commentary*, Philip J. King, Westminster John Knox Press, Louisville, 1988.
- *The Baker Book of Bible Charts, Maps, and Time Lines*, edited by John A. Beck, Baker Books, Grand Rapids, 2016.
- *The Baker Illustrated Bible Commentary*, Edited by Gary M. Burge and Andrew E. Hill, Baker Books, Grand Rapids, 2012.
- *The Baker Illustrated Bible Handbook*, Edited by J. Daniel Hays and J. Scott Duvall, Baker Books, Grand Rapids, 2011.
- *BibleCharts.org*
- *Discovery House Bible Atlas*, John A. Beck, Discovery House, Grand Rapids, 2015.
- *Halley's Bible Handbook with the New International Version*, Zondervan, Grand Rapids, 2000.
- *Insights for Living*, "Genesis," et al.
- *International Standard Bible Encyclopedia*, Eerdmans, Grand Rapids, 1982
- *Introducing the Old Testament*, L. A. T. Van Dooren, Zondervan, Grand Rapids, 1967.
- *Kregel Bible Handbook*, William F. Kerr, Kregel Publications, Grand Rapids, 2000.
- *The New Unger's Bible Handbook*, Merrill F. Unger, Revised by Gary N. Larson, Moody, 1984, Chicago
- *Why Trust the Bible*, Rose Publishing, Torrance, California, 2008

NOTES

1. Steve Law, "New Discoveries Indicate Hebrew was World's Oldest Alphabet," patternsofevidence.com, Jan. 6, 2017.
2. *Why Trust the Bible?* (Torrance, CA: Rose Publishing, 2008).
3. Ibid.
4. John A. Beck, *Discovery House Bible Atlas* (Grand Rapids: Discovery House, 2015), p. 69.
5. *International Standard Bible Encyclopedia*, vol. 2 (Grand Rapids: Eerdmans, Grand Rapids, 1982), p. 1158.
6. Brian Thomas, "Scientists Describe Job's 'Springs of the Sea,'" June 23, 2015, http://www.icr .org/article/scientists-describe-jobs-springs-sea/.
7. Philip J. King, *Amos, Hosea, Micah—An Archaeological Commentary* (Louisville, KY: Westminster John Knox Press, 1988).
8. Paul L. Maier, "Biblical Archaeology: Factual Evidence to Support the Historicity of the Bible," *Christian Research Journal, volume* 27, number 2 (2004), also available at http://www.equip.org /article/biblical-archaeology-factual-evidence-to-support-the-historicity-of-the-bible/.
9. Steven A. Austin, "The Scientific and Scriptural Impact of Amos' Earthquake," *Institute for Creation Research*, February 1, 2010, http://www.icr.org/article/scientific-scriptural-impact -amos-earthquake/.
10. Theodoros Karasavvas, "Archaeologists Uncovered an Archive that Narrates Ancient Assyria's Fall," December 18, 2017, https://www.ancient-origins.net/news-history-archaeology /archaeologists-uncovered-archive-narrates-ancient-assyria-s-fall-009306.
11. R.A. Parker and W.H. Dubberstein, *Babylonian Chronology, 626 BC–AD 75* (Eugene, OR: Wipf and Stock Publishers, 1946).
12. "Church unearthed in Israel may hold Zechariah tomb," Phys.org, February 2, 2011, https://phys.org/news/2011-02-church-unearthed-israel-zechariah-tomb.html.
13. Frank E. Gaebelein, "Malachi," *The Expositor's Bible Commentary* (Grand Rapids: Zondervan, 1982).
14. *Archaeological Study Bible* (Grand Rapids: Zondervan, 2008).
15. John McRay, *Archaeology and the New Testament* (Grand Rapids: Baker Academic, 1997), p. 72.